TOUCHING ENLIGHTENMENT

Reginald A. Ray, Ph.D.

TOUCHING ENLIGHTENMENT

Finding Realization in the Body

sounds true
BOULDER, COLORADO

Sounds True
Boulder, CO 80306

© 2008, 2014 Reginald A. Ray

SOUNDS TRUE is a trademark of Sounds True, Inc.
All rights reserved. No part of this book may be used or reproduced in any
manner without written permission of the author and publisher.

Published 2014

Jacket design by Karen Polaski
Book design by Chad Morgan

Printed in Canada

Library of Congress Cataloging-in-Publication Data
Ray, Reginald A.
 Touching enlightenment : finding realization in the body by Reginald A. Ray.
 p. cm.
 Includes index.
 ISBN 978-1-59179-618-3 (hardcover)
  1. Spiritual life—Tantric Buddhism. 2. Tantric Buddhism—China—Tibet—
Doctrines. I. Title.
BQ8938.R339 2007
294.3'422—dc22
 2007029136

ISBN: 978-1-62203-353-9
Ebook ISBN: 978-1-59179-843-9

10 9 8 7 6 5 4 3 2

Dedication

This book is dedicated to Charlotte B. MacJannet, an early and most important spiritual mentor, whom I met when I was barely eighteen and working in Europe. With remarkable prescience, "Mrs. Mac" initiated me into many of the core themes of my subsequent life and work. She gave me my first book on Tibetan Buddhism. She also introduced me to Jung, by arranging for me to meet and work briefly with one of Jung's own students. And one day she said to me out of the blue, "You need to see the world; you need to see Asia." Never one to speak idly, once I had signed on to this idea, she dug in and organized people for me to meet, work to do, and families to stay with during a year sojourn, from Japan, through Southeast Asia, to India, and then into Nepal, a journey that changed my life forever. Especially noteworthy in the present context, Mrs. Mac arranged for me to study with one of the students of Gerda Alexander, the Danish founder of Eutonie, a somatic discipline of much power and depth. Mrs. MacJannet's deep optimism about the spiritual possibilities of modern people, her commitment to relieve suffering wherever she found it, and her joy in living were priceless gifts to all who knew her. Charlotte MacJannet passed away many years ago, before I was able to realize the tremendous debt I owe her and before I could adequately thank her for her great and selfless offerings at this critical moment in my life. Belatedly, then, Mrs. Mac, wherever you may be, I send you my devotion, my gratitude, and my love.

Contents

CONCLUSION

Acknowledgments

This book owes a great debt to many people, stretching back to my youth.

I must thank my academic teachers, especially H. Ganse Little, Bill Peck, Mircea Eliade, Charles Long, Joe Kitagawa, and Frank Reynolds, for providing me the training and the tools to explore Buddhist history to great depth. When I studied with them, I never could have imagined how important and useful that education would be, not only in my scholarly life, but also and even more so in my work as a dharma teacher attempting to teach meditation—and particularly the embodied meditation discussed in this book—in the modern world.

I thank my Buddhist teachers, Chögyam Trungpa Rinpoche, H.H. Khyentse Rinpoche, H.H. the Sixteenth Karmapa, and the many other generous and gracious Tibetan lamas I have been privileged to learn from; Eido Roshi, Kobun Chino Roshi, and my other Zen mentors; and several wonderful Theravadin teachers who, in person and through their books, have taught me a great deal about meditating with the body. Thanks also to the indigenous men and women who have showed me the universality of human spirituality and its groundedness in the earth and the body—and most of all to my heart-friend, the extraordinarily gifted African spiritual teacher Malidoma Patrice Somé. In addition, thanks to the many others I am happy to count as spiritual friends from the native traditions of both North and South America.

I have been exploring and studying somatic disciplines—both Western and Eastern—for my entire adult life, beginning with the work of Gerda Alexander. In subsequent years and down to the present, I have been most fortunate to have met and worked with a succession of gifted people representing Western traditions including various massage modalities, Rolfing, and Feldenkreis and, from Asia, yoga, Qi Gong, and, of course, most significantly, Tibetan yoga. All of this has been bound together by the transformative energy work of my wife, Lee, which has led me ever more deeply into my body and its inner health, wisdom, and perfection. My somatic learning over the past forty-five years has been very gradual, but it has changed my life. This book attempts to express something of how that has been so and what I have come to.

I owe a particular debt of gratitude to Tami Simon, publisher of Sounds True, and Julie Kramer, founder of Transmission: Creating Learning Lineages, who first encouraged me to begin teaching the "body work" as a discrete set of meditation instructions and who produced the intensive Meditating with the Body residential and at-home program that has, by now, led hundreds of people into the unfolding journey of somatic practice.

In immediate relation to *Touching Enlightenment*, I must thank Andrew Merz, editor at *Tricycle* magazine, who invited me to write the article upon which this book is based. Thanks also to those who read early drafts and provided some very useful perspectives and suggestions—in particular Sari Simchoni, Al Blum, John Welwood, and my wife, Lee, who read the manuscript at several crucial stages.

I offer much thanks, again, to Tami Simon, who invited me to publish *Touching Enlightenment* through Sounds True and provided a level of attention, commitment, and editorial skill beyond anything I have yet experienced in my previous publishing experience. Thanks especially to my Sounds True editors: my main editor Kelly Notaras, who worked on the manuscript with me with intelligence and energy throughout, and Andrew Merz, who did a second, most helpful editing of the mansuscript.

Preface

To be awake, to be enlightened, is to be fully and completely embodied. To be fully embodied means to be at one with who we are, in every respect, including our physical being, our emotions, and the totality of our karmic situation. It is to be entirely present to who we are and to the journey of our own becoming. It is to inhabit, completely, our relative reality, with no speck of ourselves left over, no external observer waiting for something else or something better. In this sense, this book explores what it might mean to be fully embodied and, as such, what it might mean to be an enlightened or completely realized being, for they are one and the same.

What is presented here is an expression of the lineage of the Buddha. At the same time, it also has much in common both with depth psychology and with the various somatic methods and disciplines. But there are some important differences. While this book is an expression of the buddha-dharma, at least in relation to how that is often understood in the West, it is more somatically oriented. While my approach shares with some depth psychology and with transpersonal psychology an interest in the unfolding of the human personality as an ultimately spiritual matter, again, its methods tend more toward the body. In addition, it provides a path to fully individuated being that is available to anyone, not restricted to those who can afford long and costly psychotherapeutic work. And while this book shares ground with the various somatic schools and disciplines, it places much more emphasis on the "view" stressing that, simply in order to hear and integrate what arises in working with the body—in effect what the body is saying—a clear and accurate conceptual understanding of the subtle processes involved is necessary so we have the apparatus to receive, comprehend, and give voice to our experience.

As the reader will see, I draw deeply on Tibetan yoga, the corpus of esoteric, somatically based Buddhist meditation practices known in Tibet as *tantra* or *Vajrayana*, (the "Diamond Vehicle"), traditionally carried out primarily in solitary retreat. These I learned and have practiced for nearly forty years under the great teacher, Chögyam Trungpa Rinpoche, and other lamas in the Nyingma and Kagyu lineages. Also nourishing and deepening my understanding of the body as a spiritual reality has been the exploration of several Western modalities (the Alexander technique, Rolfing), fruitful studies with several Zen teachers, and contact with the Theravadin tradition. Also of great importance has been study and practice within several of the major "earth-based spiritualities" of the indigenous world. These include the native

traditions of both North and South America and, most impact-
fully, several years of intensive work with my friend and heart
brother Malidoma Somé, the gifted African spiritual teacher. Of
particular impact in my study with Malidoma was an all-night
"earth burial," which, through its initiatory death and rebirth
process, allowed my life to crumble and then arise in a way that
established the earth and the "body work," once and for all, as the
core of my spiritual life. My experience with Malidoma also made
it absolutely clear that tantra, or the Vajrayana, is, in essence, also
an "earth-based spirituality," though one surviving—sometimes
in disguise—within a "high" religion, namely Buddhism.

Although this is not a book about practice—most of what I
talk about here needs to be learned directly and in person from
a qualified teacher—I do express many of the perspectives and
insights of Tibetan yoga. It might be asked whether it is appropriate to be reflecting in print in this way on a tradition that has, in
the past, been surrounded with much mystery and secrecy. My
response is that the secrets and mysteries of Tibetan yoga are nothing other than the secrets of the human heart and the mysteries of
human existence. As Thrangu Rinpoche once said in another context, surely it cannot be wrong to encourage people, however we
may do so, to meet their uttermost depths, their ultimate self.

The work discussed in this book comprises a general approach
to meditation and also a corpus of what I call "somatic protocols,"
meditative practices that entail approaching, entering, exploring,
and fully fathoming the body. Simply put, these practices involve
extending awareness from the surface of the body into its interior,

extending into its uttermost ground, from its larger parts down, perhaps, to a cellular level. Central to my teaching also is use of the breath, to open the body, to carry awareness to otherwise inaccessible levels of subtlety, and to unlock the inner energy and, hence, what Zen calls the "authentic life" of the practitioner that is waiting to be lived. I want to suggest that, through this process of "the body work" or "meditating with the body," one's basic experience, not just of one's body, but of one's very self, of one's relation to others and to the natural world, opens in an unending series of discoveries and transformations. Though at first it may sound simple enough to talk about "meditating with the body," in the end I think we may find that the work eventually brings us to a new understanding and, more important, a new experience of what it means to be human and what it means to be at all.

I offer this as an interim report, rather than as anything definitive. It is the account of what I and my students have been doing, experiencing, and thinking in relation to the somatic meditation and body explorations that I have been teaching to meditators and would-be meditators for many years now. If the reader notices a certain lack of finality in my presentation, I would respond that this is somewhat deliberate and, in fact, I have tried to resist the temptation to tidy my report up too much. What I am writing about here has its own life and its own reality transcending the limits of my own experience and surpassing any attempt to talk about it. In what follows, I have tried to respect that.

One cannot really write about spirituality. Of course, one *can* write about it, but in that case it is inevitably converted into a mere conceptual facsimile. In reading about spirituality today, it is all too common for people to confuse second-order concepts about spirituality with the primary, first-order experience of the spiritual life itself, to which no thought can be adequate. Thinking then becomes a substitute for the life itself, something that is both misleading and harmful. Lecturing about spirituality is better than writing about it—the human person of the lecturer—one hopes—stands closer to the actual locus of spirituality than does the printed page. Mentor talking with student one-on-one is better than lecturing—because the spiritual journey is ultimately individual. And the singular soul meditating in solitude is better than any talking, because it is only in the depths of individual experience that the spiritual can be discovered and lived in a fully real way. Let me acknowledge, then, that writing about spirituality, as I have done here, is questionable at best. A lot of things have been tried over the past century to bring Asian Buddhism—and other non-Western forms of spirituality—to the West, and many have not worked. Attempting to write about the innermost integrity of the human person, as I have done here, may be one of them. Let the reader keep this in mind and make his or her own assessment.

—Reginald A. Ray
Crestone, Colorado
July, 2007

INTRODUCTION

ONE

Touching Enlightenment with the Body

Many years ago, while engaged in research for my book *Buddhist Saints in India*,[1] I ran across a phrase— "touching enlightenment with the body"—that instantly captured my imagination and subsequently became a prolonged contemplation extending over at least two decades. Later, unsuccessfully, I tried to determine where I had first seen these words: Was it in a Pali text? Was it in a translation or commentary from the Theravadin tradition? Did I find it in a Mahayana or Vajrayana meditation manual? Or, perhaps, did I simply dream it or make it up?

Be that as it may, "touching enlightenment with the body" has defined my meditative life for a long time. What I still find so compelling is its suggestion that we are not to see enlightenment, but to *touch* it, and, further, that we are to touch it not with our thought or our mind, but with our *body*. It is interesting

---

[1] Reginald A. Ray, *Buddhist Saints in India* (New York: Oxford University Press, 1994).

that this phrase of mysterious origin has many analogues within the Theravadin tradition itself: enlightenment, for humans, is frequently presented as a somatic experience. Dogen, the founder of the Japanese Soto School of Zen, sometimes spoke of the body as the gateway to ultimate realization, and the Dzogchen teachings of Tibet affirm that enlightenment is found in the body.

What can such affirmations possibly mean? In what way can the body be thought to play such a central and fundamental role in the life of meditation? This question becomes all the more interesting and compelling in our contemporary context, when so many people are acutely feeling their own personal disembodiment and finding themselves strongly drawn to somatic practices and therapies of all kinds.

I bring to this question my own practice and teaching of meditation over the past four decades. During this period, many things have surprised me, but none more than the growing and somewhat anguished realization that simply practicing meditation doesn't necessarily yield results. Many of us, when we first encountered Buddhism, found its invitation to freedom and realization through meditation extraordinarily compelling. We jumped in with a lot of enthusiasm, rearranged life priorities around our meditation, and put much time and energy into the practice.

Engaging meditation in such a focused way, some do discover the kind of continually unfolding transformation they are looking for. But more often than not, at least in my own experience as a meditation teacher, that doesn't happen. It is true that when we practice meditation on a daily basis, we often find a definite sense of relief and peace. Over a period of a year or two, we may feel that things are moving in a positive direction in terms of reducing our internal agitation and stress, and developing openness. All of this has value.

But if we have been practicing for twenty or thirty years, it is not uncommon to find ourselves arriving in a quite different and far more troubling place. We may feel that somewhere along the line we have lost track of what we are doing and things have somehow gotten bogged down. We may find that the same old habitual patterns continue to grip us. The same kinds of disquieting emotions arise, the same interpersonal blockages and basic life confusion, the same unfulfilled and agonizing spiritual longing that led us to meditation in the first place. Was our original inspiration defective? Is there something wrong with the practices or the traditions we have been following? Is there something wrong with us? Have we misapplied the instructions, or is it perhaps that we are just not up to them?

My own sense is that there is a very real problem, though one that is not found in any of these questions and doubts, but rather in an entirely different direction. My experience suggests that our problem is very simple: we are attempting to practice meditation and to follow a spiritual path in a disembodied state, and this is inevitably doomed to failure. To put it simply, the full benefits and fruition of meditation cannot be experienced or enjoyed when we are not grounded in our bodies. The phrase "touching enlightenment with the body," then, when understood fully, doesn't just imply that we are *able* to touch enlightenment with our bodies; beyond that, it suggests that—except in and through our bodies—there actually is no other way to do so.

TWO

What Has Become
of the Buddha's Dharma?

R eaders will notice that this book represents a comprehensive description of the Buddhist meditative path, or the *dharma*—the legacy of the Buddha—viewed from the standpoint of "meditating with the body." It is even an approach to spirituality and the spiritual life altogether. Readers may occasionally ask, "Why not write just about Buddhism? Why keep the somatic metaphor at the center throughout this account? Isn't the body really just part of the dharma, somewhat tangential, helpful perhaps, but an adjunct to the main thing?"

By way of an initial response—for it will take this entire book to respond fully—in this and the next few chapters, I would like to offer some general observations. Let me begin by referring to the various Buddhist meditative traditions that have appeared most prominently among modern, especially Western, practitioners, including the various forms of Zen, Japanese, Chinese (Ch'an), and Korean (Seon); the Theravadin-inspired Vipassana movement; and, of course, Tibetan Buddhism. One cannot help but feel appreciation for each of these great traditions and for how much of them has been transmitted into the modern context.

At the same time, as a historian of religion by training, I am also aware that religions transiting from one culture to another—particularly when they have strong ambitions for wide success and manage to become perceived as "important" in their new home—tend to become rather quickly conventionalized in the minds and even the experience of their adherents, assimilating to the preexisting values and perspectives of their new cultural context. As we study the history of such transiting in the case of Buddhism, an important question inevitably arises: Is the tradition still in some kind of recognizable contact with the identity and core inspirations of what it was before transition? Or has it assimilated to such an extent that it is tending more and more simply to mirror the values of its new environment? This is a question that many people, due to our collective experience of Buddhism for the past fifty years, are currently asking in relation to Buddhism in the West and particularly in relation to Tibetan Buddhism. If there is a characteristic quality or set of qualities that defines Buddhism as a practice and a vision of human fulfillment—and I believe there is—is it surviving in any significant way in the modern context?

To cite the Tibetan case with which I am most familiar, many of the various Western Tibetan Buddhist communities have deliberately distanced themselves from the early, somewhat freewheeling but also open and intensely exploratory and creative days of the latter 1960s and 1970s, when Tarthang Tulku, Chögyam Trungpa,

Kalu Rinpoche, and other Tibetan lamas were first teaching in Europe and America. In a trend that I suspect may be a default to our Western cultural norms, now within Tibetan Buddhism in the West, there has been a pronounced institutionalization and conventionalization. This is reflected in many communities in a strong sense of appropriate behavior, authorized approaches to the tradition, bureaucratic rules and regulations, orthodox political viewpoints, and particular attitudes, ways of speaking, and even ways of thinking that are implicitly enjoined upon members within the various communities.

Surface appearances sometimes to the contrary, Western practitioners of Tibetan Buddhism often seem enclosed in a kind of self-contained, ideological bubble that mimics attitudes and values of their Tibetan teachers. Within this bubble, there is often little interest in seriously engaging those outside of their immediate religious circle, including not only the larger religious and secular worlds of their Western context, but also other varieties of Buddhism and even of Tibetan Buddhism itself. Along with this, it is also not uncommon to come across practitioners who hold intensely derogatory views of Western culture and its religious inspirations as well as abysmal estimations of the spiritual capacities of modern people, including, sadly, themselves. This leads typically to a static, unhealthy, lifelong dependence on "the Tibetan lamas" as the source of all wisdom, power, and authority. Thus, Western practitioners find themselves "infantilized" in a kind of permanent state of spiritual—and, sadly, also emotional and developmental—immaturity.

The kind of open-ended curiosity, non-dogmatic flexibility, exploration, and creativity that particularly Trungpa Rinpoche and Tarthang Tulku envisioned when they were first teaching in America, and also their vision of the full transmission of the Tibetan dharma into the West and to Westerners, has somehow not materialized except among a few teachers and their students. Generally, one sees a strong amalgamation of Vajrayana practices with Tibetan cultural forms and values promoted as "the dharma," with other approaches that may deviate from this normalized amalgamation condemned as "non-Tibetan," "disrespectful to the lamas," "ego-centric," or even "non-dharmic." My guess is that those familiar with the Western institutionalization of the Vipassana movement and of Ch'an and Zen—including the Western teachers of these traditions—may possibly be able to report parallel observations reflecting their specific histories.

All of this can lead to some very vexing questions indeed. What happened to the Buddha's instruction to his students to remain free from fixed views? Where is his injunction to avoid overly institutionalizing and bureaucratizing his teachings? Where is the freedom from social, racial, or cultural identification and bias that so clearly characterizes his teachings? Where is his promise of the potential of each person to reach a fully realized, that is, fully mature and individuated, state of being? In short, what has become of the Buddha's dharma?

THREE

The Call of the Forest

In the Buddhist past, when questions have arisen about the authenticity of institutionalized, conventionalized Buddhist organizations, politics, beliefs, and practices, practitioners have retired into the "forest" (*skti, vana, aranya)*, the classical term for the uninhabited jungles of India. The "forest" was regarded as a place beyond the reach of conventional culture and institutionalized Buddhism, a place where the atmosphere was open and unobstructed. The forest was understood as a trackless waste, a place for all those "others" standing outside of conventional culture, such as wild animals, gods and demons, and people beyond the pale. The latter included lunatics, criminals, the terminally ill, the most extreme outcasts, and, most important, those spiritual practitioners who literally walked away from the conventionalized religious systems of India seeking "the origin of all things."

Within Indian culture, the forest was considered the ideal place for spiritual practice because, in the forest, *there are no rules and there are no presiding authorities.* The only authority is the chaos of the forest itself. The only rule is what awaits there for each practitioner, uniquely, to discover. Memories of the past and plans for the future, the psychic infrastructure of civilization, do not apply: they have no bearing and they have no footing. The forest is about something else. In the forest, there is only the ever-present possibility of events, encounters, and insights that emerge directly from reality itself, pure and unpolluted by human wants, expectations, and attitudes. Uniquely in the forest, the most radical of all human journeys can take place, one which brings us into direct contact with primordial being. Generally, the greatest saints of Buddhist tradition both in India and in larger Asia were products, so to speak, of the forest; fed up with the limitations of the town-and-village culture of institutionalized Buddhism, inspired by those who had gone before, they disappeared into the forest for years, decades, or even for life.

Increasingly in this world of ours, there is no longer any geographical forest for us practitioners to retire to. It is not just that the places frequented by lonely meditators have been overrun by modern civilization—forests sold off to multinational corporations and quickly cut down, roads built through retreat areas, social, political, and economic policies that effectively destroy the possibility of forest renunciation. It is also that even the idea of the "forest" has become largely marginalized in modern Buddhism. Every manifestation of Buddhism, it now seems, must immediately demonstrate "social engagement" and "ethical impact." It is not, as we shall see below, that these are unimportant values. But now, more and more, they have become a litmus test to determine which forms of Buddhism are acceptable and which are not. Thus, the true forest is quickly disappearing, perhaps forever, from our world.

But there is a new wilderness, a new trackless waste, a new unknown and limitless territory, a new terrain of chaos, that calls us. It is a territory—I do believe—that has not been, and cannot be, colonized and domesticated by human ambition and greed, that in its true extent cannot be mapped by human logic at all. This is the "forest" of the human body. The body is now, I believe, our forest, our jungle, the "outlandish" expanse in which we are invited to let go of everything we think, allow ourselves to be stripped down to our most irreducible person, to die in every experiential sense possible and see what, if anything, remains.

In this, I am speaking not of the body we *think* we have, the body we conceptualize as part of our "me" or my self-image. Rather, I am talking about the body that we meet when we are willing to descend into it, to surrender into its darkness and its mysteries, and to explore it with our awareness. As we shall see, this true, limitless body cannot even be entered until we are willing to leave our own thinking process behind—on the surface, so to speak. It is similar to the deep-sea diver: while floating on the surface of the sea, he knows little of what lies below, but when he descends into its depths, the limitless worlds of the ocean open to him. It was of this ever unbounded and unknown body that the great siddha Saraha spoke when he said, "There is no place of pilgrimage as fabulous and as open as this body of mine, no place more worth exploring."

FOUR

The Ultimate Challenge of Buddhism

The return to the forest of the body, then, necessitates our willingness to step beyond any and all adherence to the past and its traditions. At the same time, for me and in this book, it is the ancient and venerable Buddhist tradition itself that provides guidance and many of the means to accomplish this process. It is interesting to consider how Buddhism—itself so "traditional"—points the way beyond any and all human traditions and, right now, calls us into the chaos of the naked spiritual life.

As Walpola Rahula, in *What the Buddha Taught,* pointed out, Buddhism has always maintained that spirituality is not the possession of any one tradition. In fact, particularly in the Mahayana, spirituality is not something that can in any way be separated from human life itself; in a very real sense, the spiritual journey and human existence are one and the same. In this sense, Buddhism—particularly in its Vajrayana form— may be preserving the ancient spirituality of our aboriginal ancestors and present-day hunters and gatherers for whom—in contrast to many of the "high religions"—to be human is to be spiritual; there is no separation between spirituality and life itself.

According to the teachings of buddha nature, each of us possesses, at our very root and core, a profound and irresistible longing. This is nothing other than a longing to become fully and completely who we are, to experience ourselves and our lives, fully and freely, without doubt, reservation, or holding back. This final realization of ourselves is described as all-loving and powerful—we discover ourselves as everything that we need to be and, because of that, we become completely available to the world and its suffering beings, and discover utter trust and confidence in life.

Because it is who we are, spirituality is not something that we need to seek outside of ourselves. In a way, it is not even something that we can gain or attain. Rather, it is the depth and subtlety of our person and of our experience that we gradually uncover. Religious traditions are usually necessary for providing an understanding of our inborn potential and for showing us how to realize it. But when they claim proprietary ownership of that which we seek, they betray themselves and get in our way. Such are the teachings of Buddhism, and its warning, from its earliest days down to the present.

Buddhism, in its most subtle and sophisticated expression, is not a tradition that seeks to provide answers to life's questions or to dispense "wisdom" to allay our fundamental angst. Rather, it challenges us to look beyond any and all answers that we may have found along the way, to meet ourselves in a naked, direct, and fearless fashion. Not providing answers, as Stephen Batchelor has shown us, Buddhism instead proposes a process of radical questioning. In fact, it challenges us to question everything that we think and feel about ourselves and our reality—all our most basic beliefs, all our assumptions and preconceptions, even the way we habitually see, hear, and sense the world. We must be willing to let go of everything we have believed—every answer that we have come up with down to this moment—in order to find out the final truth of who we are.

This process of questioning may initially be conception; it may involve actually seeing something that we are thinking is so and then asking ourselves, "But is this really the case?" But quickly it moves into the silent sphere of meditative practice—thoughts, feelings, perceptions arise as we meditate. Each time, we find ourselves reacting to them, labeling, judging, pigeonholing them, based on what we have previously thought or assumed. Each time, we look directly at what is arising to see what it really is, beyond our preconceptions, as it abides in the bright light of its own being. In this process, we learn so much about how we limit even our most basic experiences. In seeing how we hold back, we are able to let go, to surrender into a greater sense of openness and being. Thus the journey begins to unfold.

While religious traditions tend to some extent to be exclusive regarding our experience, the path of radical questioning is a universally inclusive process. In this, Buddhism invites us to take seriously our entire human existence, to take everything in our life "as the path." It proposes that everything that ever happens to us is part of our journey toward realization. There is finally nothing that leads us away, no possibility of true regression, no actual mistake; everything is learning, opening, and moving forward, even when the opposite seems to be the case. This leads to a kind of fundamental and boundless optimism about what human life is and why we are here, and an underlying trust that runs through life's most difficult circumstances. Perhaps it is unrealistic to expect that any tradition could ever hold such an overflowing optimism and joy in human life and its process, but Buddhism aspires to be the exception.

Buddhism also asserts that the spiritual journey is unique to each individual. Therefore, of course, it cannot be held, circumscribed, limited, or even ultimately judged by any institution, tradition, or external authority. The unique journey that lies before us does not exist in any text, external person, or religion. In fact, it does not yet exist at all, but only lies ahead of us, to be discovered literally as we go. Thus it is that the spiritual journey cannot in any way be preconceived or predetermined; it is not humanly constructed or fabricated. The journey to ourselves is truly a journey into the unknown, a setting forth onto a sea that has never before been sailed and never before been fathomed or mapped.

The role of tradition, at least according to Buddhism, is thus not to limit the search, the experience, the journey, but to open us to it—tradition here is inspiration, challenge, and provocation, and some helpful practices, not a set of answers. It provides us with a sailing vessel, but then leaves it up to us to set sail toward a truly new world, to find whatever we may find. Yes, such a prospect is daunting. Yes, it is the ultimate human challenge, the most difficult thing any person can ever do. And yet, as noted, it is something that is written within us from the very beginning, in our genes and in our bones. As we shall see, this journey is written in the body itself, in its deepest levels and its most subtle layers. In journeying into the body, we are making a voyage toward our deepest selves. When we do so, we not only find ourselves more and more drawn to the possibility of realizing who we are, we find ourselves already deeply engaged in the journey itself.

I

OUR SOMATIC
DISEMBODIMENT

FIVE

Modern Buddhism and Global Crisis

Tibetan Buddhism arrives in the West at a time of intense global crisis. In one sense, the crisis is personal. Many of us feel sick at heart and alienated from our lives. Having lost any sense of what a truly fulfilling life might look like, we search here and there for temporary fixes and satisfactions. Acquisition substitutes for the nourishment of the soul. Spectator sports stand in for the challenge and excitement of a life lived on the edge. We go on vacation to try to find experiences of freshness and surprise that we have lost in our ordinary existence. We take time off from work to escape monotonous, uninspiring drudgery that seems, on some level, so wrong to us, so inimical to our human person. We feel increasingly separate and alienated from other people, often even in our own families. We are constantly on the move, never finding roots or ground anywhere. The icon of our culture is the jetliner, where we are flying at a tremendous rate of speed but, in a very real sense, going nowhere, a million miles from the earth, inhumanly trapped in intimacy for hours with strangers as troubled as we, against a backdrop of lurking dread that maybe we are going to die. We watch television and keep busy with ultimately meaningless activities to try to avoid, anesthetize, or forget the meaninglessness of our lives. In the end, of course, it doesn't work and we only end up feeling more unfulfilled and more hopeless. We are searching, searching, searching, but somehow we never arrive. And because of the big "lie" of modern culture—of the possibility of ultimate fulfillment through entertainment, distraction, or materialism—and because of how tightly and stubbornly it is clung to—we can't really talk to anyone about what is actually going on.

On a larger and more frightful level, though, the contemporary crisis encircles the globe. We look at our world and find degradation and disaster everywhere. Traditional societies everywhere are being overwhelmed and washed away by our modern corporate, consumeristic culture. Social chaos, now in one country, now in another, greets us on a daily basis. Natural disasters unknown a generation ago are now commonplace. Each year, we find new and potentially devastating diseases springing up. War against other nations has become a way of life, at least in the contemporary United States. The earth seems to be sinking under the weight of the poisonous presence of the human race.

I see the global crisis, in its manifestations both in the West and in the rest of the world, as a crisis of disembodiment. As I see it, the root cause of impending global catastrophe is the fact that we have completely lost our connection with our bodies and our physical existence. For reasons we shall presently explore, we have come to think that our lives, our fulfillment, lie somewhere other than where we are—in some other body, some other emotional makeup, some other age group, some other personality, with some other family, some other friends, some other job, some other city, street, and house, some other world, some other life. If to be fully embodied means to be completely present and at one with who and what we are, then modern people are the most disembodied people who have ever lived, because we are not fully present to, or at one with, anything. We are always separate and separating, always trying to find what we seek somewhere else.

We disembody, and this is intimately tied up with the fact that, as modern people, we live in a culture that survives through exploitation. Wittingly or not, we are all exploiters. Is it that we lose our sense of connection with the "others" and then feel justified in turning them into objects to exploit? Or is it that we fall into a pattern of exploitation toward our world and therefore lose our sense of connection? Either way, we find ourselves in a pattern whereby every person, every thing, every situation, and every occurrence in our life, even the earth itself, is viewed as an object that could serve or thwart our interests, our ambitions, for fulfillment. Nothing has any value on its own, but only insofar as it "serves" us. Rather than being a subject with its own integrity, it falls into the category of an object to be manipulated, used, and abused, to be exploited in order to satisfy our misplaced cravings for comfort, security, self-aggrandizement, and fulfillment.

To be disembodied is to be disconnected. The objectifying mind knows things only as lifeless concepts, as mental realities with no life, worth, or integrity of their own. When we objectify something, when we turn it into an object for our use, we lose touch with its reality as a subject. It is this tendency that explains some of the more horrific achievements of Western culture: the relentless genocide against indigenous peoples and cultures worldwide over the past few centuries; the colonial death grip on many of the world's great high civilizations and the degradation of their peoples; the more recent horrors of fascism and modern warfare; and the witless consumption and destruction of the planet that so many in the "corporate world" continue to promote as "progress." These are all symptoms of a terrible disease, the illness of having lost touch with our bodies. Many modern people are born, live, and die entirely in their heads, believing that what they think is reality and that their own feeling of complete disconnection is what life is all about.

The body presents a very different way of knowing the world and of being in it. To be embodied, to be in the body, is to be in connection with everything. When we begin to inhabit the body as our primary way of sensing, feeling, and knowing the world, when our thought operates as no more than a handmaiden of that somatic way of being, then we find that we as human beings are in a state of intimate relationship and connection with all that is. To be in the body is to know our sense perceptions as opening out into a sacred world. To be in the body is to feel our connectedness with other people as subjects. It is to know the natural world, the earth and the ocean, the rivers and mountains, as our relatives, others with whom we are in deep relation. It is to appreciate the other forms of being also as living, breathing, knowing subjects. Somehow the body's knowledge is so much more subtle, but also so much more convincing and satisfying than knowledge that is purely conceptual. Anthropology, paleontology, and other disciplines of the past tell us that this kind of primary knowing in and through the body is the ancient human way, characteristic of human life back through its millions of years of development on this planet.

We can make an important distinction between the "feel" of a life lived strictly in the head, wherein we take the world as a conceptual reality, and that of a life lived in and through the body as our primary way of knowing. To approach the world by objectifying it, to reside mainly in the head, is to put ourselves in a position of domination, mastery, and control. We domesticate the world by filtering it through our concepts, and this enables us to own and possess it, to make it subservient to our agendas and wants.

To fully inhabit our bodies, by contrast, is to discover our embeddedness in the world. We are not above the world at all, in a position of domination and control, but are embedded within it, interdependent with other people, animals, and the natural world itself. Our experience of embeddedness is much more perceptually and emotionally rich—we realize that we are existing alongside of and in connection with a multitude of other subjects, some of whom are human like ourselves, some of whom are animals or trees, some of whom are mountains, rivers, or stars. To be "with" in this way is so much more present to and respectful of creation, of what is, than the typical modern way of being "over" or "on."

Buddhism arrives in the West with much promise to address our modern disembodiment and our global crisis. Held within the texts and the traditional practices especially of Tibetan Buddhism is a clear and realistic path back toward embodiment. The tradition shows us how to burn through the dehumanizing, objectifying tendency of human thinking, so rampant today, and how to recover a life that is indeed open to the knowledge of reality that arises in and through the body, wherein we see others as subjects, as coinhabitants of this world, as "all our relations," as the Lakota Sioux say.

While the potential of Buddhism to address our modern disembodiment is powerful, it is also true, as we shall see, that modern Buddhism has not taken full advantage of this most important aspect of the tradition. Why has it fallen short of its potential to bring us back into full embodiment and, thereby, to deeply address and heal our personal and global crisis? To repeat: Modern Buddhism has, in my opinion, been so worried not just about its own survival in the modern world, but also about its social and economic success, that it has unwittingly overassimilated to modern Western corporate, consumeristic values. It is in danger of becoming another modern, organized religion. While entanglement with its surrounding political and economic cultural context is certainly not new for Buddhism, in the modern case, this entanglement may be far more lethal to Buddhist spirituality than in the past, because to succeed in the modern marketplace, as Buddhism is trying to do, there is an almost irresistible temptation to become one of the oppressors, one of the exploiters, one of the utterly disembodied.

SIX

Our Physical Divestment

T hose of us who live in the modern world, then, generally exist in a state of extreme disembodiment. Most of
us spend our lives with very little actual awareness of
our bodies. In some cases, we seem to feel and act as if we were
divested of our bodies entirely. It is not that we don't *think* we
have a body. In fact, many people spend a great deal of their time
thinking about their bodies, in a self-congratulatory, apprehensive,
self-deprecating, or even self-destructive way. However, even when
we are supposedly attending to our bodies, we are usually still in
our heads. We are not in contact with our actual bodies. We have
thoughts about our body, but very little direct experience of our
body itself. In this way, in relation to the body, we modern people
are narcissistic: we are so enamored of our ideas about the body,
our concepts of it and designs on it, that we have little awareness
of the body or relationship to the body as an actual reality in our
lives, independent of what we think.

There is no more telling example of our modern disembodiment than the way in which we use, misuse, and exploit our bodies simply as part of our modern lifestyle. If our idea is to be socially and sexually attractive, we diet, work out, make and dress ourselves up, continually seeking ways to appear physically more and more appealing. If we want to succeed athletically, we typically overtrain, pushing our bodies beyond all natural limits, using chemicals to artificially enhance results and to block our awareness of injury and physical pain. If our ambitions are tied to work, we may put in sixteen or eighteen hours a day over decades, punishing our bodies mercilessly, using stimulants to keep our energy up and antidepressants to avoid impending letdowns. If socializing and party "highs" are important to us, we may take "recreational" drugs, often to the point of disrupting and permanently damaging our brain chemistry. Or, if our goal is to avoid genuine human contact and commitment, we may engage in compulsive, random sexuality to distract ourselves from our own loneliness or spend our free time "vegging out" in front of the TV. In all these cases, the body is the vehicle and the body is the victim.

If we fear physical pain or find any level of it unacceptable, we may regularly turn to over-the-counter painkillers or prescriptions. If we feel unwilling to tolerate emotional pain, always somatically located, we may smoke, drink heavily, imbibe marijuana or other similar illegal substances, or resort to our psychiatrist. If we find ourselves with seemingly irresolvable psychological issues, we may make psychiatric medications a routine part of our daily lives over a period of years or even a lifetime.

Again, to handle emotional suffering, we may follow the path of anorexia, starving ourselves to death, or bulimia, making ourselves disfigured, anemic, and eventually nonfunctional. In all these cases, we are aggressively interfering with the body's processes and compromising its attempts to regain its own internal balance and heal itself. In all these cases, the body has become an object, a slave to what we want.

These ways of relating to our bodies may yield some kind of satisfying results in the short term—sometimes the very short term—but in the long term, they hardly lead to the freedom from suffering and the happiness we are seeking. Because all these behaviors are, to one extent or another, exploiting and abusing the body, they lead us eventually to increased physical distress, injury, disease, or chronic disability, or to deep and irresolvable emotional confusion, pain, and anguish. But, strangely, often the deeper our misuse of our bodies and the more intense our resultant suffering, the harder we push against the body, increasing our abusive behavior.

So deep is our modern disembodiment, then, that many of us have no trust in the body whatsoever and content ourselves with disregarding it on every occasion and at every possible level. In all of this, not surprisingly, there is rarely any sense that the body, on its own and from its own side, might have something to offer us; that the body might, in some sense, be more intelligent than our conscious self or ego; or that the body might have its own designs from which—if understood—we might stand to benefit a very great deal.

SEVEN

Our Emotional Disconnection

One facet of our disembodiment mentioned in the previous chapter deserves further comment because it is often so problematic to modern people, namely our increasing inability to experience our own emotional life with any degree of openness, trust, or confidence. Emotions are, at root, a somatic experience: they arise out of the darkness of the body, they are felt intensely in the body, and they call us—sometimes with great insistence and even grisly intensity—back into the body. To be fully embodied involves an unconditional presence to our emotional life, not separating and not distancing ourselves by retreating into our heads into judgments, recriminations, or self-loathing. At the same time, if, as suggested above, we are continually attempting to move away from the body and its life, if we are seeking greater and greater disembodiment, then our emotions—which are one of the primary expressions of the body—are going to present a terrible threat to us.

We live in a world that is becoming more and more structured, where, for many people, the day is tightly scheduled from morning until night with work, family obligations, prearranged phone calls (to which we often assign specific time limits), and entertainment, and where even intimate time with families or partners has to be put on the timetable for it to have any likelihood of happening. In the work environment, for example, each day is often exhaustively programmed and filled with detailed expectations before—and sometimes long before—it arrives. Driving time is an opportunity for important phone calls and even checking email; and, especially in business, cell phones are not infrequently kept on the bedside table, and 4:00 a.m. phone calls with coworkers about the next day's activities are not so unusual.

All the planning that goes into managing our lives is the function of the reasoning, managerial mind. Our planning is often so tight that there is literally no room for the unanticipated or unexpected. Often we judge the success or failure of our day in accordance with whether we have managed to accomplish everything on our "to do" list. In fact, those who are best able to move through their days without being derailed by the unexpected are regarded as the most reliable, efficient, and "successful" among us.

Emotions, however, do not follow any predetermined timetable. They are not predictable, and they operate beyond the mechanisms of our control. Many find emotions quite distressing and frightening precisely because they arise within us, sometimes powerfully affecting us, and yet seem to have a life of their own. As psychotherapist, teacher, and author John Welwood observes, "[Emotions] are our most common experience of being taken over by forces seemingly beyond our control. Usually, we regard them as a threat, imagining that if we really let ourselves feel our anger or depression, they would totally overwhelm us. Maybe we would be unable to function or go berserk."[1]

Why do so many modern Western people feel uneasy in the face of strong emotion? Is it because our highly structured and rationalized mode of existence simply requires that we ignore the unpredictable and potentially disruptive and destabilizing energy of emotion? Or has our highly routinized way of life itself developed as a fear response to emotions and to their inherent power and compelling nature, a kind of unconscious defense mechanism against their non-scripted reality?

An argument can be made for each of these two possibilities. Obviously, given our modern lifestyle, it is clear that the unpredictability and overpowering force of emotions are potential threats to the necessary routines of the kinds of lives we live. On the other hand, many trends in Western culture express a fundamental distrust of emotions that goes back a long way. Again, as Welwood points out, "From Plato on, the 'passions' have been viewed as our 'lower nature.'"[2] And popular Christianity has tended to view the emotions and the body from which they arise as "the devil's domain," as something uncontrollable, frightening, and potentially threatening to the strict moral requirements of the religious life.

---

[1] John Welwood, *Toward a Psychology of Awakening* (Boston: Shambhala, 2002),182.
[2] Ibid.

Be that as it may, many of the major realities and trends of modern life may be seen as attempts to override emotions and even eliminate them from human experience. The frenetic speed and "busyness" of modern culture—its reliance on work habits where there is literally no unstructured time as well as on entertainment by distraction, such as TV, videos, sports events, compulsive shopping, and so on—can be seen as attempts to keep emotions at a distance or even negate them completely. In a similar vein, the vast array of psychiatric medications seem designed to limit and control the emotional states that people go through, reflecting a medical environment in which any strong emotion is likely to be viewed as pathological and in need of "treatment."

Whatever the reasons, it is clear that many modern people view raw emotions with a mixture of distrust, anxiety, fear, and even loathing. Because emotions are known in and through the body, our strongly negative attitude toward them drives us further and further away from our bodies. And, leaving our bodies further and further behind, we become even more distrustful of our feeling life, which always seeks to pull us back into our embodiment. It is a vicious cycle, then, in which our fear of emotions and our physical disembodiment fuel, reinforce, and exacerbate one another.

In the following chapters, we shall consider the way in which reclaiming our human embodiment enables us to reconnect with our emotions and reenter the warmth, richness, and subtlety of a full emotional life that many of us thought we had lost forever.

EIGHT

Some Historical Roots of Our Modern Disembodiment

O ur modern disembodiment, reflected in so much of our lives and our contemporary society, raises an all-important question. What might be the ultimate source of our alienation from the body? It is not uncommon for modern people to trace our physical disconnection back to the Christian heritage and to see its negative attitudes toward the body, the emotions, and sexuality as a primary cause. My own sense, and that of many historical anthropologists, historians of religion, paleontologists, human ecologists, ethnobiologists, and historians of culture, is that the roots of our disembodiment are far older and more general, and that Christian deprecations of the body are symptoms rather than the causes of our alienation.

The appearance of agriculture some ten millennia ago marked a cataclysmic shift in how our species lived and experienced existence. Prior to that time, from the time our primate forebears descended from trees and began walking upright some five million years ago, our ancestors followed a lifestyle defined initially by foraging and scavenging, subsequently developing what we understand as a hunting-and-gathering way. The inception of agriculture and its gradual growth to dominance marked the slow but steady erosion of hunting and gathering as our primary means of livelihood. This had an enormous impact on the disembodiment of our species—the full effects of which we are seeing only today.

From contemporary anthropological studies, we know that the sense of self of hunter-gatherers is fully embedded in the more bodily cognitive functions, including feeling and the sense perceptions, and that it is highly relational and interactive with the natural world. Hunter-gatherers roam the landscape on an annual cycle, reading with their feeling, senses, and intuition the ever-changing patterns of animals and vegetation, and the "inanimate" worlds of landscape, water, and weather. Through myth and ritual, they find connection, communion, and even identification with the concrete, physical world given to sensation, feeling, and intuition—a world experienced as filled with living energies, intelligence, and presence. Conceptual thinking plays an important role, but it is very much in balance with the more somatic functions, and also serves them—thinking is embedded in and is in service to the interpersonal and natural worlds accessed through sensation and feeling.

The kinds of knowing predominant among hunter-gatherers were clearly a matter of survival. As Jungian psychoanalyst Esther Harding has pointed out, if you were walking through the jungle and didn't see the poisonous snake lying under the leaves on the path in front of you or sense the danger of a boa constrictor about to drop out of the tree above, you didn't live very long. The more you were rooted in your senses, your subtle feelings, and your intuitions, the more chance you had to survive. Those without such sensitivity and awareness were simply factored out of the genetic pool.

But these kinds of knowing were not only a matter of survival; to be in dialogue with a world filled with intelligent, powerful presences—including not only the animal and vegetal worlds, but rivers, lakes, mountains, valleys, and the earth and sky themselves—was to discover one's full humanity. Hence the importance of initiation ceremonies among hunting-and-gathering peoples, in which the entry into adulthood was marked by rituals introducing the cosmos as a living reality with which one needed to be in appropriate communication and within which one found the meaning of one's life.

The birth of agriculture marked a cataclysmic shift away from the hunting-and-gathering way. So great and, in some ways, so negative was its eventual impact on our species that Paul Shepard, a founder of human ecology, calls it "the single most catastrophic event ever to befall the human race."[1] Agriculture led to an increasing separation of human and world and, eventually, to our present disconnection and our personal, social, and ecological disembodiment. Agriculture gave rise to ownership of land, ever-increasing

---

[1]   Michael Thoms, New Dimensions, radio interview.

population growth, accumulation and unequal distribution of wealth, slavery, social hierarchies, armies, warfare, and patterns of physical disease and social dislocation previously unknown, all of which we now understand as coterminous with "civilization." And it led to the increasing destruction of our earthly habitat, the effects of which we are seeing today. Most important in the present context, agriculture set in motion the development of a self-concept and way of relating to the body very different from that characteristic of hunter-gatherers.

The agricultural person, in contrast to the hunter-gatherer, survives through the continual attempt to control the natural world. This continual effort at control, particularly as it has developed down to modern times, has involved the gradual loss of nature as an independent, freestanding "other" with whom one must be in intimate and respectful dialogue. The farmer not only has to control the natural world, but also all his property—which, at least for the elites, came increasingly to include wives and children, more and more people, wealth, and territory. While the senses, feeling, and intuition all have their roles to play for the agricultural person, the primary function through which this kind of management is achieved is the thinking function—conceptualizing what needs to be controlled, making plans, convincing others to align themselves with projects, evaluating what worked and didn't work, keeping track of assets, and so on. You can't really grow crops in a sustainable way without a lot of thinking and planning.

It is often said that feeling unites while thinking separates. We can perhaps go further. Sensation brings us into intimate contact with the world around us; intuition opens us to our context in an instantaneous, non-thinking way; feeling reveals our deep connections with others—human, animal, and vegetal. These functions are immediate, often subtle, and largely non-conceptual; and they are essentially somatic, experienced in and through the body.

Thinking, as we have already seen, tends toward disembodiment: it separates in that it involves a disengaged stance whereby—based on past experience—we abstract from the living and invaluable other, think him as an object, ignore him as an independent actor, conceptualize him, and consider how to manage our relation with him. It is cool, apart, and noncommittal—in other words, disembodied. Thinking, when it stands as the primary or sole function of interrelation with the other, leads us, in the words of philosopher Martin Buber, into an "I-it" rather than an "I-thou" relationship. The most important human cognitive function since the invention of agriculture, thinking has come to be more and more predominant, while the other functions or ways of knowing have, in many modern people, atrophied.

This is not to say that hunter-gatherers did not attempt to control the conditions of their lives or that agricultural people did not engage in dialogue with their world. Rather, the invention of agriculture brought with it a shift in emphasis away from a modality characterized primarily by dialogue and a balance of cognitive functions. In agricultural times, the managerial function of thinking became more and more desired, from a survival standpoint. The agricultural lifestyle has provided a way for the human desire for security, comfort, control, and predictability—in short, for control of our environment—to fulfill itself to greater and greater degrees and to a level completely unimaginable in pre-agricultural times.

To say this is not to idealize the hunting-and-gathering way. We know from modern anthropological studies that this way of life, while open, flexible, and adaptive, was also uncertain and could be painful and difficult on a physical level—serious physical injuries from the hunt, hunger from time to time, the ever-present reality of premature death when the small nomadic communities could not support the very young, the frail, and the old.

In modern times, urban people have increasingly succeeded in creating an alternate reality: we spend our time in buildings—homes and workplaces—that shield and separate us from direct contact with the elements; we reside in cities, often at great remove from the natural world, that embody our collective human ideas and projects; we often have little direct relation to our food sources; and, mesmerized by the prospect of complete control over our lives, we regard even our bodies, as mentioned, as an object to be managed in the service of our ambitions.

This move from the body to the head in terms of primary survival function is clear today—in contemporary societies, the vast majority of us get ahead not through the acuity of our sense perceptions, the subtlety of our feeling, or the farseeing-ness of our intuition (which, in modern contexts, are often seen as liabilities), but rather through a highly differentiated, conceptual type of intelligence. We do well in this modern world if we are able to function as disembodied brains—"brains on a stick," in philosopher Ken Wilber's evocative phrase—largely disregarding emotions, the sensory world, and the vast spaces opened up by intuition.

All of this is understandable: In a corporate culture, emotions must be factored out as much as possible because they don't run according to the time clock. Sense perceptions must be regarded as distractions. And intuition, which tends to bypass conceptual reasoning to arrive at its knowledge, to uniquely see into the future and to often call into question the status quo, must be written off as "wacky." All these "other" ways of knowing are generally thought to be insufficiently "bottom-line oriented" and tangential to the "real concerns" of corporate culture. All these ways of knowing are—or so it is often thought—"unproductive." Thus we arrive at the curious state of affairs in which the more disembodied we are, the more likely we are to survive and to gain social approval, success, and material wealth in our modern world.

How fundamental or inevitable is our modern disembodiment? Is it something that can be addressed by us modern people with any realistic hope of remediation? When we reflect that our disconnection and alienation from our bodies reaches back beyond the origins of Christianity to the beginnings of settled agriculture itself, we might be inclined toward a pessimistic conclusion. Let me suggest an alternative view.

Consider that the seemingly long period of time since the inception of settled agriculture has little significance from an evolutionary standpoint. It represents a miniscule fraction of our history as a species, which has been in recognizable evolution for five million years. If we take as a benchmark the inception of stone tools over two and a half million years ago, the period of time since the discovery of agriculture represents .04 percent of our evolutionary history. From an evolutionary standpoint, this is a very small period of time, a tiny fraction of the blink of the evolutionary eye. While our human genome has continued to evolve throughout this long period, in its most fundamental aspects, it remains the same. From an evolutionary perspective, then, we modern people are genetically and biologically still the hunter-gatherers we were when agriculture arose, and the full embodiment of our essential being remains as incumbent on us as on any of our forebears. Because our basic makeup is so little different from theirs, full embodiment, while obscured in modern people, is entirely accessible and recoverable. In our genes and in our cells, it is ultimately who we are.

It is my belief that we modern people can arrive at the full embodiment that has always been a possibility for our species. The impact and the implications of such a recovery are nothing less than revolutionary. For to recover our original or primary body as our own involves experiencing the totality of oneself, without judgment; living with a directness that is not filtered or distorted by the thinking mind; rediscovering ourselves within the network of relations with others; coming to awareness again of the primordiality of the natural world as a subject; and, perhaps most surprising, beginning to sense and see what has been called the "unseen world," the "other world," the world of "others" who, while not flesh and blood, are nevertheless living presences around us and with us, to inspire, guide, and protect. Recovering our basic, inborn body has, then, profound implications for healing the self, mending our broken relationships, restoring a healthy relationship to our world, seen and unseen, and healing the planet. All that we need is a method to enable us to reclaim our original body, the body that is our most basic being at this moment, but that we cannot clearly feel or see. That method is offered to us in the body work introduced in this book, the somatic practices of Buddhist meditation.

NINE

Meditating without the Body

The Buddha lived in northeast India at a time of increasing agriculturalization, urbanization, and political centralization. Accompanying these changes, people were already becoming increasingly disembodied and were coming to view spirituality as a process of overcoming, dominating, and subduing "nature" and the human body. The Buddha saw himself as turning back to an earlier mode of being, declaring, "I follow the ancient way." He left aside the compelling social changes around him and retired to the jungle, which—as mentioned—was thought of as the nonhuman locale where the primordial might be discovered. When the Buddha affirmed the importance of nourishing and caring for his body as essential to his spiritual development, and when he touched the larger body of the earth as evidence of the legitimacy of his path, he separated himself decisively from the increasing disembodiment sought by so many spiritual teachers and traditions of his day, including his own previous meditation masters and the dominant Samkhya-Yoga system. Having renounced spiritual paths that involved the renunciation of the body and their goal of separation from "the material," the Buddha discovered and followed the way back to full embodiment.

The method that the Buddha discovered was meditation, but, at least according to the tradition, it was unlike any other kind of meditation being taught in his day. The meditation taught by the Buddha and practiced in subsequent Buddhist history is deeply somatic—fully grounded in sensations, sensory experience, feeling, emotions, and so on. Even thoughts are related to as somatic—as bursts of energy experienced in the body, rather than nonphysical phenomena that disconnect us from our soma. In its most ancient form, Buddhist meditation is a technique for letting go of the objectifying tendency of thought and entering deeply and fully into communion with our embodied nature. And hence it leads to "touching enlightenment with the body" or to "touching enlightenment in and through the body."

It is quite surprising, then, that among many of us modern people, the somatic teachings of Buddhism have not crossed the cultural divide that separates Asia and the West. This lack of transmission may be due to our own extremely disembodied state, in which we are literally unable to hear the call to embodiment present within traditional Buddhist practice. It may also be traceable to the fact that our Asian teachers, who come from very different and much more physically grounded cultural situations, do not always understand the full extent of our own somatic alienation or the tremendous limitations it imposes on our ability to meditate and pursue the path. Perhaps again, this lack of transmission is partly due to the classical Buddhist texts, which, at least as we tend to read them, do not always provide a clear, direct, and effective remedy to our disconnected situation either.

Whatever the reasons may be, in the West, meditation is often practiced as a kind of conceptual exercise, a mental gymnastic. We often approach it as a way to fulfill yet another agenda or project—that of attempting to become "spiritual," according to whatever we happen to think that is. We may try to use meditation to become peaceful, less confused, sharper and more clear, more "sane," more effective in our lives, even more conceptually adroit. The problem with this is that we are, once again, attempting to be managers, to supersede what is given, to control the "other." In this case, the "other" is ourselves, our bodies, and our own experience. Ultimately, in our meditation practice, it is often our own somatic experience of reality that we are trying to override in the attempt to fulfill, once again, our ego aim.

In a Western context, this might not sound like a bad thing. We talk about people taking responsibility for themselves: we have to have a life, have boundaries, proceed with our plans, become an adult, and so on. But if that is all that there is, then what often ends up happening on the meditation cushion is this: We have an ideal of what meditation is or should be, what we like about meditation, which might be some experience that we've had somewhere along the line. We then end up using our meditation as a way to recreate that particular, desired state of mind.

Rather than being open to whatever needs to arise right now, we are basically trying to recreate the past, instead of stepping out of it, toward the future. To put the matter in bald terms, we end up using meditation as a method to perpetuate and, in many cases, increase our disembodiment, to separate ourselves even further from the call and the imperatives of our actual lives.

This is what John Welwood calls "spiritual bypassing": meditation becomes a way to perpetuate self-conscious agendas and avoid impending, perhaps painful or fearful, developmental tasks—always arising from the darkness of our bodies—that are nevertheless necessary for any significant spiritual growth. And this is what Trungpa Rinpoche called "spiritual materialism," using spiritual practice to reinforce existing, neurotic ego strategies for sealing ourselves off from our actual lives in the pursuit of survival, comfort, and security. When we use meditation in such a way, we aren't really going anywhere, just perpetuating and reinforcing the problems we already have. No wonder when we practice like this over a period of decades, we can end up feeling that nothing fundamental is really happening, because it isn't.

Consider, for example, the meditation technique that is so central in the texts and so often given to modern meditators: pay attention to the breath at the tip of the nose, feeling the in-breath and the out-breath. For a fully embodied person, this is an effective technique by which the practitioner can connect more deeply with the body and progressively open up his or her awareness. But the practice has a very different feel for someone who is somatically disconnected and habitually already abides almost entirely in his or her head. For such a person, using a technique that requires attention on the nose can easily reinforce the tendency to remain entirely invested in the head and continue to be unaware of the body. If we are already out of touch with our body, its sensations, its feeling, and its life, carrying out a practice that involves attending to the breath at the nostrils often continues and even strengthens our disconnection.

Those of us meditating in such a way are locked into a cycle and genuinely trapped in a dysfunctional way of practicing. The more we analyze the situation, the more trapped we feel; the harder we work at our practice, the more we feel the whole thing closing in on us. We feel desperate, that we have to get out, but we can't see how to do it. As in this previous example, the practices that we are using often just don't provide the right key. If we don't abandon the practice entirely, which is an all-too-common result these days, we know for certain that we need help; we need outside intervention. But where the help will come from is a big question.

I would like to suggest that the help we are looking for may very well come from incorporating principles of the Tibetan yoga tradition into Western Buddhist practice. Though complex, esoteric, and often held in secrecy in their original context, I believe their basic principles and some of the more central practices can be taught to Western practitioners, even at a beginning level, with immediate and strongly positive results. Interestingly, very advanced practitioners can benefit from the same perspectives and practices as much or more. These practices, I believe, offer the best chance available for us modern people to reverse our disembodiment in a deep, thorough, and lasting way. The next chapter provides a brief summary of the somatic view and methodology of Tibetan yoga and the challenge it provides to our disembodied conceptions of meditation and the spiritual life.

TEN

The Somatic Challenge of Tibetan Yoga

The term "Tibetan yoga" refers to advanced, esoteric, somatic Vajrayana meditation practices traditionally carried out by men and women hermits spending much or all of their time in seclusion, in solitary retreat. Although this tradition is preserved within Buddhism, an organized, institutionalized (and thus an agricultural) religion, its roots and its essence are far older. In my Ph.D. study at the University of Chicago, my dissertation advisor, the internationally renowned scholar Mircea Eliade, contended that the Vajrayana, though nominally "Buddhist," in fact represents a "survival" of the aboriginal spirituality of humankind, in other words, the pre-agricultural, paleolithic religious orientation of our forebears of perhaps a million years. It is quite interesting that Chögyam Trungpa in his Shambhala teachings said more or less the same thing: there is within each person, irrespective of his or her historical period, culture, tradition, or orientation, an inherent human spirituality that lies at the very heart of the human being as such. My own practice of Tibetan yoga (Vajrayana)—carried out in dialogue with the study of earth-based spiritualities, as mentioned—has confirmed this fact on an experiential and practical level.

While the actual practice of Tibetan yoga in its more esoteric aspects requires much preparation, it is nevertheless important in the present context for two reasons. First, it presents a thorough challenge to any and all notions that meditation can be practiced in a disembodied state or in any kind of separation from the body. In fact, Tibetan yoga holds the opposite point of view: *to attain realization, we have to practice in such a way that we become fully and completely embodied.* This is why, in Tibetan yoga, *virtually every practice is aimed at recovering the body.* This book and the somatic practices it describes are specific responses to Tibetan yoga and especially to its viewpoint that realization is the result of greater and greater embodiment. Second, Tibetan yoga is important in this context also because it provides me with many of the specific insights, gates of entry into the body, and methods for exploring the body that make up the body work on which this book is based. For these reasons, it may be useful to provide a brief summary of some of the primary perspectives and practices that characterize this ancient, esoteric, "primordial" tradition upon which I am drawing here.

The journey that one makes through the practice of Tibetan yoga unfolds according to a series of stages. In the first, one learns how to identify and abandon the myriad body concepts that we all carry around. In other words, each one of us has a package of mental images of our own body that make up what we think our body is. The first step on the Tibetan yoga path is to progressively strip away everything we *think* about what our body is. Eventually, we arrive at a point where we have no mental picture left and we actually *know nothing* of what or how the body may be. Now we are ready to take a look and see what our body actually is, as revealed to the eye of direct experience.

In the second phase, when we turn our awareness to the body to see what it is, we notice various things occurring. There are moments of what we might call sensation: intensities of warmth and coolness, hot and cold; flashes of energy; strands of moods that flow gracefully through; upsurges of energy, pleasure, and pain; waves of light and chasms of darkness; and so on. Two things are particularly interesting about what we notice when we look within the body. First, every experience is, in some very real sense, unique. There is no naming it; no idea or concept seems adequate. Second, there is nothing permanent in our experience of the body: everything is ever-changing and fleeting.

In the third phase, we learn how to abide for longer and longer periods of time within the fundamental emptiness of the body (the fact that we have no idea what it is) and the continual patterns of energy that arise within the body (phase two). Rather than touch these experiences of the body and then quickly (and anxiously) exit back into our conscious thinking process as a way of escape, we simply learn to abide in the body.

In phase four, we learn to "read" the manifestations of the body, to understand in a nonverbal way the energy that is occurring within us. And, in the fifth phase, we discover within what we see as imperatives to action. In other words, we discover that the life that we need to live is actually being born, moment by moment, within the emptiness of the body (phase one), as the energy that arises (phase two), which we can abide with (phase three) and eventually learn to understand (phase four). In this way, the spontaneous life of the body becomes the source of our actions and engagements in the world. These are, according to Tibetan yoga, nothing less than expressions of the great compassion of a realized person.

At each stage, we find ourselves continually running up against what we have been thinking about our body and being challenged to let go of our ideas in order to see more nakedly and directly, in order to go deeper. As we let go, we are gradually dismantling all the presuppositions and conceptual overlays that are getting in between us and our full, complete, and naked experience of our body.

These stages all involve attending more and more closely to our body, feeling into it, sensing and discovering what it is really like. As we progress, we are becoming more and more identified with our actual body, the body we meet in our actual experience; we are becoming more embodied. The more we progress along this path of profound embodiment, the more we realize that our actual experience of our body is, in fact, the experience of enlightenment. As we become more and more embodied, we find ourselves approaching the awakened state.[1]

---

1   In Tibetan yoga, this process takes us through many stages and levels of increasing

It is sometimes said that the intent of the Vajrayana is to redeem matter, redeem the most gross, physical, ordinary, down-to-earth aspects of our human situation. It might be better to say that the Vajrayana invites us to explore what our bodies, our physical existence, and the earth are really and truly like, when we look directly at them and see them nakedly, with the eye of non-conceptual wisdom. When we do so, it is proposed—as we may read, for example, in the classic Samdhinirmocana Sutra—that we will see that every aspect of our world, our life, and ourselves is and always has been a free, liberated, and completely pure expression of enlightenment. In this sense, we have not redeemed matter, but we have redeemed ourselves from the terrible error of thinking that matter is ultimately not spiritual, that somehow realization is found somewhere else.

The challenge of Tibetan yoga to modern practitioners of meditation is thus simple. Consider the possibility that true spirituality is not a matter of distancing ourselves from our bodies, from all the aspects of our physical life, or from the earth itself. Consider the possibility that our true and ultimate realization actually lies in and through matter, in and through the body, in and through the earth, and that, *to discover, to attain our own enlightenment, we simply have to allow ourselves to be fully and completely embodied.*

---

realization. Toward the end, so we are told, we make the astounding discovery that even the appearance of physicality that our body has for other people is itself dependent on our own incomplete embodiment, our inability to identify fully with our body's ultimate experiential truth. When we do finally let go of any and all ideas of our body as something that is solid and conceptually identifiable, so it is said, our body simply dissolves into light, the famed "rainbow body" described in Dzogchen. Many are the accounts of reliable witnesses reporting, even in modern times, their experiences of advanced practitioners who took this final step on the journey and whose bodies dissolved into the empty, clear radiance of a rainbow.

II
ENGAGING THE PROCESS:
MEDITATING WITH
THE BODY

ELEVEN

The Call to Return

For some of us meditators, our disembodiment reaches excruciatingly painful and completely unacceptable proportions. It is almost as if our practice itself and the sensitivity it develops have brought us to a level of awareness in relation to our somatic situation that is unbearable. We feel out of touch with our body, our emotions, our sense perceptions, even the basic experience of being alive. Perhaps this awareness has been slowly growing over many years; perhaps it happens upon us one day, rather abruptly. We realize that we are not really living our life, not really going through our relationships and our experiences in anything but a numb and mechanical way. Although everything may seem fine with us from the outside, inwardly these experiences, just in and of themselves, plunge us into the midst of a profound personal crisis. We really feel lost. Perhaps without even knowing exactly what is wrong, we begin looking for ways back into our body, our world, and our life. The sense of personal crisis is, itself, the call of the body to return, our inspiration to try to find a way to recover our embodiment.

For others of us, the body calls us back through the fortuitous intervention of an external event or circumstance: injury, illness, extreme fatigue, impending old age, sometimes emotions, feelings, anxiety, anguish, or dread that we don't understand and can't handle. Depression is one of the most powerful ways the body calls us back—a terrible darkness, an unbearable hopelessness and despair that settles over us, wherein we are so pulled down that we barely have the energy to think a single thought, let alone rise to do anything or engage anyone.

Either way, we hear the call of the body and feel an inexorable pull toward it. It is pulling us down, one way or the other, sometimes with a terrifying crash. After a period that perhaps feels like death, which can go on for years, something in us, some new life, begins to stir.

For those of us with knowledge of meditation, it is natural that we eventually attempt to see what or how meditation may bear on the intensely somatic call that we are hearing. Whether we are injured or ill, encountering debilitating psychological states of mind, or despairing over a life that is slipping by us, it is likely that we will initially be extremely tentative in bringing meditation to our situation. Perhaps we will take a few moments now and then to let our mind relax, rest, and open to our feelings and our situation. If we do, we may find that there is some kind of shift— not necessarily in the content of what we are experiencing, but in our relationship toward it.

Generally, in experiences such as those described above, there is an underlying feeling of "problem," an ongoing anxiety, and a resistance toward what is happening. When we open our minds in meditation, though, we suddenly find our "problem" becomes the focus of our meditation. Without even thinking about it, we find our body's call to be the subject of our attention. Our meditation is naturally turned toward the body. Without even knowing, we are receiving our first lessons in "meditating with the body."

As we turn our meditation toward the body, as we open our awareness to it, we will find that the frozen-up quality around our physical or psychological problem, or our general feeling of disconnection, suddenly has more space; moreover, it begins to communicate itself to us in a way that could only be described as "active." At this point, we are likely to find ourselves receiving healing and transformative information that we had not previously noticed or even thought possible. This can be extraordinarily subtle at first, perhaps just barely sensed. But at some point, we perceive that something new is coming toward us. We begin to gain increasing clarity, recognizing that our debilitation, when viewed from the point of meditation, is a learning situation for us with great possibilities. We sense that our meditation has become an invitation for the body to begin showing us things. At this point, we are "meditating with the body."

Thus it is that we find that we have a partner on the spiritual path that we didn't know about—our own body. In our meditation and in our surrounding lives, the body becomes a teacher, one that does not communicate in words but tends to speak out of the shadows through sensations, feelings, images, and somatic memories. No longer able to force the body to adapt to our conscious ideas and intentions, we find that we have to begin to learn the language that the body itself naturally speaks. Having thought we knew what was going on, we discover, over and over, that we have completely missed the point. And, having supposed that we were completely confused, we come to see that we have understood something far more profound and far-reaching that anything we could have thought. It is all very puzzling, but, with the body as our guide, we begin to feel, perhaps for the first time in our lives, that with our body, we are in the presence of a force and intelligence that is filled with wisdom, that is loving, flawlessly reliable, and, strange to say, worthy of our deepest devotion.

TWELVE

How Do We Proceed?

As we engage our somatic crisis, whatever it may be, we realize that embodied meditation is a very different and far more fruitful way to practice than the disembodied path we had been following. But this leaves us wondering just how to carry out our meditation in an embodied manner and inhabit our body in practice. Most fundamentally, meditating with the body involves paying attention to the body in a direct and non-conceptual way. This calls for very focused work and requires regularity, steadiness, and an ongoing commitment. In fact, I would say that once we "catch on" to what meditating with the body is all about, we enter a path that will unfold as long as there is life. At the same time, the experiential impact of the work is immediately felt, so there is confirmation of the rightness of what we are doing and an evolving natural trust in the process that is beginning to unfold.

Meditating with the body involves learning, through a variety of practices, how to reside fully within our bodies. What we are doing is not quite learning a technique, not quite learning how to "do" something. Rather, we are readjusting the focal length, the direction, and the domain of our consciousness. Thus, we gradually arrive at an awareness that is actually *in our bodies* rather than in our heads. It's not something you actually learn to do; it's a way of learning *how to be* differently.

Forming the core of the training is a corpus of perhaps fifty "somatic protocols" that are arranged in several main groups. One set of practices has to do with learning how to begin developing a pattern of relaxation within the body. Another focuses on cultivating a relationship with the earth underneath. A third attends to discovering awareness of the interior of the body. A fourth concerns locating internal tension and learning how to release it. A fifth group involves cultivating a sense of the inner space or silence of the body. A sixth is oriented toward bringing *prana,* or "inner breath," down to the cellular level. And so on. The practices lead people through a rich and multifaceted process of relaxation, developing presence within the body, opening interior awareness, reading the information the body gives forth, learning how to let the body come more and more to life, and finally surrendering to the body as the guide of one's life. All these aspects are treated in detail in the following pages. A brief summary of the protocols is given in the appendix.

As one enters the process of the body work, it becomes critical to learn how to see in a new way. As an illustration, I would cite an example provided by Malidoma Somé. Malidoma had been away from his village for a long time. At the age of three, he had been kidnapped and brought up in a Catholic boarding school. When he escaped and returned to his home nearly twenty years later, he wanted to get the light going one night. In the West African village where he was born, though the people didn't have electricity, they had ways of creating light at night if they wanted to. Still, at night they might say, "Let's turn the lights off so that we can see." When Malidoma wanted more light, he was told, "No, if we light the lamps, we won't be able to see." As the village elders explained it, you can't see anything real in the daylight. The only thing you see in the daylight is what you want to see. When you turn the lights off in the night, you see what wants to be seen, which is a whole different story.

It is very much the same way with our body. We need to turn off the light of what we think, of our diurnal consciousness. We need to descend into the night, the darkness that is our own body. When we do so, we discover that it is not neutral or dead, nor is it a space that is just simply there for our consumption and our use. Within the deep shadows of the body, within its darkness, we begin to discover a world that exists in its own right, quite apart from anything we may consciously think, expect, or want. We begin to find that the body has it own wants—in a sense, it wants to be seen on its own terms and within its own frame of reference. This can be a rather surprising discovery for many of us who, as modern people, are so very alienated from the body. We can't imagine the idea that the body might be a living force, a source of intelligence, wisdom, even something we might experience as possessing intention. We cannot conceive of the body as a subject. And yet, to carry out the body work, this is exactly what we need to do.

As we move further into the work, it quickly becomes evident to us that we are going to have to let the past die. We must not be derailed by some past idea of our body or our life that we have in our mind. Of course, this is what the body work is all about. Discursive thinking is basically a set of memories that we are now recycling as "us." That's why it's such a problem. It's coming from the past. We've picked it up from here, there, and everywhere. The only thing that is truly ours is the life that's in our body that wants to unfold. Everything that we think, all our plans and all our values, all our projects, our self-image, our sense of personal identity—all of that is beside the point of what needs to happen right now.

In letting go of the past, are we losing anything essential? Consider the example of relationships. When we let go of the past in relating with another, it doesn't mean that we are letting go of the person, not at all. Rather, we are letting go of the habitual, often tedious patterns that have defined how we are together, opening the way for the mystery of the present to unfold with our friend. In a similar way, we have to let go of all the habitual patterns that define—and so severely limit—how we relate to our own life as a whole. It doesn't mean that life goes away, but our body will start to show us how we need to be and what can happen. This is why the body work is so powerful and so profound: it is training in forgetting in a good way, in how to let go of the past.

Sometimes letting go in this way can seem risky and engender fear. We may feel that, through the work, we are going to lose something essential, even lose our self. But losing our solid and continuous sense of self—our ego—is what this journey is about. It can be helpful to contemplate the fact that we are eventually going to die. Once we realize this and the fact that our death is obviously going to involve ego death and *completely* losing our hold on the past—then there's really nothing to lose. At that point, we can say to ourselves, "What's the worst thing that could happen?" That we'll die. And not only is that the worst thing that *can* happen, it's something that's *going to* happen. So letting go of the past at that point can be a great relief and bring much peace.

THIRTEEN

Entering the Gate

We begin to make a relationship with our body through meditation practices that direct our awareness to its various parts. In undertaking this practice, it is initially very much as if we were looking at the body from the outside. For example, we might direct our attention to our hand or our foot. We are a somewhat removed observer attempting to discern what might be there.

When we do this, initially we find we often cannot find anything at all. Though we may begin with absence of feeling or with numbness, as we continue, the place we are attending to will begin to show signs of life. Let us take the example of the big toe. At first, we may have no sensation at all in the area of our toe. We may continue for some time, trying to feel, with no results. There is simply no feeling in the location of the big toe. It is as if we are missing that part of our being.

Then, at some point, we will begin to detect a very faint sensation in the general area of the big toe. As we continue, we begin to feel a kind of increasing sense of something being there. Going further, the big toe will begin to take on signs of definite life, and we begin to feel that there is something here to find out about. Further on, we feel the big toe as a rather complex entity, with much going on within it. Beyond this, we find ourselves increasingly sensing the big toe as having a kind of vividness, energy, and intensity never experienced before. Finally, the big toe is discovered as a universe unto itself, with patterns of tension and relaxation, frozenness and openness, pains and feelings of well-being, humming with life, with a particular character and demeanor unique to itself.

One begins with the more obvious and identifiable parts of the body, such as the big toe of our example. Since the lower belly is a key center from which both tension and energy radiate out, one might also begin practice there. But then we begin to develop more subtlety, and we gradually become aware of places within the part we are attending to, of tendons and ligaments, tiny muscles in out-of-the-way places, organs, bones, the circulatory system, the heart, and so on. As we proceed, we come to realize that virtually anyplace we look within the body, we are going to find an open field to explore.

As we continue further in our practice, increasing interiority develops. At first, we put our awareness into our abdomen or our heart center or our limbs, our feet, our fingers or our toes. Initially it feels as if we are *putting* our awareness into those places. But as time goes on, we sense that what is *really* happening is that those places themselves are *already aware*. We direct our awareness to a certain part, and we find ourselves discovering that what we experience is actually much larger than the awareness we have put there. It is as if this larger, preexisting awareness of this part of our body is coming back toward us. As we experience it we come to realize that what we are doing is actually tuning in to the awareness already existing, not just in these particular places, but throughout the entire body.

Through this practice, there arises a shift in the emphasis and shape of our awareness, a shift in the way we are aware as people. Habitually, we experience a highly conceptual form of consciousness, the "daylight consciousness" already mentioned, which most people experience in their heads and even in their frontal lobes—a kind of being up front and "out," "toward" the others, the environment, toward what we want or consciously or unconsciously intend for our lives.

This kind of restricted consciousness is actually a way of being very focused based on what we think, of trying to bring into being things that are in some way important to the project of "me," to my self-image and my life. In this highly focal, intentional consciousness, we exclude a huge domain of potential information—information that is actually already at the periphery of our awareness. In fact, part of the process of being aware in the "daylight" way includes pushing against and marginalizing—or repressing—the much larger field of potential awareness.

But when we start to place our awareness in our body, something different begins to happen. Usually fairly early in the practice, we come to realize that there is another way of being aware. The more we work with the body, the more we are able to see within the body. This seeing is quite different from the daylight variety: we increasingly come to attend to the periphery of our daylight awareness rather than strictly to the center. It is almost as if we learn how to disregard what is sharp, clear, and right in focus, and receive what is happening on the boundary. This is not only the boundary of our awareness, but it is also the boundary between our "mind" and our "body." We are learning to see more in the body's way. This process begins as soon as we begin the somatic meditation work, but it continues on and on, to greater levels of subtlety, seemingly without end.

Over time, the way in which we are aware as people undergoes a basic change. To reside beyond the periphery of ego awareness is to reside in the body. The more we reside in the body, the more we find ourselves living in the penumbral awareness of the body itself. In time, we find ourselves knowing our world not so much through thinking about it, but by sensing it and feeling it, not just as the body does, but as the body. We begin to experience moments when we realize that, fundamentally, "we" *are* the body. As we find ourselves in greater and greater somatic embodiment, we discover deeper and deeper contact with the world. At this point, our conclusions about it recede into relative unimportance. Life is then less and less about thinking and more and more about simply *being*.

The body work described here is the path toward this goal. Through the somatic awareness practices, we are able to arrive at greater and greater alignment—and finally identification—with the body. As we seek to bring awareness to various places in our body, the breath can be used to great advantage, as a vehicle. To continue the previous example, one of the somatic exercises I teach asks meditators to bring their attention to their big toe. Initially, as mentioned, people often can't feel anything; there is just a complete numbness. But in the teachings of Tibetan yoga, it is suggested that we can use our breathing to enhance somatic awareness.

Tibetan yoga speaks about the outer breath, our normal respiration, and also about the inner breath, our life force, or prana. The outer breath holds the inner breath, as a sheath of a plant might hold its pith. When we bring our attention to the outer breath, we gain access to our inner breath.

According to Tibetan yoga, our inner breath, or prana, can be directed in various ways. For example, our outer breath fills our lungs. But we can also visualize ourselves bringing our outer breath into any place in our bodies. Thus, we use the *visualization* of our breath—rather than the physical breath itself—as a way to bring our attention in a strong and focused manner to any place in our body. Now, it is of the nature of prana that, to whatever location in the body we direct our attention, there the prana will go. So when we visualize ourselves bringing our breath into a certain locale, what we are doing is bringing our prana, our inner breath, to that place.

We might do this by visualizing that we are bringing the breath into our body from the outside, through the skin. In the example of the big toe, we can visualize that we are bringing the breath in through all the pores of the big toe, top, bottom, the sides, the front, all at once. Alternatively, we might visualize that we are just breathing directly into a location, such as the interior of the lower belly or joint such as the knee. Here we are not moving from the outside to the inside, but just breathing directly into the interior location, from the inside to the inside, so to speak. It is as if our entire attention is within the lower belly and we simply find the breath arriving there. Although this cannot really be described in words with much accuracy, a little practice quickly shows how it works.

And here is the key point: wherever our attention goes, the prana goes, and *the prana carries awareness right to that point.* By directing the prana, we are able to bring awareness to any location within our body. The practitioner breathes into the big toe and is able to bring awareness to it. This kind of breathing greatly enhances the process of developing our ability to be aware of virtually any part of our body. Breathing into the big toe enables our direct knowledge of the big toe to develop much more quickly than it otherwise would. It facilitates our ability to receive the impressions of our sensations without impediment and opens us directly to the experience of the self-existing—that is, already present—awareness of the big toe.

This breathing practice also helps us uncover the energy that ultimately *is* the big toe, when considered strictly from an experiential standpoint. In other words, our seemingly solid physical sensations of the big toe are a substantialized and solidified experience of a more primary experience of the toe: that it is actually a vibrating, scintillating field of energy. By directly feeling this, we are opening to a kind of communication with that part of our body that is without impediment and even without any duality at all. When we leave aside our usual conceptual image of ourselves and of our body, when we are able to identify completely with the energy in the big toe, there isn't anything else. In a sense, we become the energy of the big toe; we *are* it.

This kind of "non-dual" experience of the big toe is clearly a dynamic process. Somehow, the more we sense the energetic world that is the big toe, the more we find flowing into our consciousness in the way of input, grounding, revitalization, and nourishment. Somehow, simply through developing this awareness, we feel that we ourselves are changing on some fundamental level. All this is "information" of a sort, but not a kind we could objectify or name in any way.

FOURTEEN

Discomfort in the Somatic Practice

The somatic meditations are often experienced as deeply satisfying, leaving us with a profound sense of well-being. At the same time, the actual work of developing awareness that occurs through our practice often carries with it an edge of discomfort. For one thing, the sheer energy and intensity we uncover in a particular location in our body, or in the body as a whole, can be quite uncomfortable. Our experience often seems to be too much, out of bounds, even verging on unbearable. Since the habitual tendency of the ego mind is to seek comfort, ease, and control at all costs, this intense energy can cause us to feel distress. This distress reveals just how much we have marginalized and even completely repressed the actual, markedly intense experience of our body and its energies. Now that intensity is beginning to disclose itself to us, with some force.

As we work with the body and explore the various parts of it, we are likely to begin discovering painful *tension*. The word "tension" is a general term used in this book to cover a wide variety of difficult somatic experiences. Tension can be viewed from either of two angles. In one sense, it refers to an experience in the body: we feel tension in a certain place. In another sense, it refers to the result of an activity on the part of our ego mind, the activity of holding, tensing, or freezing in a certain location. In fact, these two meanings are the same thing perceived from two different angles. Initially, we are aware of a tight part of our body. Later, through practice, we discover that it is actually *we* who are holding, *we* who are tensing the body—that there is no tension "out there" in the body independent of us and what we are doing moment by moment.

The term "tension" as used here refers to these forms of somatic discomfort:

- Numbness: the body or a part of the body feels numb, insentient, dead.
- Solidity: a part of the body feels heavy, dense, and solid—as if it were a brick or a stone.
- Tightness: we notice a kind of overly constricted quality to a place in our body—it feels unnaturally tight.
- Pain: the body or a part of the body feels soreness, achiness, dull pain, throbbing pain, acute pain, a kind of locked-up tension that signals the body's more or less acute distress.
- Strong emotional states that seem immobile and unmoving: anxiety, dread, depression, fear, etc.
- The subtle tension we feel when we withdraw from any experience, whether of the senses, the emotions, or anything else.

On a general level, all these forms of somatic discomfort share one feature: they imply some kind of holding, stuckness, locking, or other lack of movement. As we shall see, simply becoming aware of the discomfort means that movement has begun. But the existence of the discomfort in the first place reveals that the open field of awareness and its accompanying flow of energy are somehow impeded. Let us look more closely into these forms of tension and the processes they suggest:

- Numbness implies that our consciousness is split off from that part of the body. Energy, when cycling freely, moves through the awareness of the body. When a part is numb, the energy is dammed up.
- Solidity suggests that we are no longer completely numb, but that we are running into the seemingly outer, unyielding boundary of this part of our body. Our awareness can penetrate no further, hence the feeling of "solidity."
- Tightness brings us face-to-face with the inner immobility of the area, its resistance to any softening or movement.
- Pain is the next step above tightness. It is the first glimpse of specific content—calling to be explored—heretofore trapped in the body, that is now surfacing into our awareness. This content has been dammed up to the breaking point and is now demanding the psychic attention that pain calls forth. All forms of physical pain would be included in this category, whether from illness, old age, or injury.

- Emotional states that seem immobile and unmoving are experienced somatically in various parts of the body or in the body as a whole. They are a kind of holding that has finally come to the surface, though this "holding" expresses itself in a more overtly energetic way than the other kinds.
- The subtle tension we feel when we withdraw from any experience is known, in Buddhist psychology, as the "suffering of conditioned states" and refers to the tension that accompanies our retreating from the things that we experience, not seeing or sensing their freshness, as we fall back to and into our centralized self.

Again, we may refer generally to these various forms of somatic discomfort as tension because they express themselves as some kind of immobility or restriction in the body and also because, ultimately, as we discover through the practice, we are the creators of the immobility or restriction.

At the same time, it is important to recognize that such attempts at labeling are no more than crude approximations. Ultimately, every experience is unique. Whatever category or set of categories we may use to label a form of discomfort, it is always going to transcend those categories, being its own thing above and beyond any term we may apply. It is the recognition of this that makes the body work always fresh and endlessly fascinating.

As we engage the somatic practices, we find many forms of discomfort arising—some extremely subtle, others more vivid; some momentary, some ongoing. Discomfort is something that we have already been aware of, but on a subliminal, previously unacknowledged level.

So it is that this discomfort may be a feeling of being numb, shut down, and emotionally and physically dead. We might feel disembodied, as if we are floating. Our discomfort may take the form of tightness or tension in a large tendon, muscle, or muscle group. Or it may express itself as a frozenness or holding in a small area, say, a tiny muscle on the inside of one thigh, a point under a shoulder blade, something in the tip of a finger. Whatever its size or location, we feel the tautness and the need to release, but we cannot let go. The discomfort may also be experienced as physical pain, possibly little sharp points of pain, a dull achiness, or something more intense.

Our discomfort may also arise from somatic experiences that are inconsistent with our preexisting concept of what our body is or should be. We may discover, for example, that our body is not the unitary entity we thought it was, and is, in fact, in a state of complete disarray. Thus, some places may feel very hard and armored; others, incredibly vulnerable, unprotected, shaky, and weak. Some places feel stuffed and bloated; others, starved and emaciated. One side may feel shorter or smaller than the other. One side feels alive; the other, dead. Everything may seem out of kilter, which itself may fill us with distress or even dread. We might want to scream or run, or jump out of our bodies.

On a more subtle level, however, tension may include feelings and sensations that do not feel strictly physical at all. We may notice that there is a kind of emotional or feeling density in certain parts of our body, energy that feels in some way locked up, though not quite in a physical way—and yet we feel it somatically, in our body, and sometimes very intensely. Such feelings might include a sense that our heart is very tight, as if encased in armor. We may feel that our throat is constricted and we are gagging or choking, or that our head is dizzy, our belly feels nauseous, or our sexual center is uncomfortably claustrophobic with its energy. There is a feeling of solidity and stuckness, though it may be very subtle. We feel a call to let go, to release, but we cannot do so.

Again, our discomfort may be experienced as painful emotions: We may suddenly feel deep heartache, unpleasant agitation, dreadful anxiety, or extreme nausea. We may feel fear, panic, groundlessness, anger, irritation, paranoia, desire, pride, and so on. The list is endless. These emotions are expressions of tension because we find ourselves locked in them—they won't move and we are unable to escape.

This initial, most crucial step in the body work involves discovering a body that is in a lot of discomfort, holding, or tightness. As our awareness develops, we begin to realize that our habitual, if subliminal, response to all this somatic distress is an unconscious or barely conscious pattern of freezing: we are holding on for all we are worth, fearful and paranoid, tensing our body so we won't have to feel. We begin to realize that we have been walling off all this discomfort for years, decades, or even our whole life.

FIFTEEN

The Background and Process of Discomfort

In a teaching known as "the birth of ego," Buddhism offers a theoretical explanation of discomfort. Initially, discomfort arises on a purely spiritual level: all kinds of phenomena burst upon us in our lives—sense perceptions, feelings, thoughts, people, situations, and so on. In the very first instant of their appearance, they arrive unexpectedly and with much vividness, and our initial experience of them is one of shock. They challenge our small, restricted sense of self because they always come out of nowhere and are always initially independent of what we think or want. Momentarily, they shatter our self-concept. In that first instant of any experience, we find ourselves floating in the open space and emptiness of non-self. Typically, seeking to reconstitute our "self," we retreat into primal feeling reactions to the open space: fear, anxiety, dread, or even panic. This is the beginning of ego.

Fear and these other basic emotions are also, in their turn, challenges to our solid self—they are so distressing and so uncontrollable. We usually resist the intensity of these feeling reactions by solidifying them into more gross and tangible emotions, such as irritation, anger, neediness, pride, desire, paranoia, and so on. To these, we usually attach some kind of ego "narrative," some story line that locates them in reference to our "I." These more gross emotions also represent challenges to our sense of self, because they are so powerful and painful. We may further try to deny the intensity of these emotions by tensing or freezing our body against what we are feeling. We freeze so we won't have to feel the intensity of what is occurring.

In the somatic work, as we become more and more aware of our own process, this theoretical outline becomes a matter of personal experience. We can see exactly how "we" come to be: (1) something disquieting arises; (2) we feel an instant panic; (3) we react with sudden anger, jealousy, pride, etc.; and (4) we tense our body against it—our chest tightens up; we feel our belly drop; our shoulders hunch up. Although all of this happens in a matter of a second or two, the more somatically aware we become, the more we can discern the stages quite clearly.

There is one final stage in this process. We should remember that the experience of tensing, tightening, and solidifying is itself most unpleasant, involving sometimes intense somatic distress as we recoil from our experience and freeze. How do we handle this very unpleasant somatic feeling of freezing up? If we are skilled practitioners, we may know how to read what has happened and to relax through the layers of reactivity that have been building.

Most of us, however, will deliberately turn our attention away from the unpleasant tensing and tightening. We will shut out our body's feeling and retreat into our conceptual thinking process. Will Johnson, in his writing on the posture of meditation, has noticed this critical movement. Our way of shutting out our body and its discomfort is, in fact, by retreating into our obsessive thinking process. The more we shut out our body, the more we retreat into thinking. The intensity of our compulsive thinking is in direct proportion to the extent that we are unwilling to experience our body in a full and direct way. We have, in fact, dissociated from it.

This final stage, where we are more or less entirely disconnected from our bodies, where we are physically numb and not even aware of our numbness, is the state in which many of us modern people live. Once we have retreated so fully from our somatic life and our physical embodiment, about the only thing that will help us reverse our direction is the kind of somatic crisis described above: we fall ill, experience some injury, or are overwhelmed with some other uncontrollable somatic situation. At that point, we have little choice but to take seriously the message the body is sending us.

Within the framework of the body work, the appearance of discomfort is thus good news. This is because it marks the beginning of reversing the process described above, of the development and fortification of the ego, the ultimate cause of our disembodiment and alienation from the deeper self. By working with the body, by engaging the discomfort, the tension is present to our awareness, and we are able to engage the process of unraveling the layers of our self-concept.

The first step in this process is that we move from a state of insentient numbness backward into a state of discomfort. Then, as the work progresses, we move through layer upon layer of discomfort, sometimes feeling great freedom and fulfillment, but often just finding another layer to peel away, as if we were an onion. The discomfort becomes more subtle and transparent as we move deeper and deeper into the body, through each successive level of emotion, feeling, sensation, mood, and felt-sense. Finally, we arrive at our core, the empty space at the center, which is open and free but, at the same time, the basis of our entire being. At that point, our embodiment is complete, our realization is actual, and the solid "ego" has become a distant dream.

In order to work in an open and creative way with the discomfort that is arising, then, it is important to understand that, far from being a problem, it is what we have been looking for. If we believe that our discomfort is an indicator that something is wrong, it will be natural for us to resist it and push it back again into the shadows of our body. If, on the other hand, we see it for what it is—a positive development and marker of our progress in the somatic work—we are far more likely to welcome it and approach it with an attitude of openness and curiosity.

The discomfort that we are experiencing in the body work is, then, a sign that our somatic practice is beginning to succeed. It means that the body is communicating information that has needed to come to our awareness, perhaps for a long time. We begin to understand that distress itself is an expression of the "wisdom of the body." It is the body's way of letting us know there is work that needs to be done and life that needs to be lived—and our discomfort shows us the way in. Discomfort, then, is always a *message*—that we are holding on too tightly to our sense of self—and an *invitation* for us to relax, open, and surrender to the fire of larger experience.

SIXTEEN

The Process of Letting Go

Within the body's tension itself is found an invitation for release. This invitation brings with it critical information: as we become more and more aware of the uncomfortable tension, we also find ourselves beginning to sense that it is actually we—the conscious, intentional, focal awareness we are constantly trying to maintain—who are responsible for the tension in the first place. It is our own overlay, so to speak, that is creating this phenomenon of freezing.

This is not a conceptual kind of understanding, but something that suggests itself on a much more primary, even physical level. By doing the body work, we start to "feel" some pattern of our investment in the tension, our contribution to it, our maintaining and reinforcing of it. As this sense becomes more and more palpable, we begin to discover that we are coming into the capability to take responsibility for the tension, to enter into it consciously, and to let go.

It is as if, at first, we are on the outside, looking at the holding. Next, as we look more closely, we can feel a boundary between us and the holding. Then we find that boundary dissolving, and, as this occurs, our awareness begins to dissolve into the tension itself, so that, in a manner of speaking, we find ourselves inside it, discovering that it is actually we who are holding on. There is, at this point, a sudden, though often quite subtle, somatic fear, almost a panic, that arises—there is a trembling, a shaky, unstable feeling. For a moment, we are both holding on and releasing. We oscillate back and forth. On one hand, we can't seem to let go, but at the same time, we feel we *have* to let go—to open, relax, and surrender. We hover on this excruciating edge for some time, and then—as long as we don't back off and run away—we find ourselves somehow moving through it and releasing.

This process of release is repeated in virtually all the body work exercises, every time we do them, whether we are just beginning practitioners or have been at it for years. Sometimes the identification of tension and its release form the core of the somatic protocol we are doing. At other times, we may be focusing on something else, but even then, we are continually finding places where we are holding and that are calling for release. At certain points, when our awareness is deep within the silence of, say, the lower belly, we are aware that release is still occurring on some outlying periphery, and we are able to incorporate that into the work we are doing without moving off-center. Often, the release occurs in a very small region of our body, but there are times when we locate a tension, enter it, and let go, only to find an entire side of our body letting go and opening up. The process of release seems to go on and on because the journey into full embodiment, and the accompanying dismantling of the solid, pathological self, offers no endpoint in sight.

Our holding on is both physical and psychological. Ultimately, what we are holding on to is some kind of fixed feeling of being; that is the psychological dimension. It manifests in physical holding but is ultimately driven by psychological fear and insecurity, by our grasping after personal solidness and security, personal territory that we are trying to maintain. When we let go, then, it is thus not just a physical letting go but, at the same time, a letting go of our fixed sense of being. This represents a leap into the unknown.

The moment of release is a leap into the unknown because, in that instant, we can't take our thinking mind—the mind that objectifies our experience and knows conceptually—with us. When we leap, we just find ourselves there, naked and stripped of any way to conceptualize our body—or anything else—at all.

In this moment, there is an abrupt and complete shift in the way we are experiencing our body. Prior to release, we felt an intense solidity, an unbearable claustrophobia, related to our somatic holding and our frozenness. In the moment of release, however, it is as if this intolerably suffocating claustrophobia has suddenly disappeared completely.

Abruptly, we experience ourselves as nothing but empty space, with no one commenting or even observing. We find our body still present, for this is not a disembodied state. In fact, it is quite the opposite: we feel completely in and at one with our body while at the same time feeling empty of any solidity or objectifiable reality. And, with nowhere to land, nothing to latch on to, our mind falls into a state of utter silence. We may feel relief or freedom—we may burst into laughter or uncontrollable sobbing—to find that there is, in this moment, no longer any sense of "me" at all.

This experience of "unknowing," as we may call it, goes by in a flash. Soon enough, we come back, reconfigure ourselves, and engage in the process of holding and freezing, of thinking and objectifying our body once again. But such an experience leaves its imprint—we are left longing for it, longing to return to that "nowhere" space of our body, which, strangely, is what we have been seeking all our lives.

SEVENTEEN

The Unfolding Journey

As we continue with the practice, the process of exploring our physical being and unlocking our somatic tension goes on and on, to more and more locales in the body and to deeper and deeper levels of subtlety. In each new experience, we bring prana, life, and awareness to our bodies, we feel the blockage, we meet the invitation to release, we surrender our hold, and finally, we experience the relaxation, the sense of unknowing, and the open space that result.

In this process, we become acquainted with our body in ever new ways. As we proceed, we may feel as if each particular part of our body is opening like a flower. As we go further with our breathing, we increasingly discover a sense of energy, life, and vitality in, for example, our hand.

Beyond this, we sense that the hand has a particular kind of awareness that is quite unique to it. As we perform this same exercise with other parts of our body, we realize that each part likewise

has its own very specific and unique *awareness profile*, if you will, its own personality, its own knowledge, its own living truth. It has its own reason for being, its own relation to the "us" of our conscious awareness, and its own things to communicate in an ongoing way.

Thus, if we can tune in to it, we find that each part of our body has its own way of being that is alive, intelligent, and fundamentally independent of our conscious mind. For example, people who go barefoot a lot may comment how intelligent the feet are, how much they know, and how much information and vitality they receive from the earth. Such folks are continually receiving information and energy through their feet—or rather their feet are receiving these as aspects of their own awareness—just from walking on the earth and feeling the continual energetic exchange that occurs with each step.

With each part of the body a whole world opens up and is available for discovery when we begin working with it. With each new discovery, who "we" are grows deeper, more subtle, more complex, more connected, and more open and extended. And more unknown. All of this unfolds from that first experience of numbness, frozenness, and claustrophobia.

As we continue, we realize that each part of the body is a living force, an individual galaxy unto itself. Each part is, in some real sense, an entity unto itself, an individual with its own intelligence, its own voice, and even its own will. Each is a galaxy floating in ever-changing relationship to the others parts, other galaxies, within the vast, unknown universe of the body.

This discovery can be startling and even quite unsettling for those of us who think of the body as a unitary entity that somehow belongs to "us," conforms to our ideas, and is "ours." By contrast, we now see that the label of "me" and "my body" is an imprecise and finally inaccurate label given to this universe of individual and somehow interrelated worlds, the parts of our bodies, perhaps down even to individual cells. This realization can be disturbing because we realize that the idea of the body as part of a unitary, consistent, definable "me," at least as far as the body is concerned, has little or nothing to do with the actual situation.

EIGHTEEN

The Body's Own Agenda

A s we move through the process of discovery, it begins to dawn on us that the body has an agenda of its own that it wants us to follow. The agenda begins with some region or part of the body coming forward to meet our awareness, alerting us to our holding, and then inviting us into the process of release and relaxation.

The interesting thing here is that we are not imposing our ego's agenda on the body. We are not saying, "Okay, I have a back problem, and I'm going to use this bodywork to solve my back problem." Instead, we are taking our lead from the body. The body says, "We are going to start with the arches of the feet. This is where we are going to begin." The next day, we will be back at it, with the body calling us once again to the arches of the feet, this time perhaps focusing on the interior of the foot behind the arch. And so it may go for some time. Later, it will be the calves, then next it's the neck, and then the next day or the next month, it's the region under the shoulder blades, under the clavicles, within the interior of the chest, along the interior of the spinal column. In other words, the body itself actually gives us the routine. It gives us the protocols and it gives us the journey. And perhaps, somewhere along the way, our back problem is ameliorated or disappears entirely.

At the time we are following the body's directive, we usually do not understand why the body work is going in the direction it is. As we explore the body, we do feel very specific invitations and callings, but why it is that *these* invitations and callings are foremost at this particular moment remains a mystery.

Thus it is that we are called to let go of what we think we want or think we need, and instead to listen deeply; we are invited to surrender to the invitations to awareness, openness, and letting go that come forward from the body. Through that process, there is a deepening understanding that the body, far from being an object or a tool of our personal ego, is actually calling to us constantly with a primal voice. It commands our attention and engages us in a process that we find extraordinarily compelling even while we do not and cannot fully understand the larger pattern of what is going on.

At the same time, there are periods in the work when we do see something of what is occurring and why. To give one example, it is quite interesting that when people do this body work thoroughly and deeply, whatever unresolved personal tasks they may have tend to turn up somatically. These tasks may be momentary or ongoing—even tasks of a lifetime.

It is sometimes amazing how literally these tasks can manifest in the body. People who have difficulty with self-expression may feel at a certain point that they are being strangled because they sense the energy collecting at the throat; they feel unable "to find their own voice." If we have difficulty "swallowing" our situation, we may find tremendous distress at the mere act of trying to eat or drink. People who are unaware of their emotions may experience their heart as if in a vice grip. Someone who is just beginning to become aware of negative aspects of themselves that they are unable to digest may continually feel that they are about to vomit. Somebody who is going through a reorientation in relation to what they think about themselves, their relationships, or their lives, may feel dizzy, as if they can't think or even perceive in a clear way. Someone who is avoiding getting their hands dirty with the concrete, earthy aspects of life may have rashes, even eczema, on their hands and arms. In these vivid expressions and even in less dramatic ways, we may be able to see something of what the body is up to in drawing us into a particular somatic territory.

These tasks are clearly brought forward by the body, always in accordance with its own developmental timetable. Even if we happen to have some clarity about what somatic/emotional development issues are at stake, most of us are in the dark about how the work is going to unfold, what may be required of us, what other dimensions, both smaller and larger, of our lives may be implicated or affected by the work, and what kinds of changes the body is calling for.

It is important to trust the painful moments of confusion and chaos in the work just as much as—and, perhaps, even more than—the more acceptable moments of peace and clear comprehension. It would be accurate to say that whatever is happening in the work is what the body needs us to feel right at this moment. The periods in the work when we experience a great deal of clarity about what is going on and why are not inherently superior to these others; just like the more difficult moments, they are being offered up by the body because they are what is most needed. Most of the work occurs in the dense, dark clouds of our own unresolved relative truth. We find ourselves called down into the darkness of the body, into an open, uncertain, and unsettling realm of reality that has no particular allegiance to the current standpoint of our conscious ego.

However, at certain points, so the body seems to judge, it seems important that all our understanding be opened up and our trust renewed. In these moments, the clouds part; suddenly, we see the vast landscape that we are traveling through and glimpse the brilliant and majestic mountains toward which we have been heading all this time, even when we have been most lost and unable to see anything at all. Through this process, there slowly develops a deep confidence and joy in this human body of ours, and in the journey it infallibly enables us to make.

In what the body offers us, then, in its timing, sequencing, and particular intensity of experience, the body is completely and entirely trustworthy. The body doesn't just know us flawlessly; the body is—as we shall see—nothing other than our own totality. It is our deeper self calling us home, and it knows exactly how this journey needs to unfold, just what we can handle, how the necessary information can best come through, and in what way the needed transformation can best occur. In a sense, then, if we are able to be open to it and listen with clarity, the body is more trustworthy than the therapist who is often having to guess what our problem is and how to best work with it. It is more reliable than pharmaceutical intervention, which is so often random and experimental, injecting foreign and often very disruptive chemicals into our system. Thus, again, if we are able to receive its wisdom, the body is the ultimate teacher, the trusted guide on the journey.

III
UNDERSTANDING THE
PROCESS OF MEDITATING
WITH THE BODY

The Importance of Non-conceptual Understanding in the Body Work and Where Concepts Are Needed

As I have already suggested, the somatic work requires that we be willing to let go of our ideas about the body and enter into the domain of its direct, non-conceptual experience. This is a requirement of doing the body work because we cannot enter the body in an authentic way if we are still trapped in our conceptual versions of it. These need to be surrendered at the door, so to speak, as the price of admission to the somatic mysteries. We also need to let go of our thinking, if only temporarily, in order to be open to what the body itself reveals and to fully profit from what is revealed. Even beyond this, enlightenment or realization involves learning how to live in the body in a non-conceptual way, no longer relying on what we think in order to live our life, but rather on what the body knows and communicates in an immediate and utterly naked way. Given the tremendous importance attached to conceptual thinking in modern Western culture, it will be helpful for us to examine the central and critical role of non-conceptual knowledge in the work. In addition, we need to consider whether conceptual knowledge may have a legitimate, if subordinate, function to perform.

Within modern Western culture, most people believe that the only valid and reliable knowledge is that which is conceptual. Other kinds of knowledge—feeling, intuition, sensation, images, dreams, visions—are thought to be secondary, as they are only able to yield their meaning and value when they are "interpreted" into a conceptual frame of reference.

Occasionally, of course, one meets modern Westerners who reject the assumption that conceptual knowledge is the only truly valid kind of knowledge. But even those of us who are of this opinion, when push comes to shove, tend to operate out of what we *think* about the world. Though we may be of the *opinion* that conceptual knowing is subordinate, we do not, in fact, function in that way. Especially when feeling discomfort or threat, we habitually fall back into conceptual ways of knowing as our primary reference point, our method of safety and reliable orientation.

The meditative traditions of Buddhism—the source of the body work described in this book—take a rather different approach. For them, direct experience, unmediated by concepts, is held to be the primary and, by far, most important kind of knowing. Conceptual understanding is considered essential, of course, but seen as strictly secondary. First we have our life; *then* we think about it and come to conclusions about it. The conclusions are thus always secondary and after the fact. For Buddhism, concepts are not reality itself, but are merely abstract conceptualizations of our experience and therefore greatly reduced versions, only slivers, mere memories of our actual life. I may think that I know my wife of thirty years pretty well, but often what she sees or says or does truly surprises me. What I think about my wife, Lee, is the conceptual abstraction—it's not her; who she actually is as a person is quite different from my idea, and reveals itself fully only in surprise. The surprises bring me into contact with the real person, and, to receive this real and actual person, I have to be willing to let go of my previous conceptual ideas.

For Buddhism, concepts—which are memories of past experience—are always superseded by what is occurring now. The conceptual abstractions constantly need correction and reformulation in light of unfolding experience. This is why, in Buddhism, conceptual versions of reality are called "dreams." Finally, in relation to the actual, immediate, concrete fullness of reality, they have no substance.

Why, then, do most of us take the conceptualized abstractions, the conclusions we come to, to be reality itself? Because our non-conceptual life is ever unpredictable and open-ended. It can leave us feeling uncertain, insecure, and unprotected. When we are able to "pin things down" and put them in definite and definable terms, we suddenly feel more safe and secure. We know who and what we are—or so we think.

In taking our conceptual versions as reality itself, we have lost touch with the substance, the reality, the abundance, and the freedom that is always available in the present, preconceptual moment. The process of meditation involves gradually shedding our multitude of opinions-built-upon-opinions of how things are, and becoming more and more aware of the literal, non-conceptual substratum of all our thinking—the substratum which is reality itself.[1]

In working with the body, this fundamental principle—that the non-conceptual precedes and is more fundamental and meaningful than the conceptualized version—is critical. In the work, we must take as our ground our literal, direct somatic

---

[1]   For the scholars among my readers, it may be helpful to mention that a discussion of these issues forms a primary focus of the philosophical work of the great Buddhist master Asanga, the renowned fifth-century CE Yogacarin meditator and thinker so very important to the somatic work of Tibetan yoga. According to Asanga, conceptual thinking represents an abstraction from more primary reality. Asanga calls these conceptual abstractions *parikalpita*, ("imagined reality"). Because we habitually take them as identical to the reality of which they are abstractions, they are ultimately false. They are ultimately all lies. Asanga says that in order to conceptualize something, there must be some more primary experience that is the basis, the substratum, in Sanskrit, the *vastu*, in relation to which we are conceptualizing. To create a conceptual abstraction, you have to have something you are doing this to. This vastu is nothing more than *however and whatever is appearing* at each given moment. It is ineffable, that is, non-conceptual, experience. It is simply the causes and conditions that are ripening in this moment in appearance. Asanga calls this non-conceptual substratum *paratantra*, the continuity (*tantra*, the non-conceptual experience that is continually unfolding as our life) that is ultimately "other" (*para*)—that is, it resists any attempt to make it part of our conceptual inventory. Can we give a label to this ineffable experience? Yes, we can, but then we have left the domain of paratantra and reentered parikalpita. Asanga describes the mind that is able to abide in the non-conceptual as *parinishpanna*, "the fully ripened and perfected awareness." He summarizes it in a simple way: when we see paratantra, the non-conceptual substratum, as it is, without attaching labels or concepts to it, that is parinishpanna, our own full perfection; when we overlay that substratum with concepts, then we are dwelling in parikalpita, not seeing things as they are but as we want to see them, and this is the source of all the confusion and the suffering of *samsara* (the prison-like existence of the centralized, solid ego). It is important to realize that Asanga is not theorizing here. Like other great Buddhist philosopher-yogins, he is taking his foundation in what he has experienced, over and over, in the course of a lifetime, in Buddhist meditation. As many Western commentators have point out, Asanga's "philosophy" is actually more of a psychological description of how things work, more of a phenomenology, if you will, than a "philosophy," at least as we usually think of it.

experience, whatever it may be. That is why, in this book, we have begun with the *process* of body work rather than with how we may understand it. In the work itself, practice and the experience that arises from it precede conceptual understanding. And even the conceptual understanding we arrive at must be considered never more than provisional and approximate, always subordinate to and in need of correction by what we actually find when we explore the body. There are no "right answers." Each person's experience is ultimately going to be different from anyone else's.

At the same time, however, once the primacy of the nonconceptual is established in our understanding and, even more important, in our meditation, then it becomes worthwhile to consider the conceptual geography surrounding our somatic explorations. It is not only helpful, but crucial to the body work to have some grasp of the historical and cultural contexts in which the work is being carried out (as in section I) and also a clear understanding of why we do body work, what happens when we do it, and how we may understand what happens in both practical psychological and theoretical terms (the present section).

This conceptual kind of understanding is important because, as human beings, we are always formulating conceptual maps of our reality. Especially when we approach an area as intensely experiential as somatic meditation, it becomes important to understand what we are doing and why. Without this understanding, we would lack the clarity and trust to fully receive what we are going through. However, when our conceptual understanding is sufficiently broad, clear, and sophisticated, then we can accommodate our discoveries, whatever they may be, and learn in a full and complete way from them.

An accurate conceptual understanding can also sensitize us to greater subtlety in our forays into the shadows of the soma and actually help us to see more. For more experienced somatic voyagers, what we or anyone else currently thinks about this kind of work can be an *agent provocateur,* giving us a language to then critique and reformulate from the viewpoint of what we ourselves are discovering, a ground for our own creative expression, which can then be shared and explored with others. In the present section, then, we are examining some of the traditional and modern perspectives on "touching enlightenment with the body."

TWENTY

What the Body Knows

W hat does all this somatic work have to do with spirituality and, frankly, with meditation? We need to realize that when we develop somatic awareness and enter into the process of relaxation and release described above, we are not just making peace with our physical existence. In fact, we are entering into a process that lies right at the heart of the spiritual life itself, something the Buddha saw a very long time ago. He saw that while spiritual strategies of disembodiment—such as trying to turn away from the body, the emotions, sexuality, pain—may yield apparent short-term gains, in the long run, these strategies land us right back, and perhaps more deeply, into the confusion and suffering we began with.

In meditating with the body, what's going on is that the awareness itself is being retrained and reeducated. We begin to live our life as a continual welling up from the depths of our soma, of our cells, our bones, and our tissues. Rather than thinking that the conscious mind is or should be the engineer of our lives, we begin to realize that the conscious mind is actually more appropriately the handmaiden of the body. The body becomes the continual source of our inspiration, creativity, direction, and engagement with others—what we need in order to live authentically. The body itself is the unending font of the water of life.

Our constant attempts to maintain the "integrity" of our continuous, solid sense of ourselves lead us to be very resistant to—in fact, to ignore—information that is inconsistent with that image. And this means that we have a huge amount of information, moment by moment, to block out.

When we live our lives, the body itself is a completely nonjudgmental receiver of experience. These days there is much talk about creating effective personal boundaries. The interesting point here is that you actually can't put up boundaries around your body. The boundaries happen up top, in the head. There are no boundaries in the body. The body is open and porous; it is sensitive and vulnerable; it is already in interconnection with everything in the universe. The body is intelligent, and the body's knowing operates completely outside of and beyond the realm of our very limited conscious ego awareness and its desire for "boundaries."

From the body's viewpoint, whatever occurs in our world—whether we like it or don't like it, whether we find it a bad situation or a good situation—is perceived with complete openness. Whatever occurs in our environment, our body receives. On a somatic level, we receive the full experience in that way, always. There are no boundaries around the body and there's no way you can protect yourself, unless you go into a dark dungeon and shut the door and try to hide under your bunk, and even then your body's going to be receiving all the energies that are going on around you. No matter what the mind thinks or wants, the body receives and the body knows. It is always and without fail in immediate and direct contact with the naked, non-conceptual experience of life. In fact, in a real sense, the body is that experience—the non-conceptual substratum that precedes the overlay of concept, labeling, and judgment. As we discover in and through the body work, the body—in what it senses and what it picks up—abides in the ineffable reality of what is; it is unobstructed in its wisdom and its knowledge.

So, the body receives experience in a completely open and nonjudgmental way, but because of our investment in who we think we are or want to be, in relation to our hopes and fears about "me" and our attempts to maintain this self, we refuse to receive a great part of what the body knows and feels and understands. (Here, "we" means our conscious self, our conscious mind, our ego.) This is the process: something happens, the totality of experience is registered on a somatic level, and our conscious mind says, "No." Or we say, "I want this part of what happened but not that part." Thus, our ego consciousness doesn't simply receive what the body knows; we don't receive the somatic information it is trying to deliver in a complete and straightforward way.

This is what Buddhism calls ignorance (*moha*). This ignorance is not being unintelligent or uninformed. It is the act of blocking out knowledge and wisdom—received by the body and abiding in it—that is inconsistent with our self-image. Ignorance is actually incredibly intelligent. The activity of ignorance knows exactly what to accept and what to reject in order to keep the illusion of our unity and consistent self intact.

In Buddhism, ignorance is considered one of the three basic mental poisons that operate to protect our "self." The process of ignoring described above also involves the other two poisons, passion (*raga*) and aggression (*dvesha*). Using passion or desire, we try to draw in and latch on to those small portions of our somatic experience that seem to reinforce our "self" toward our consciousness. Using aggression, we try to deny, negate, or destroy whatever in our body's knowledge is inconsistent with what we are trying to maintain. Our aggression especially sets up a deep conflict, not so much with outside situations or other people—though we may view it that way—but with our body itself, with information about reality that it is trying to deliver. This is why people who are overcome with strong, habitual aggression so often live in a hellish experience of life and die in misery—they are at deep war with their own physical embodiment.

TWENTY-ONE

What Happens to What Is Rejected?

This leads to another most important question: What happens to all that denied and rejected experience that our body has already received? To put it simply, all that somatic awareness and experience is walled off from our consciousness. As we have seen, we literally freeze the body—which knows and is aware of the totality—so that we don't have to feel more than that very small portion we can accept.

The experience of the body, however, has not been destroyed by our rejection nor has it somehow disappeared. Rather, it continues to live in the patterns of mental avoidance and physical tension that we have developed around it. In fact, the ego—along with the physical freezing and holding that maintain it—is a large, ongoing activity of avoidance and denial. As Freud noticed a long time ago, if we know how to look at the ego in the right way, we can see that all the rejected experience that is held "down below" is actually visible in a kind of compressed, impacted, and pathological way, in the very nature and structure of the ego itself.

Thus, the experience that our body has taken in but our conscious "self" has been unwilling to receive dwells in a kind of no-man's land or *bardo* ("intermediate") state, in our body. There, we do subliminally feel it, primarily as an abiding threat and source of subtle anxiety that runs throughout our life. Thus, perhaps surprisingly, what we fear or are anxious about is never the external world in itself—rather, it is our own body, what it already feels and what it already knows.

Our ego maintenance, then, represents the ongoing activity of rehearsing and repeating, over and over, the "narrative" of our personal "self"—who I am, who I should be, who I want to be, who I must be, to survive as "me" and escape annihilation. It is very serious business, indeed. The more this continuous conceptual narrative is cut off from what the body knows, the more delusional we could be said to be.

We might think that the process of "walling off" experience is fairly simple, manifesting through obvious physical tension—a tight back, frozen shoulders, a rigid pelvis, and so on. The experience of Tibetan yoga suggests that this is a vastly oversimplified view. In fact, the "repression" that occurs when we push back against the body's knowledge involves every part of our body—not just our muscles and tendons, but our cartilage, all our organs, our nervous system, our bones, and even our blood and lymph systems. According to Tibetan yoga, when we push back against our experience, the totality of the unreceived knowledge is "held" in every part of our physical organism down to our very cells. In this way, the body is literally "petrified" and locked up, unable to perform—in relation to our consciousness—its genetic function, the natural function of its original "design." And what might this be?

The body's natural or genetic function is to take in the totality of its experience of reality. This totality becomes— for an ego-consciousness that is open to it—the ever-changing and reformulated basis of how the human being thinks about him- or herself, other people, and the world. Let us consider this process in more detail. In our usual state of disembodiment, when something occurs that is, in any way, jarring or threatening to our sense of "me," we can see our mind freezing against what our body is implying. As we saw above, we literally tense up so we won't have to see or feel. We are resisting and turning away from the somatic information coming our way.

However, the somatic work enables us to approach this situation differently. When we have gained the ability to reside within the body in an ongoing and continuous way while living our life, we notice how much information comes to us that, under other circumstances, would be highly troubling and cause us to turn away. But, abiding within the body, we find we can receive this information, however inconsistent it may be with what we had thought or want to think about ourselves. The next thing we notice is most interesting, even astonishing: as we receive this information, we find that we can easily and simply, sometimes with humor, sometimes with sadness, let go of what we thought, abide in the "unknown" space mentioned above, and sometime later arrive at a different way of thinking about situations, our lives, and who we are.

The more aligned with our body we are and the more we are able to receive its totality of experience, the more our conscious self, what we think about ourself and our world, will exhibit a loose, porous, and flexible nature, readily able to undergo transformation. We will be able to let go of what we thought; we will receive the new information the body is bringing forward; our preexisting concept of self will be able to dissolve; and we will be able to reconstitute our ideas of ourself—for that is part of our human way of being—but in a more informed, more realistic, more easy, and more up-to-date way.

It is important to emphasize that the body's way of communicating information, and the ego's relaxation, letting go, and reformulation in light of the new experience, is very different from the ego's habitual way of "processing" information. In our habitual way of operating, any new piece of information is put through the ego's sieve, the ego's way of picking and choosing. It is "processed," trimmed down, manipulated, and filtered so that the end product can be assimilated by the preexisting self-concept. The integrity of our preexisting "self" is thus maintained by basically destroying the life of our "new" experience.

Consider how people become our "enemies." Initially, someone does or says something that implies they do not like us, would like to undermine us, want others to think poorly of us, or are against us in some other way. Our usual response is to feel deflated or angry and to think, often obsessively, about what occurred until we have "figured it out." For most of us, what we figure out is to place this person in the category of "enemy" or adversary, a person who is defined by their hostility toward us and our revulsion toward them. Maintaining this conclusion inevitably involves ignoring the information of our body in several ways. For one thing, particularly if this is a person we have previously known, we begin to wall off any positive qualities or experiences that may have been part of our experience of them in the past. In addition, from now on, we are unwilling to allow in, to see or acknowledge, anything good in them. Thus we arrive at a caricature of the person, a greatly reduced version of who they have been, are, and could be.

In our habitual ego operation, then, our experience is unable to complete the circuit: body to flexible self-conscious ego, to dissolving of the previous self-concept, to reformulation of the "self," keeping it current with our true somatic experience of the world. Being unable to complete the circuit, the literally organic journey our experience is making toward consciousness is aborted, and it gets jammed back into itself, impacted as described. And there it stays, in a kind of unhealthy stagnation, where, in some instances, it may be unlocked through the kind of somatic work described here, or by some other form of somatic intervention or discipline, years or even decades later. In contemporary society, we talk about these as a release of "trauma." But actually, for our ego, all naked experience is "traumatic," meaning unacceptable. As with our traumas, so with virtually every moment of our lives—the full range of our experience is not admitted, but is pushed back, jammed down, and walled off, where it abides in the body as conscious or unconscious tension.

In the somatic work, the process is exactly the opposite: the integrity of the body's communication is retained. This leads to the breakdown of our previous way of conceiving of ourself and our world. In the previous example, rather than try to come to any conclusions about our apparent adversary, rather than try to actively "figure out" what happened and how it fits into our idea of our "self," we simply abide within the body, in the sting and the pain, and perhaps the humiliation and confusion of what occurred. Abiding in that way, we let all of it work on us, in the shadows and the darkness.

If we can resist forcing the process, over time we will inevitably come to a much richer understanding of both ourself and the other person. We are likely to see what we may have done or may have been in relation to them that contributed to their hostility. We may come to see their own pain in relation to their life and how we became an occasion for them to express it. We may see qualities or attitudes in our self that are somehow part of the mix that we had missed. All this information was, prior to the upsetting incident, unavailable to us. But, through opening to the experience itself as we feel it in our body, and being willing to let the body show the way, the incident may well become a catalyst to a larger way of being for ourself and a greater sympathy for this person and for other people. Through this process, we have irrevocably lost our previous way of being and thinking and have come upon something unprecedented, a new "self" and a new way of being, born from the ashes.

Many strands of contemporary research suggest that this open, free-flowing relationship between body and mind is, indeed, part of our genetic heritage and fundamental biological inheritance. Certainly, anthropological studies suggest that this kind of open, porous, flexible, ever-changing, body-centered self-concept characterizes contemporary hunting-and-gathering societies and characterized the peoples and communities of the Paleolithic Age. In light of this, it appears, as suggested above, that the increasing emphasis on having a solid, continuous, relatively isolated "self" through the agricultural, industrial, technological, and cybernetic ages represents a pattern of mounting dysfunction that is inconsistent with our genetic makeup, with how we are biologically set up to function. If so, then the kind of body work proposed here perhaps offers a way, without our necessarily trying to become different people in a different time and place, for us to reclaim a far more healthy and satisfying relationship to our body and rediscover our "original nature."

TWENTY-TWO

An Example

I would like to illustrate these points with a personal example. Although there are many different examples I might use in this context, this one seems especially fitting for the wealth of practical insights it affords into the processes and principles of the somatic work being described here. I describe the example here and will then draw out some of its more important implications toward the end of this chapter and in those that follow.

Many years ago, I was on a long solitary retreat. At that time, my mother was dying of cancer. One day, while I was sitting on the porch of my little cabin, eating lunch, completely out of nowhere, I felt a terrible and hopeless despair fall over me. Somehow I knew that this was not a feeling of my current self, but a long-buried memory that had surfaced, and yet the experience was completely fresh, vivid, and absolutely real. After a few moments of unbearable intensity, the despair abruptly vanished.

But it was immediately followed by a recollection from earlier in my life. When I was in my teens, my mother had confided in me her opinion that babies should be allowed to cry themselves to sleep because it "made them tough" and was "good for their lungs." She went on to say that when I was a baby, she had engaged in this practice, allowing me to cry in my crib, night after night, unattended. At the time she reported this to me, I reacted very negatively, becoming unaccountably angry. The moment I remembered my mother's report, I realized with utter clarity that what I had felt was the despair of myself as a baby crying for his mother, to no avail. I realized exactly how I had felt at that time, helpless and hopeless, abandoned to death. I also understood why I had never been able to bear to leave my own infant children crying and unattended for long and also why, when other parents left their children crying with seeming unconcern, it always upset me greatly. After my retreat, I filed this experience away as another retreat lesson, and that seemed to be the end of it.

A number of years later, long after my mother had died, I was leading a meditation program at a Buddhist center when chronic back problems seemed to intensify. I sought the help of one of the participants, who was a network chiropractor. Network chiropractors work with precise patterns of unconscious holding in the spine and elsewhere in the body. She gave me a few treatments, which seemed to relax and open much of the tension in my back.

One day, while I was receiving another treatment, I suddenly found myself in my crib, as a baby, experiencing the same terrible and hopeless despair that I had previously felt on retreat. On this occasion, however, it wasn't my adult self experiencing those feelings—it was the infant himself. Although I was not someone comfortable with or accustomed to showing much emotion, especially in front of other people, and especially with my own students, I broke into uncontrollable sobs and wailing, calling for my mother, pleading for her to come, begging her not to leave me alone. For the next two hours, this geyser of emotion continued unabated. The terrible pain of abandonment alternated with intense anger and rage toward my mother for leaving me and not coming to my rescue. My wife and one of my teenage daughters were in the house where we were staying and where I was being treated. My daughter later commented to my wife, "I thought Dad had gone completely insane. It was crazy. I have never seen him express anything like this, and, in fact, I don't think I have ever seen anyone express such intense pain and anger."

The experience of abandonment had somehow been stored in my back. At the time of the original abandonment and in subsequent years, it had not been processed; it was unable to complete its destined circuit of experience. Perhaps it "waited" until after my mother's death to fully emerge, because my mother was always a somewhat cold and unemotional person, and also quite fragile, and to experience the pain during her lifetime might have disrupted our relationship in a way that was unacceptable to me. Perhaps through the assistance of my chiropractor, in the context of a meditation retreat, with my mother gone, and with strength and confidence coming from many years of meditation, the experience was able to come to the surface and be experienced in all its intensity.

Things began to move in new ways for me after that. My back was not frozen in the same old way, and a dark shadow that I now saw had been with me all my life, as well as unexplained appearances of sorrow and sadness, now became somehow less threatening, more fluid, transparent, and workable. I also noticed that when feelings of black hopelessness arose, I was able to go fairly directly, and with confidence, back to being that baby in my crib, to stay with the small child's primordial despair for as long as was needed, until the feelings, in their own time, completed their work and moved on. Always, I found myself emerging refreshed, deepened, and with renewed openness and joy in just being alive.

This example illustrates the previous discussion in a number of interesting ways. First and most obviously, the terrible experiences of the small child in his crib—and quite likely other similar traumatic experiences of early emotional abandonment—had somehow become buried in my body, making their appearance initially in back pain. Second, this unacknowledged experience, though hidden from conscious awareness, contributed in some major way to a shadow that lay over my whole life. Third, the hidden traumas of emotional deprivation as well as their impact on my conscious experience had remained inaccessible to me: I did not recognize their shadow until I had moved beyond it. Fourth, we can also see here the impeccable timing of the body: my back pain reached an unacceptable level precisely in the context of a meditation retreat, when my mother's previous death and my own development allowed the buried traumas to be opened to consciousness. In that context, the original traumas could be experienced and lived through, and the emotions of anger and rage against my mother could be fully felt and integrated into my feelings about her, my understanding of our relationship, and my own, ongoing life. Strangely enough, the needed outside resource—my doctor—appeared just at this climactic moment.

Subsequently, I found myself with much appreciation for what my own journey toward embodiment and my lifelong meditation practice had offered to me in this process. In this regard, I was grateful for the sustained, physically present openness that Tibetan yoga cultivates, as well as the ability, nourished through embodied meditation, to experience very intense emotions and extremely painful mental states in a full and grounded way, not only without being derailed by fear, but with confidence and freedom from judgment. In these ways, I felt that my training and practice had enabled me, once the moment was ripe, to open simply and swiftly into the full chaos and terror of the small child's limitless despair; to remain in those feelings for as long as was needed; to go through the profound rage against my mother without holding back; and to exit the experience without getting caught by afterthoughts or judgments, but simply letting the whole thing go and moving on with my life.

TWENTY-THREE

Karma of Cause, Karma of Result

The concept of karma, the principle of cause and effect, stands as a philosophical centerpiece of Buddhism generally, and more specifically, of Tibetan Buddhist yoga. When the Buddha developed his teaching on karma, he primarily did so not by speculating about it, but by carefully and closely observing exactly how things worked in his life. It continues to be true today that the deepest insights into karma come from inspecting with focus and clarity exactly how things go for us. The experiences described in the previous chapter have been a fertile source of insight for me into what karma is, how it reveals the functional relationship of body and mind, and how somatic meditation opens the way for its purification and transformation.

The principle of karma may be divided into two parts: *the karma of cause* and *the karma of effect or result*. The karma of cause refers to *the way of acting and the acts* that create the unresolved karma, while the karma of result refers to *the totality of unresolved karma that we have created.* The karma of cause refers to the production of what we may term "unfinished business." In other words, there are certain ways we act in our lives that leave some kind of hangover, that will haunt us until it is resolved. To give a very simple example, if I leave the house for work in the morning in a rush and I am short with my wife without acknowledging it, much less apologizing for it, there will be some cloud in our relationship that will stay there until it is resolved. I have created unresolved karma. If it continues to be unresolved, it will contribute to a gradually increasing cloud bank of similarly unresolved situations that will haunt the relationship until dealt with. If none of this is ever dealt with, it could end in a relationship that is either dead or in the divorce court. According to Buddhism, each of us has created a nearly infinite mass of unresolved karma in this and countless previous lifetimes—the karma of result.

When we attend to the karma of cause, we look at how we relate to our life and experience to see how karma is being created by our way of acting. When we attend to the karma of result, on the other hand, we contemplate the entire bank of unresolved karma that accompanies us in each moment—recognizing that all of this is actually the result of our own previous actions. "Owning" the karma of result, the totality of our relative situation, as our own creation, empowers and enables us to take full responsibility for our life and who we are.

We can view the karma of cause and the karma of result in somatic terms. The unfinished business created by the karma of cause comes about through the incomplete mind-body process previously described, that results in holding patterns of tension. As we saw, when something occurs in our life, we tend to accept a small part of the total experience into our consciousness and block out the rest, so that it remains trapped in our body in the form of unacknowledged feeling, emotion, sensation, insight, and so on, held at bay by unconscious tension, holding, and freezing. When we resist our body's experience, we increase the backlog of incomplete experience and our somatic frozenness. In order to hold the increasing backlog at bay, we must develop more and more sophisticated ego strategies of avoidance, denial, and rationalization, and also increase the force of the energy we put into locking up and numbing our bodies to maintain our repression. This process is what is meant by creating karma, the karma of cause. As our ego situation becomes more and more at odds with what is held in the body, our karmic backlog, our karmic debt, and our bodily dysfunction increase. The karma of result is the totality, at any given moment, of what we have been unwilling to fully experience and the way in which we have managed to avoid it through short-circuiting the natural cycle of life.

According to Buddhism, each baby is born into particular circumstances that are in accord with its karmic situation, that is, its unresolved karma, at the end of the previous life. The entire complex of the baby's gender, physical makeup, general strength and constitution, experiences during pregnancy, family, local region, country, and culture, and even its birth as a human baby, reflects the baby's final karmic situation in his or her previous incarnation. Also included is all the unresolved karma from all of the person's previous lifetimes, stretching back into the illimitable past, which cannot be readily seen in the immediate situation, but rather resides below the surface, in the universal unconscious (*alaya*), in the form of mental traces and tendencies that will emerge at some later time. All of this is the totality of the baby's relative situation, the baby's karma of result. In this life, based on how we live in relation to our already existing karmic situation, we affect our karma of result, exhausting some karmic seeds and sowing others.

Some of the individual's karmic situation becomes evident during infancy and childhood, first to his or her family, then gradually to him- or herself. However, much of the unresolved karma—the part that is hidden in unmanifest form in the unconscious—will only emerge during later life, as the infant moves from infancy into childhood, adolescence, adulthood, and finally old age and death. According to Buddhism, most of the individual's unresolved karma will not surface in any given lifetime, awaiting another time and place, another birth, for the moment when its appearance becomes timely and necessary.

The small child is just a recipient of his or her accumulated karmic situation and, at least according to Buddhism, does not yet have the tools to actively engage and resolve the unfinished business of the past. When the child reaches adolescence, however, he or she begins to engage this karma in an active way and work with it more or less consciously—and this process continues from then until death. In a sense, all of life—whether or not one is a self-conscious practitioner of some spiritual tradition—involves engaging the unfolding of one's karma, creating new karmic seeds and perhaps resolving some old ones.

TWENTY-FOUR

Our Unlived Life

As we have seen, we create karma by never fully relating to anything that we ever experience or do. We experience things openly up to a certain point in the body; then, before it has been delivered fully to our consciousness, before it has completed its own process, in fear, we separate and exit into our thinking mind. As we have seen, this leaves a surplus, an overhang, unfinished business that remains pending, perhaps for a few moments, perhaps for a million lifetimes.

In the example described above, as a small child, I was unable to integrate—to maintain conscious connection with—either the horror of abandonment or the ferocious, murderous rage I felt toward my mother for her neglect. To have felt those emotions as a small child would have been overwhelming and, in relation to my need, would have made impossible the developmental tasks, in relation to the mother, incumbent upon a growing child. So I managed to "forget" the small child's despair and his rage for the time being, which enabled me to focus on the kind of maturation needed in order to continue the genetically given ontogenic process, to grow into life and its various stages. But, as we saw, the experiences of the infant were not really forgotten, for they remained alive and active though trapped in the body, expressing themselves in the shadow that hung on the periphery of awareness and in periodic sadness. It was perhaps also active in particular challenges I felt at that time in trying to help students who also experienced depression and despair in their lives.

We can speak of our unresolved karma, our rejected somatic knowledge, as our "unlived life." It is that very large part of our human existence that we do not consciously feel, engage, accommodate, or incorporate. It is something that has come to our body, something that is an expression of our karma ripening and coming to the surface, but that we have allowed to go no further. Many of us feel that we are missing life, that life is passing us by, that we are missing what our life could be. We don't know why we feel this way or what to do about it. However, when viewed from the point of view of the body, this unlived life is the life that is already ours, that is already happening, but that we are ignoring and avoiding out of our fear and desire to maintain our status quo. Of course, we long for this life, and, of course, our sense of missing it can be excruciating. It is our habitual way not to ever live through anything. We only live through things up to the point that we know what to do with them, and then we shut down. We don't allow experience to flow through all the way. Thus, we are continually creating karma and remaining locked in the grip of restricted awareness and incomplete experience. Meditating with the body provides a way for us to reconnect with our unlived life and, gradually over time, to learn how to live in a more complete, satisfying, and fulfilling way.

TWENTY-FIVE

The Body and Its Dimensions: The Full Extent of the Karma of Result

This precise physical body of ours—human, male or female, tall or short, and so on— is, as mentioned, the result of all previously created karma. In understanding the karma of result, however, it is important to realize that our body is not restricted to the envelope of our immediate physical person. In fact, when explored deeply through the body work, our body is discovered to have an interpersonal, and even a cosmic, dimension. The interpersonal body refers to the other people with whom we are interconnected; and the cosmic body refers to the "body" of the natural world, both animate and inanimate. While we shall explore each of these three in more detail later, it will be useful to touch upon them here because, *together, they compose the karma of result.*

In the modern world, we generally think of our bodies as being discrete entities separate from other people and from the larger world. This view is an expression of the disconnection we feel between ourselves and the interpersonal and cosmic dimensions of life. Through the somatic work, though, as we fathom the body through deeper and deeper layers, we come upon the somewhat startling discovery that, as far as our body is concerned, we are not separate from these larger communities of being at all. We see that our apparent separation was simply due to our unawareness of what our body knows, the result of residing in our head and experiencing our life from there. We realize that our body feels, senses, knows its interconnection with all things. In fact, we *are*, we exist, only in and through interconnection; ultimately, we are nothing other than "interbeing," in Thich Nhat Hanh's beautiful phrase. All of this becomes increasingly clear the deeper we enter into our somatic existence.

Our physical body, the one seemingly bounded by the envelope of our skin, is the first somatic "layer" we encounter in our practice. It forms the main focus of our somatic explorations in the beginning. The second body, the "interpersonal body," represents a layer that gradually begins to make itself evident after we have explored the more individual aspects of our body quite extensively and developed a relatively open and free relationship with them. This interpersonal body may be defined as the nexus of relationships we have with other human beings, of which we are an incarnation and an expression. The third body, what I call the "cosmic body," really only becomes accessible to us at a fairly advanced stage of our somatic practice, after much work with the physical and the interpersonal bodies. The cosmic body is the primordial "body" of the earth, of the natural world and its nonhuman creatures, of which we are, at an even deeper and more subtle level, embodiments and expressions.

Thus it is that the more deeply we explore this body of ours, the more we discover that what it "really" is, is not just this immediate individual body, but actually an interpersonal phenomenon, and then, beyond that, a cosmic phenomenon. Through this work, we discover that it is not possible to be fully embodied, fully present to our body, if we remain only within the confines of our physical bodies. If we want to be truly "grounded," fully real, and completely embodied, we will find ourselves needing to open to our body's interpersonal and cosmic dimensions.

Our physical body is the portal, then—the one and only gateway that exists—to the totality of our embodied existence. Our individual, personal body is the outward layer. The interpersonal network and the living energies of the primordial world abide at more and more subtle levels within us. The deeper we journey into our body, the more we come upon the infinite worlds of other sentient beings and of the cosmos itself. In this way, the physical body is the all-important access point to our embodiment in its various dimensions and layers, the incomparable, sacred gate. This is why the great siddha Saraha could sing:

> *Right here [in my body]*
> *Is sweet Yamuna [river],*
> *Right here the Ganges sea;*
> *Right here*
> *Are [sacred cities of] Prayag and Banaras,*

Right here the moon and the sun.
Holy places, shrines, and lesser places
All right here—
I've been there in my travels,
But I've seen no place of pilgrimage more blissful than the body.[1]

It is worth noting that, even though we modern people tend to think of our body otherwise, as an entity that is separate and distinct from the interpersonal body and the cosmic body, modern science is showing us that there is no solid, impermeable, discrete envelope to our individual body and that we are in constant and open-ended exchange with the larger bodies, just as our brain is with our lungs, our bones with our circulatory system: the same principle, just a larger scale. This growing modern acknowledgement of the profound interpenetration of our physical body with the social and cosmic bodies is certainly moving in the direction of ways in which the body is understood and experienced in Buddhism and Buddhist yoga, and also in many indigenous cultures.

---

[1] Jackson, Roger R., *Tantric Treasures: Three Collections of Mystical Verse from Buddhist India,* (New York: Oxford University Press, 2004), 80-81.

TWENTY-SIX

The Moment of Greatest Alienation

T he body, in its own wisdom and with its own impeccable timing, gives rise to some manifestation of unresolved karma in the form of a physical sensation, a release of energy, an injury, an illness, a dream, the powerful upsurge of emotion, a charged thought or memory, or, perhaps surprisingly, an event apparently from the "outside" world, such as a chance human encounter or a "natural" event. When some aspect of our unresolved karma surfaces in this way, when it comes into our awareness, it is said that that particular karmic trend is "coming to fruition." It has come to fruition in the sense that it has now appeared along with an inevitable invitation, sometimes a demand, for us to receive it, experience it fully, and thereby resolve it.

According to Buddhism, such gifts arise from the darkness of the body where all our unresolved karma is held. In Buddhist philosophy, the "holding tank" that the body represents is called the *alaya,* the universal unconscious. As the unconscious, the body holds all the karmic seeds that we ourselves have sown and that must, on our journey to realization, eventually ripen into the light of consciousness to be fully engaged, felt, and thus worked through and completed.

Such "gifts" of the body arrive, for all of us, moment by moment throughout our lives. According to Buddhism, there are two very different ways in which we can relate to such arrivals. In the first, we do not accept the gift, which arrives in the awareness of our body; rather, we turn away from it into the avoidance, the escape represented by discursive thinking. As we have seen, in this case we create further karma, the choice that most of us make most of the time. This leads to what Buddhism considers the perpetuation and even deepening of samsara—of our habitual evasion of our experience through somatic disembodiment. In the second approach, in accord with genuine spirituality, we accept the gift fully; we abide in our bodies with the gift, allowing the experience to make its full journey through our lives. In that way, we resolve the karma it embodies.

As discussed, we short-circuit our experience somewhere in midstream. There are two ways by which we do this: repressing it or acting it out. In the example given earlier of my despair as an infant, I blocked out awareness of the threatening feelings; I repressed the memories of what had occurred and what I had felt, simply to avoid psychic annihilation. It was through the wisdom of my own state of being that these experiences were temporarily marginalized—because I was so small and with as-yet-undeveloped ego strength. At the same time, it is the mystery of our incarnation that nothing is ever lost—everything, as a manifestation of unresolved karma, must, in fact, be retained because we will eventually need it on the spiritual journey to full realization. And so the infant's experiences were retained within my body for later attention and integration.

If I had been older—perhaps an adolescent—and had experienced the same kind of nearly lethal abandonment by my mother and felt the same kind of murderous rage, I might have attempted to manage the overwhelming emotion, to deal with its terrible intensity, through open rebellion against my mother, other authority figures, and society in general. Again, there is an accurate wisdom in such actions, because they defer the full intensity of experiences for which the time and opportunity of assimilation have not yet arrived. Though understandable and "wise" in its own way, each of these approaches—repressing the threatening feelings or attempting to get rid of them by acting them out—nevertheless clearly produce their own karmic results that can profoundly impact a person's life and create additional obstacles.

According to Tibetan yoga, there is a more creative way—than either repressing or acting out—to relate with our karma as it comes to fruition. This alternative is shown by the ability, gained through embodied meditation, to experience openly and fully the unlived and unintegrated feelings and emotions from earlier times. With those tools came the ability for me to stay right in the middle of the inferno of the horrific experiences of the infant self, to stay there while the fire burned through its own fiercest intensity, and to continue to remain until it reached its own conclusion, died down, and finally abated.

It is not good enough to experience the surfacing karma at arm's length, remaining at a safe distance from what is occurring. It will not work if, when the threatening contents arise, we step back and observe from the secure standpoint of our current self. If we remain removed, nothing fundamental is going to change. What we have to do is to become the damned—become that part of our self that has been rejected and cast out. We have to allow ourselves to enter whatever hell our despised experience has been cast into, taking on its full identity and reality, and its full human experience. Only when we are willing to do that is redemption possible.

This, I think, is one of the profound insights of Christian spirituality. The example of Jesus shows us that only when we allow ourselves to fully experience the criminal, the condemned, the utterly banished and exiled within us, only when we are actually willing to surrender to and identify with all that darkness and all that hell, can salvation occur. St. John of the Cross, always our mentor and our guide in these matters, tells us that the moment of the deepest, most complete alienation and separation from everything that is good and holy, from everything we know and trust, *is none other than the moment of redemption.* This is the only way; there is no other! In the body work, we must be willing to go even that far; otherwise, there can be no fundamental transformation. And the only way we can go that far is through our ever-increasing embodiment—the body work gives us the understanding, the methods, and, above all, the strength and confidence to do this.

To put this in general terms, the way to resolve karma is to experience what is arising—whether it's from the inside or from the outside—fully and completely, with no reservation, judgment, or hangover. For example, in the previously mentioned example of my leaving for work in a rush, being short with my wife, and then walking out with no further words, we can see that I am not relating with my experience in a complete way and that this is creating further karma. I am simply not present to the totality of my situation, of my feelings and my interactions with my wife. When I "rush," I have disengaged; I am in a disembodied state. I am running from the painful feelings of my situation—of having gotten up late, not having left enough time to get ready, fearing being late for work—and from being with my wife, who looks for some basic level of decency and emotional presence from me. In my disembodied state, though the anxiety is coursing through my body, I am only dimly aware of feeling it. The anxiety has me by the throat, and I am trying to deal with it by ignoring it and everything it reflects. I do this by going faster and faster, as if I could outrun the situation and outrun my anxiety. So, driven by my fear, I am skimming the surface of my life, dropping my tube of toothpaste, leaving my pajamas on the floor (for my wife to pick up), stubbing my foot on the bedroom door, spilling my coffee, all capped off by being short with my wife. I am in a state of complete disembodiment and in such a mind of confusion that I am unconsciously acting as if being on time is of more consequence than respecting the tender and open feelings of my wife, my life partner and truest friend.

At that climactic moment, if I had really let myself abide in my body and feel the anxiety and aggression toward this person whom I deeply care for, I would simply have stopped, looked at her, been present to myself, and opened to the uncertain future of what might be needed right now. And maybe I would have burst out laughing or found myself tearful. But, no: completely ignoring the somatic knowledge that was right there on the verge, I just kept going. Hence the creation of new karma—of additional karmic debt and additional karmic pressure, additional (if subliminal) guilt, and twisted feelings and compromised relationship. All this new karma, most likely, is going to be more painful and more difficult to resolve later than if I had just stopped at some point and begun to be fully somatically present to what was going on. We can generalize this approach to everything we do in life. Because we always have some agenda that we are engaged in trying to fulfill, we are never really there, never fully present in our bodies and to our lives, to its situations and our emotions, its people and its events. And not only do we resist the opportunities to resolve past karma that the situation offers, but, by resisting, we also create more and more karma, more and more unfinished business.

From the Buddhist standpoint, what is arising in our lives is never random, no matter how "out of the blue" it may seem; it is always the expression of unresolved karma. This means that everything that ever happens to any of us in our human lives, however "religious" or "mundane" it may seem, whatever our religious commitments or lack thereof, is thoroughly and profoundly spiritual.

It is also important to realize that the surfacing of karma calling for resolution is always experienced as a challenge to our current self-concept. This is because, in the past, we have sought to maintain our idea of our self by refusing to experience what is now surfacing. So the karma that is coming up calls us now to live through it fully, let go of the self-concept that has refused it admission, and become something else and something more.

This is the deeper meaning of the Buddha's teaching on the First Noble Truth, that life is suffering. Life is not inherently suffering. However, when we try to maintain a solid sense of "self" and to keep at bay the backlog of the karma we have accumulated, we experience stress, anxiety, and pressure from "the other side," from the unconscious, from the body. When we continue to wall off the karma arising in each moment, calling us to open, assimilate, and change, we are going to experience a constant struggle with life—a constant conflict with whatever is occurring and a continual war with our own bodies.

It is literally as if we are locked in a room with someone we have mistreated all our life and, though this person is trying to tell us how bad they feel, we refuse to listen. The pain of trying to shut out what is true about us and our life, which our body already knows in depth and in full, is what the First Noble Truth points to. When we actually open and listen, then an entirely different relationship to life comes into being. Life continues to unfold as before, but because there is no one resisting it and no one turning away from it, there is no suffering, only the experience of openness, freedom, and joy—the experience of full embodiment.

TWENTY-SEVEN

Beyond the Reactivity of Ego

When we do the body work, we drop down below our thinking process, meet the body in its own space, and explore what is there. Through this process, we find out a lot of things. First, we uncover the actual experience of having or being a body—the physical sensations; the currents of energy; the aches, pains, and positive feelings; places where we feel open and others where we sense constriction; areas of density and areas that are more porous and transparent; regions of coherence and regions where we feel in pieces; and so on. The discoveries are very literal, and they are endless.

Through this work, we also find out more about who we are as this *specific* human being. It is not that we uncover information in the usual, conceptual sense, to somehow enhance our mental image of our self. Rather, through what can only be called non-conceptual knowing, we begin to tap into a process that feels as if it lies very close to who—or what—we are.

This process unfolds as a succession of contents. Feelings, images, emotions, thoughts, sense perceptions, memories, hopes and fears, begin to flow through us. Sometimes the flow is relatively unimpeded; at other times, something will come up that catches our attention, catches *us,* for a period of time—a particular memory, a certain person, something of which we are especially hopeful or fearful, some impending event, and so on.

What is it that governs what arises for us in the body work? Again, what we meet is determined by the unique totality of unresolved karma held in our bodies. We owe a debt to the past, and this debt makes itself known in the form of some present experience expressing the burden of the past and needing to be attended to just now. As mentioned, all people, whether they are "spiritual practitioners" or not, and whether or not they work with the body, experience this very same process.

As we have seen, the arising of situations based on past karma is always more or less unexpected, because it contains at least something of what we have previously been evading or been unwilling to experience fully. Thus, for Buddhism, all experiences are, to some extent, unanticipated, unwanted, and, in fact, potentially, if not overtly, threatening. We didn't experience them fully in the past because they were threatening to our self-concept, so now here they are again.

According to Tibetan yoga, each moment of our experience appears initially as the abrupt appearance that is literally outside of the mind; at least it is outside of our conceptualizing mind. When experience initially appears, there is something there, but it first arises in the body as somatic knowledge that has not yet been "processed" by the thinking mind; it has not yet been "recognized" as one thing as opposed to another, and it does not have a label or a story attached to it. There is a feeling of totality to it, and accompanying it is also the experience of a mind that doesn't know what to think.

For example, the next time you hear a loud noise that you were not expecting, pay very close attention to your mind. You may notice that, at the moment of the noise, first there is this big thing that happened and instantly your mind just falls completely open. Startled, you find yourself momentarily lost. You aren't thinking anything—your mind is just empty. Very shortly, though, a succession of mental images and thoughts arises as you try to regain your orientation. Thus, you might first realize that what startled you was a noise. Then you may briefly scramble for where the noise came from: "Oh, the kitchen." Then you try to know what it was: "Oh, the flowers I put by the open window must have blown over." Then finally it's, "Oh no, I bet my beautiful vase broke." All our experience arises in the same way. Initially, in the first instant, there is no ground, no thing to be recognized, not even an observer. Each moment of our experience, in its first appearance, arrives as nothing we can know in a conceptual way; it is too much and we are too empty.

Thus it is that when something first arises, it appears from outside of our existing framework, and we have no idea whatsoever of what to think. So, for a moment, we don't think anything; we experience just a completely open and receptive state of being.

This is known in Buddhism as the "pre-thought moment," a moment of experience that is empty (in terms of our mind) but, at the same time, fully embodied; that is, it is being received by our body before "we" think or do anything with it or about it.

Our ego—paranoid, fragile, and reactive as it is—immediately responds with panic, with fear of the unbounded experience that has suddenly presented itself to us. In Trungpa Rinpoche's experientially precise and accurate description, we recoil from the experience of this undefined "something," and we try to figure out what it is and where it fits into our mental inventory. We begin to size up this experience, to develop attitudes toward it, label it, fit it into our own ego narrative, and weave it into our existing self-concept. The important point is that we have literally created the bounded and definable "thingness" that we eventually arrive at out of the seemingly limitless totality of what our body initially received.

For most of us, this process happens so quickly we don't even notice it. All we see is our own process of reaffirming me, me, me. We don't see the totality against which we are constantly reacting when we continually reaffirm ourselves in this way; the basic experience of our body, our preconceptual, somatic awareness, is lost. In fact, for most people, only the most catastrophic event, such as a car crash, sudden news of the death of someone we love, coming to the boundary of death ourselves, or a serious psychological breakdown can slow our ego process enough for us to notice, in any sustained way, the somatic awareness that underlies our incessant "egoizing" of everything. Such experiences, however, when they do occur, have the potential to alter one's life direction forever.

One thing about receiving experience as our body knows it, as a kind of totality, is that we discover that our experience itself is, in and of itself, actually neither "for" nor "against" us. It is inherently neither desirable nor undesirable. It is so vast and limitless, so complete and ungraspable, that we can, in fact, form no attitudes about it at all. This discovery enables us to receive and appreciate the karmic fruition of our lives in a much fuller and more complete way. At this point, we no longer avoid our karma. We no longer meet our karmic fruition with reactivity, selectively appropriating and rejecting it, and thereby leaving unpaid the karmic debt that our experiences hold or sowing karmic seeds productive of future suffering. In meeting our karma in the body, where it arises, we have, in a very real sense, turned our life around.

TWENTY-EIGHT

Empowerment

The ability to meet our karma in the body, where it arises, is extraordinarily empowering for people. According to Tibetan yoga, there are several important aspects to this empowerment:

- We hear the call. Whatever karma arises brings with it a clear and powerful call to us to experience it fully and thoroughly, without reservations and without pulling back. That is the very nature of human experience itself—that it arrives with such a compelling call. Every human being, on some fundamental though usually implicit level, feels the imperative to fully feel and fully experience. When we descend into the body and find ourselves increasingly able to heed this primal call, it leaves us feeling empowered and fulfilled on some very basic level.
- We trust the process. The more we understand the somatic work, the more confidence we have in the process it unlocks.

We see that our body already holds everything we need for the journey: all our past that we need to work on, all the present wisdom that we need to connect with, and all our future possibility that needs to unfold. We simply need to be willing to give up the arrogant, ignorant, and all-controlling attitude of the ego and surrender to the guidance of the profound wisdom the body already holds. All that is required now is for us to move beyond the reactivity of hope and fear, in order to accept our life in its spontaneous totality. Realizing this, we can discover a deep sense of trust.

- We trust the timing. Through repeated experience, we come to the concrete and personal insight that all karmic invitations are timely. The fruition of past karma arrives at just the moment when we need it in order to go further in our development. Past karma never comes to fruition too early or too late. Again, this instills a deep sense of confidence and an all-trusting openness in our life and its unfolding.

- We appreciate the opportunity. Astonishingly enough, we come to understand that each karmic invitation brings with it, always, the ultimate opportunity of our life. Through experiencing our life fully, as it is born moment by moment in our body, we not only feel the freedom of experiencing things completely and to their fullest extent, we begin to gain some basic understanding of the purpose of our human life. There is, in this, a profound sense of fulfillment.

- We recognize that we are unfolding. Whatever arises now does so because of ground that we ourselves laid in the past. Like all sentient beings, in the past, we partly received and partly did not receive what was going on for us. What we were able to take in was based on our maturity at that point, and, in a similar way, we rejected what we rejected because we were not yet ready for that next step. In other words, we are and always have been moving along a path toward ultimate fulfillment, toward the person that we are needing to become; moreover, we make this journey according to our own impeccable timing.

- We see that there is no problem. Within this perspective, we are able to take full responsibility for ourselves and to view everything that occurs in our lives, no matter how positive or how negative, as steps on the path toward our final realization. In a very real sense, we have never been separated from our self or alienated from who we truly are. There is not and never has been any mistake or any fundamental problem. This is what Trungpa Rinpoche once called the "ultimate positivity."

Understanding the karmic process within this somatic perspective has some important implications. For one thing, ultimately there are no victims. All of us, throughout our countless lives, have been "victimized" innumerable times. Difficult as the experience of "victimization" may be—whether it is at the hands of another person, a natural disaster, a disease, an accident, or some other life-altering circumstance—in every case, the experience is understood to have an ultimately positive meaning: it holds unique and irreplaceable opportunities for our own learning process and spiritual unfolding.

This does not mean, of course, that we should not do everything in our power to alleviate the suffering and the victimization of other beings. The fact that, in the life of a "victim," there are others willing, inspired, and able to help is critically important: it is part of the mitigating circumstances that may provide just the sense of compassion and literal assistance they need in order to understand and make the most of what they are going through. Our mere existence, and the fact that we are touched by another's suffering and are able to help, are all part of his or her positive karma. We should never shrink from the obligation another's victimization implies, even if, as is said over and over in the Mahayana, it costs us our life.

The teachings on karma suggest that, in a very real and most empowering sense, we are the willing, creative agents of the trouble that we so often seem to find ourselves in. This is true of the smoker who gets lung cancer, the philandering husband whose marriage breaks up, the workaholic who comes down with chronic fatigue syndrome, the heavy eater who gets a heart attack, the person whose angry words create hurt and chaos in his or her personal relationships, the person who rushes to work and gets a speeding ticket, and so on. In each of these situations, on some level, we know we are flying in the red zone. We are setting ourselves and others up, so to speak, for something to happen that will engage our pained and perhaps remorseful attention. How often do we think, "He brought it on himself," or even, "I brought that on myself"? We get into trouble on purpose, and we do it for our own good, for the learning process and the growth it leads to. In Goethe's words, "People in their deepest, most primal urges, unerringly know their own best course."

So, in some sense, behind all our most meaningless and most senseless activity, and behind all the chaos we create for ourselves, there is something profoundly intelligent. There is a life purpose unfolding, a directionality to our lives. That directionality doesn't come from an external deity but, somehow, from the very depths of our own human person, the most hidden recesses of our body. We could adapt Goethe's phrase to read, "In the deepest, darkest mystery of their bodies, people discover their own salvation."

Karma, then, is the arrangement of our life so that we learn. It is not some impersonal mechanism that just lands on us. In this sense, we go through everything we go through because something very deep within us requires it, in order for us to become who we ultimately are and need to be. It is, always, the ultimate reality of the universe flowing through us, being us, and coming to its own fruition in and through us.

This understanding of karma is able to emerge in a unique way through the body work. Through descending into the creative chaos of the body, through approaching the font from which our life constantly flows, we begin to see our own continually emerging karma "as in God's eye it is," to use G. M. Hopkins' wonderful phrase. In other words, rather than being entirely wrapped up in and preoccupied with *our reaction* to our karma, we are in a position to fully receive and taste it and also to contemplate why and for what it may be. When we do, we begin to see that, in a certain way, everything that comes about in our life is bringing something very definite, utterly real, and extraordinarily helpful to us. This discovery leads us to feel that our life itself is an unending process of blessing and goodness for us.

This understanding of karma also leads us to a place of genuine sympathy, compassion, appreciation, and deep respect toward others. We are sympathetic because we understand from the depths of our own being just how very difficult life is for all people. We feel compassion for others because we know very well how compelling is the reactivity we all engage in most of the time and also because we know it is not necessary. And we find much appreciation and deep respect for others because we can see that their trials, their suffering, and their struggles embody the very same path toward fulfillment and liberation that we find ourselves right now traveling.

TWENTY-NINE

Impersonal and Individual

As we arrive at a fuller understanding of karma and how it works, we find ourselves coming to understand our life as both less personal and more individual than we had thought.

THE IMPERSONALITY OF OUR LIVES

Before we learn how to engage the body fully and deeply, we tend to view our life in largely individualistic terms. We have a more or less governing concept of who we are—a concept that is finally individual to ourselves—and we tend to evaluate and judge everything that occurs from the vantage point of that centralized viewpoint.

When we do the body work, however, we discover that the karmic fruition that arises as the occurrences of our life, the totality of experience that appears to the body moment by moment, has a fundamentally neutral character. The way we experience this neutrality is that our life has a quality of "givenness." Things arise just as they do; they appear, independent of our personal expectations, judgments, or evaluations. Any questions of judgment or control come up strictly subsequent to the arising of experience. First, there is the totality in its givenness; second, there is how we may react to it.

In this process, we become aware of the distance—which is a great and impassable divide—that separates our somatic experience, over which we have no control, and our personal assessment, which we construct after the fact. The more we become aware of this disjunction, the more what arises in our lives gains a feeling of inevitability. Conceptually, within the framework of Buddhist philosophy, our experience *is* inevitable, because it is the natural result of prior causes and conditions. But the important point is that we *feel* this inevitability as a quality—the most striking quality—of our experience.

This experience of inevitability, just by its very nature, cuts off our usual, habitual stream of discursive judgments. So striking and "as it is" do we find our experience, that we literally do not know what to think and often do not care to think anything. And so our judging mind weakens and begins to dissolve. When our experience appears with this intense feeling of inevitability, it is as if we are viewing a brilliant and beautiful weather pattern that is so striking that all words and even all thoughts fail us.

Because of this, we find ourselves very much more present to what is occurring. And, owing to this, we begin to find within our experience a meaning, a direction, and a reason for being. In other words, we begin to find that our experience—completely independent of what we think or want to think—has its own inbuilt character, meaning, and purpose.

This purpose is discovered in the specific momentum and directionality of experience, its urge toward expression, and its impact on our environment, animate and inanimate, among which the human social environment is particularly prominent for us. We discover that, left alone, our experience will unfold according to its own inner nature. But we see more: our experience, left to follow its own course, has the most profound of all possible impacts on ourselves and others.

At this point, we begin to sense that our experience, and thus our immediate life, is ultimately not *about* us nor is it *for* us. We begin to sense that we are vessels or vehicles for something that is much larger—in fact, reality itself, in all its vastness—and that our lives are unfolding rather completely independently of our own personal sense of "self," with its various hopes and fears, its ambitions and agendas. We begin to realize, in other words, that our own life is ultimately not a personal phenomenon at all.

THE BIRTH OF OUR INDIVIDUALITY

Ironically enough, the realization that our life is not a personal phenomenon marks the birth of our true individuality. Our true individuality is quite the opposite of our life as personal. The reason for this is simple. To think of our life as personal, there must be some concept of a *person* or "self" in reference to which everything that occurs is viewed, understood, and evaluated. In other words, we can't think of our life as personal unless we have some notion of a "self" or a coherent, centralized "me."

As we have seen, this concept of "self," this self-conscious "me," is an abstract mental construction that we have fashioned out of the various encounters and events of our life. In our search for the comfort and security of a definable and locatable identity, we attempt to maintain this self-concept in the face of our experience. To do this, as we have seen, we have to continually negate our actual experience. In this way, the attempt to maintain a personalistic interpretation of our life involves denying our experience. When we drop below our conceptual fantasia, as noted, we encounter a level of experience that offers itself as genuine, unique, and powerful. When we let go of what we think, we meet in our body a being or a kind of being that is informative, self-affirming, and satisfying.

We experience this "being" that we meet in the body as completely and utterly unique. Of course, if we retreat to the level of concept, we can attach labels to what we experience and then compare and contrast it with our ideas about the experience of others, as the conceptual mind will do, and arrive at an assessment of what is the same and what is different. At that point, all uniqueness is lost. This is not because there was no uniqueness in our experience, but rather because the conceptual mind is, by its nature, unable to register the experience of uniqueness. Even to say "unique" is to identify what we have seen with our non-conceptual eye under a general rubric. As Kierkegaard noticed a long time ago, when we do this, we betray the very nature of reality.

But when we stay within the domain of the body, the striking appearance of everything that arises is that it stands apart from, and resists, any kind of conceptual categorization. In its vividness and abundance, in its illimitable, empty, yet arresting, character, our experience discloses the fullness of its being. It is self-defining—any attempt to provide an external identification inevitably involves losing it. Only when we remain fully present to our experience, within the body, can we be said to know it as it is.

If our experience arises as the fruition of past karma in accordance with causes and conditions, does that not negate our true individuality? When we understand karma fully, then we will see why every moment is and must be unique. Consider that the causes and conditions manifesting in each moment of experience of ourself and others are literally infinite, arising from all space and time, without beginning or limit. For this reason, no two moments of experience can ever be the same. This is the teaching of the Buddhist psychology (the Abhidharma), deepened in the most important and influential Mahayana Buddhist philosophical school, the "central philosophy of Buddhism," the Madhyamaka. Each moment is a distinctive appearance, a distinctive fruition, of the life of the universe. In each moment, the universe delivers itself in a fresh, complete, and unprecedented way. This is the core teaching of one of the most important Buddhist texts in East Asia, the *Avatamsaka Sutra*.

Again, when we abandon the idea that what we "really" are is a centralized self corresponding to our ideas, we discover ourself as the unceasing, ever-changing kaleidoscope of experience that arises as our life. So we discover that we are, in each moment, a truly individual phenomenon, not limited even (or especially) by any notion of a continuous or coherent "self."

As we have seen, these unique moments of our experience contain an inbuilt way, or *Tao,* an energy, intelligence, direction, and mission in the universe; and so it is that we find ourselves becoming—more and more effortlessly—the vehicles or conduits for this "intention" of our experience, of the universe, to fulfill itself. Amazing as it may seem to us, this intention—and we see this as it arises, as it finds expression, and as it impacts others—is utterly pure, untainted by any self-serving agendas or personal politics. We experience it as being in the service of, and as an expression of, reality or being itself.

This realization, of course, can only occur when any self-conscious "I," even any sense of "me" being me, has ceased, if only for a moment. When it does occur, this realization is accompanied by a very powerful and life-transforming awareness. Undeniably and astoundingly, we discover that, when life flows through us in such a pure and powerful way, utterly beyond any preconception or idea that we may have, we have found our true life. With an overwhelming sense of recognition, freedom, and gratitude, we feel, "This is why I was born. This is what my life is for. This moment shows me, finally and ultimately, why I am here." This marks the realization of our true, incomparable individuality.

THIRTY

The "Good News" of Chaos

Our exploration of the somatic foundations of the spiritual life leads us to an important discovery: The spiritual journey is not accomplished by disconnecting our self from the relative reality of our lives and "attaining" some "higher state." Nor is the journey made by ignoring the actuality of our life and seeking a bypass, a passage around it, to some distant goal. The spiritual journey of the human person is made only by meeting our relative experience with absolute directness and complete nakedness, and by allowing relative reality to ground, inform, and guide us, and bring about the transformation we ultimately seek.

But what *is* this relative reality that is so central to our journey? It is certainly not our self-conscious ego, with its inflated ideas of who we are and our place in the universe, and its agendas and strategies for self-perpetuation and self-aggrandizement. It is also not our preconceptions and concepts about the emotions we run into, the situations we encounter, or the people we meet. It is not our hopes, expectations, or fears. In short, this relative reality is not *our* version of things, things seen from our ego-centered point of view. When we stay mesmerized by our own versions and completely absorbed in trying to maintain those versions, we are avoiding our true relative reality, our karma. The more we avoid, the more we simply recycle our habitual patterns of avoidance and remain trapped in a lifeless and disembodied *bardo*, in which nothing can happen.

But what else is there? Some might argue that there is nothing else, that everything we experience in the relative way is just our own distorted version—that there is nothing at all beyond that. Buddhist yoga, however, says that there is another kind of relative reality—standing apart from and beyond our self-absorbed version—that is the world itself, abiding in its own purity, power, and integrity. This is the relative reality known in and through the body, the somatic knowledge that is the basis of our spiritual path.

The relative reality that is so central and essential to our journey is found in all those emotions, people, and events—before we interpret them—that seem to arrive from some unknown source, that crash in on us and throw our ideas about everything into disarray. We experience this "pure" relative reality as something that destabilizes us, drops us into a space of uncertainty, and disrupts plans and expectations. It is that which instigates chaos in our lives. This relative reality is what the body already and always knows and what we meet when we enter the body in our somatic work.

It is the partner who announces one day, out of nowhere, that the relationship we had thought was so secure is, in fact, not working at all. It is the mysterious pain that turns out to be a life-threatening disease. It is the "ideal" job that suddenly turns sour and becomes unworkable. It is the "sure" investment that evaporates with a market shift. It is the flat tire on the way to an important meeting, the coffee spilled in the boss' lap, the computer that crashes for the third time this week. It is the baby who wakes up early from his or her nap, just as we are about to sit down to practice, and the parent who falls ill and needs our help, just as we are about to go on retreat. All these things cause us simply to stop. We then find ourselves just abiding in the body, present to its somatic knowledge, with nothing to say or even think. We are back to square one, feeling freshly what our life is and how misguided our thinking about it has been. At that moment, we are abiding in the body's knowledge and are in touch with the world as it is.

The arrival of unexpected chaos also occurs with events that we would classify as positive: the "hopeless" relationship that abruptly becomes workable; a dead-end life that surprises us with an unanticipated burst of possibility; becoming pregnant after being told—and accepting—that it would never happen; financial disaster that turns around, leaving our depression and negative thinking nowhere to land; illness to which we have become habituated that resolves itself; the dull boring job that suddenly turns on a dime with new, open, and creative challenges. Again, what we have been thinking about our life—our mental picture—is suddenly revealed to be off-kilter and out-of-date; we have to let go of what we had thought, surrender to the complete and silent knowledge of the body. We need to go back to the beginning, reassess from the ground up—literally from the body upward—and see what's what and who we are, now.

It is these situations that represent our actual karma as it is known in and through the body. This knowledge of the body is quite apart from anything we may want or choose to think about it. Such situations are expressions of the body's knowing and are real and concrete in a way that our wishful thinking and biased interpretations are not. When we are willing to relate to this somatic knowledge, when we are present to and able to engage our actual karma in this way, our journey can begin to unfold.

The hallmark of the chaos brought about by meeting our actual karma is our emotional response. When things transcend the expected, we feel what we might call "open-ended" emotions, emotions that are somewhat out-of-control yet fundamentally somatic, felt in and through the body. The somatic emotions are very different from the disembodied ego emotions, which always contain an overriding mental overlay such as dullness, security, validation, self-satisfaction, arrogance, pride, certainty—more or less dead-end emotions that are limited in their role of ego self-congratulation, justification, and glorification, and have literally nowhere to go.

But there are other emotions or feelings that arise in the body and abide in it, that are open-ended because they do not have any particular boundaries or limits; they are not subject to ego control. These include feelings such as angst, anxiety, depression, hopelessness, fear, groundlessness, and emptiness, and also feelings of boundlessness, inspiration, and joy. Meeting, seeing, or encountering our actual karmic situation always represents an invitation to grow further. This has two major aspects. In the first, there is a growing realization that the person who we have thought we were or have been trying to be is inauthentic, phony, shaky, and of no real substance. We feel what we identify as our very self dissolving, disintegrating, and dying; we are falling back into the body. In the second phase, we recognize the claustrophobia and restriction in our "self-image" and sense the relief and freedom that begins to arise in our bodies, even as we are dissolving. If this is a process we have become familiar with, as we are dying, we are able to connect with an expansive experience of openness of our person, and we feel a dawning inspiration and joy arising from within.

In order to illustrate these points, it may be helpful to examine some of these emotions in more detail and to consider, in particular, the kind of sequential development they often hold.

- Angst: Most of us live with a perpetual, underlying angst, a feeling that whatever may be going on in our surface life, underneath it all, things are not right; they are not secured, and something is or is about to be awry or "off." We may appear to "have our shit together," but underneath, we know we don't.

- Anxiety: Beneath the angst, we may feel a more explicit kind of trembling of the soul, a strong, somatic sense that our foundation is shaky, our life is vulnerable, that really anything could happen at any moment. We often envy the security others appear to feel.

- Fear: Beneath anxiety, we may sense the ego death that is impending or actually occurring, and we are desperately afraid of letting go.
- Groundlessness: We begin to feel that everything is dissolving. We can find nothing to hold on to to provide a feeling of security or a reliable reference point. We may feel as if we are falling down, down through empty space.
- Depression: We feel some kind of strong inner pull—we are compelled inward and downward, into the darkness of the body, the darkness of the unconscious. We are approaching the totality of somatic knowledge, in which ordinary hopes and fears, ordinary judgments, have no footing and cannot survive. Of course, to our struggling ego mind, this feels terrible. We can no longer participate in life because we see how delusional and futile our own attempts at doing or accomplishing anything have been, how inauthentic our previous hopefulness toward life was. There can no longer be any emotional investment in the way we were and the way we saw life, because it is now seen to be empty and pointless. This descent into the body is a very powerful experience of ego death, though it is especially difficult for modern people because it is so stigmatized in the contemporary world and because it makes it difficult or impossible to participate in the "big lie" of modern culture and its materialistic values.
- Emptiness of non-existence: Finally, if we are courageous enough to let go of even the quite subtle judgments and evaluations implied by depression (I am worthless; the others

are making their lives work in a way I cannot), then we fall through the floor, even of the depressed mental state, into a space that is open and empty. Here, we arrive at an experience of complete embodiment, gained through descending deeper and deeper into the shadows and then the darkness of the body itself. We arrive at a place where there is no thought at all, just the total knowing of our soma.

- Openness and boundlessness: Then we may feel our mind open into a much larger sense of being than the one we have been used to. This can be experienced with a great sense of shock, then a huge relief.

- Inspiration: We may now sense something arising in our body—a kind of freshness, lightness, and possibility emerging quite of its own accord out of our openness.

- Joy: At such transition points, we can feel an energy in our bodies that can only be described as joy, at both the feeling of life within us and our own emerging being opening out before us.

We can view this whole process as one of sacred descent, descent into the body. We begin with the subtle discomfort and apprehension of basic human angst, the surface of human life, and feel a call—which may be experienced as a pull—to descend into something deeper. As we do so—perhaps mostly unwillingly—we encounter the deeper feeling strata, finally falling into depression and through to non-being. This is the last stop in our somatic embodiment, and, fully embodied, we experience the spontaneous life that then begins to birth.

This entire process unfolds from the initial experience of chaos, itself arising as somatic knowledge. When we are rigidly attached to our disembodied state, the advent of chaos is experienced as purely threatening. But when we have some understanding of the invitation that chaos brings, we can experience it as "good news."

When we try to meditate in a disembodied and disconnected state, we are unable to handle or relate with the chaos our body presents, and so we turn from it. While we may be able to arrive at some relative peace, the scope and depth of that peace is going to be severely restricted and limited. This is because, when we reject the chaos of somatic knowledge and exit into discursive thinking, we are turning our awareness against itself. We act, think, and feel as if the knowing of the body did not exist. In retreating into discursive thinking *about* something rather than just receiving it in its naked, somatic, and chaotic form, we have retreated from the experience; we interpose our discursive thinking—which is a kind of jammed-up awareness—as a buffer or screen to insulate ourselves from the direct experience. This, in effect, ties up our awareness in the ongoing efforts of resisting, pushing away, and walling off somatic knowledge.

By contrast, when we open ourselves to the "good news" of chaos, we are resolving or exhausting our karma and, in so doing, liberating our awareness into its natural, boundless condition. By fully experiencing what is here, without reservation, withdrawal, or repression, we are, in effect, dismantling the patterns of mental avoidance, resistance, and grasping that have characterized our relation to this aspect of our relative reality in the past. Through this process, we gradually release our preoccupation and investment in our thinking, and our awareness can return to its natural state.

Until we are willing to receive the chaos of the body and live through some of the wealth of information and emotions that have been offered to us but rejected, our awareness remains imprisoned. According to Tibetan yoga, somatic meditation brings us in touch with the fire of direct experience, a fire of all the vivid and intense pain held by these previously rejected aspects of experience. That fire of experience gradually burns, burns, burns up the structure of our ego. It is a visceral inferno, one that is said to purify awareness, to make the field of awareness very, very bright. The more we do the work and enter the fire, the more our awareness actually opens up. According to the tradition, enlightenment itself is when there is no more residual karma left. Then awareness, no longer tied up in the evasionary tactics of ego, is set free and liberated to its fullest extent.

THIRTY-ONE

The Body of the Buddha

A t this point, I would like to connect the previous discussion back into Buddhist history, with, in particular, Shakyamuni Buddha, who founded the tradition. Let us begin by considering what it is that makes a buddha. How might we define such a person? One very interesting definition given in the life stories of Gautama, the man who became Buddha Shakyamuni, is that a buddha is not someone who attains some ethereal and disembodied state. In particular, a buddha is a person who is fully embodied, one who is present to and remembers all his former lives, all his previous births. Not only does he remember them, but he *feels* and lives through them *as if he were living them once again*. In other words, to become a buddha, a fully awakened one, Gautama had to inhabit everything that he had ever been through, each event in every lifetime he had ever experienced. For a buddha, the unconscious, composed of all unremembered, unlived, unintegrated experience, must be brought to consciousness and thus exhausted. The bringing into awareness all the contents of the unconscious, the alaya, is what enlightenment is.

THE FIRST WATCH OF THE NIGHT

On the night of his enlightenment, during the four watches of the night, Gautama brought to awareness the knowledge held in his body at ever deeper levels. In the first watch, in the words of the *Buddhacarita,* the earliest full-length biography of the Buddha, he reflected, 'There was I so and so; that was my name; deceased from there I came here'—in this way he remembers thousands of births, as though living them over again."[1] Gautama's path to enlightenment, then, involved bringing the buried memories of his present and former births into awareness in a complete form, as though he were "living them all over again."

Why was it so important for Gautama to remember? According to Buddhism, in their full, uncensored form, *experiences are inherently nothing other than pristine awareness.* In Tibetan tradition, the matter is described thusly: "Whatever occurs is the expression of the awakened state." This is a traditional way of saying that experience, in and of itself, in its untrammeled form, is nothing other than the display of wisdom. When, however, we choose to forget all but those small fragments of our experience that are consistent with our concept of our "self," then—as we have seen—the energy of that wisdom is turned against itself; in opposition to

---

[1] Edward Conze, *Buddhist Scriptures* (New York: Viking Penguin, 1986), 49.

itself, it produces ignorance, and we lose touch with the vastness and freedom of the awakened intelligence within.

To attain enlightenment, Gautama had, therefore, to remember in this specific sense: he had to relive everything that he had ever gone through. In a very real sense, he gained a fullness of experience of his own history that he had never before had. He experienced something that had already occurred, yet he did so as if it were the first time; in a way, it *was* the first time, because his previous experience had been incomplete and left a residue in the form of karma. Now, he had to return to those long-lost worlds of his past with an openness to the totality of what he had gone through. His journey to enlightenment, then, represented an ever-increasing transparency to the most ordinary, mundane, and painful aspects of his previous existence, all those things that before he had managed to forget. He had to surrender to what had been, whatever had been, and give in to the devastating (from the ego's viewpoint) truth and reality of everything that had ever happened to him and his uncensored experience of it.

According to the *Buddhacarita,* Gautama's emotional openness and his intimacy with his own life experience had two profound impacts on him. For one thing, they obliterated any notion of a continuous, substantial self. The more he remembered, the more he saw that "he" had been so many different things at different times, that any idea of a coherent, ongoing identity made no sense at all. This "totality" that was his experience was all so vast, so chaotic, so intense, so contradictory, so overwhelming, so fathomless, and so endless that any attempt to make sense of it, to find any single and coherent "person," was futile. The Buddha's story shows the rest of us *why we must forget so much* in our struggling to stay in samsara; to do otherwise would shatter the very self-identity that we are trying so frantically to maintain.

In addition, the more Gautama remembered, the more he lost any sense of his difference or separation from other suffering beings. Over his countless births, he had, as the text tells us, been through everything that every human who has ever lived has gone through. He remembered—in the sense of bringing it all to present awareness—that we are all awash in a cosmic sea of ever-changing experiences, with no hope ever of finding any definitive footing, any dry land of a "self." The more Gautama remembered, the more he saw that he and others shared the very same joys and sorrows, the same life conditions, the same confusion, as well as the same hopelessness of resolving or coming to closure about any of it. The pain they felt—all of it—was pain that he knew, directly, right at that moment, as his own. This realization marked the birth of unbounded love, empathy, and compassion toward others.

From this, even more profound levels of remembering unfolded for Gautama. According to Buddhism—in both early biographical and also later tradition, particularly the Avatamsaka Sutra—we are all so thoroughly interconnected with one another that what any of the others experience is known to us in deep and subtle ways. We may remain oblivious to our intimate interconnections and interrelations only by ignoring, forgetting, and repressing this knowledge. And yet the information of what others experience is held within us, in our bodies; though implicit and unacknowledged, it is still alive, active, and impinging on us.

THE SECOND WATCH

On the path to enlightenment, though, this kind of ignorance must be overcome. The enlightenment story makes this point vividly clear. In the second watch of the night, Gautama looked into his own heart (*citta*) and saw the world "appear to him as though reflected in a spotless mirror."[1] He saw how beings endure the continual flux of death and rebirth, all in accordance with their karmic actions, and that nowhere can any of them find respite. He saw directly and in his own heart, in his own body, that nowhere, from the top of samsara to the bottom, is there any resting place, any security, or any escape from ever-present impermanence, from ever-present suffering and death. This served to confirm in Gautama just how futile and fruitless the pursuit of lasting or satisfying samsaric happiness is. And this insight, in turn, roused further the spontaneous compassion he was feeling toward all the suffering beings in his sight.

THE THIRD WATCH

In the third watch, Gautama's remembering deepened once again, and he called to mind what further things he already knew, in the depths of his own unconditioned mind, but had previously been unable to acknowledge. He saw that "living beings wear themselves out in vain.

---

[1] Conze, *Buddhist Scriptures*, 50.

Over and over again they are born, they age, die, pass on to a new life, and are reborn. What is more, greed and dark delusion obscure their sight, and they are blind from birth. Greatly apprehensive, they yet do not know how to get out of this great mass of ill."[2] Like all of us, Gautama already knew this on some deep, previously unacknowledged level; now it had risen right to the surface.

THE FOURTH WATCH

Gautama now remembered the ancient, inborn knowledge of karma that he had been blocking out: in the fourth watch, he saw how everything that occurs does so in accordance with the creation and ripening of beings' actions, including all mental and physical phenomena, even those ideas of a substantial personal "self" that we take for granted, habitually carry around, and take for real. This realization led him to this liberating insight: "From the summit of the world downward he could detect no self anywhere."[3] He understood that all the struggles that make up samsaric existence, all presupposing of a "self" that needs to be protected and maintained, are groundless, fruitless, and without reality.

Gautama's prior spiritual training and practice had involved a process of progressive disembodiment, a movement away from his mundane, relative experience as a human being. His two primary teachers, Arada Kalama and Udraka Ramaputra, had each taught practices by which one ascends through ever more disembodied

---

2 Conze, *Buddhist Scriptures*, 50.
3 Conze, *Buddhist Scriptures*, 50.

and ethereal trances, arriving first at the experience of nothing at all and then of neither perception nor non-perception. In his subsequent journey with five renunciant companions, Gautama sought to disembody in another way, by annihilating his body through extreme ascetic practices.

Gautama, however, finally realized that all of this was going in the wrong direction. He saw that in abandoning the relative, he relinquished the ability to attain the realization he sought. Whether one is trying to use the relative for purposes of ordinary pleasure and security (as most beings do), or trying to push it away in search of some ideal spiritual state (as his teachers and ascetic companions had been doing), it is always the ego's game, the same old game of forgetting, ignoring, repressing. He saw that only in remembering without limitation or reservation, only in identifying with the relative and embodying it fully, only in present awareness of the totality of relative reality, where ego has no foothold, may the ultimate awakening and freedom he longed for be found.

So Gautama reversed his direction and remembered. He opened himself to the full truth and reality of his relative experience, finding intimacy with everything he was and ever had been, and with the infinite array of others' experiences as well. The closer he drew to the concrete experiences of human life, and the more embodied he became in this way, the less room there was for any sense of a separate or discrete self. Finally, at the moment of enlightenment, there was no one at all, just experience itself fully displayed, free, complete, and beyond question. Truly, he realized himself as the world, as the process of reality unfolding in and as his human person.

When the Buddha arose from the Bodhi tree, awakened, so present and naked was he to "what is," and so at one was he with the experience of all beings—that he decided to share his discovery far and wide. With his person not being separate from others, his discovery of the liberation that alone comes from unreserved intimacy with relative reality was as much theirs as his. It was a human discovery for all. How could he not keep going, bringing the freedom he had found to others?

It is within this context that we can understand the well-known "universalism" of the Buddha. On one level, this universalism is that his way was applicable to all beings, of whatever station or circumstance. His discovery was of the human spiritual capacity, as such. But more deeply, his universalism is the realization that there is no truth, no final reality, that can be separated out and extracted from the totality and set up as some kind of landmark, some kind of special domain.

Conventional religion claims that "our truth, our reality, and our way are better than yours, so you should abandon yours and come over to ours." But the Buddha saw that *whatever our relative reality,* openness and transparency to it, surrendering to the wisdom it embodies, is the preferred, the ideal, and the only path to full awakening for human beings. In other words, the path to enlightenment for every sentient being is already implied in the totality of his or her karmic situation, the entire array of his or her life experiences, which ultimately includes everything that is. To attain to the ultimate is to open to, make one's peace with, and find resolution in being fully embodied in that way.

IV
DYNAMICS OF THE PATH: PRINCIPLES, PRACTICES, AND EXPERIENCES

THIRTY-TWO

Developing Peace: Somatic Shamatha

B uddhist meditation is generally described as having two phases: first, mindfulness, and second, awareness. In the first phase, that of *shamatha,* or quieting the mind, we select an object of attention and, through directing our mind to it, aim to gradually diminish our inner turmoil and arrive at a state of mental stillness. In the second phase, out of the stillness developed in shamatha, we seek to develop awareness, or *vipashyana,* clear seeing. The somatic approach to meditation and its practices, in some respects, recapitulates this basic shamatha-vipashyana structure of all Buddhist meditation, but with some significant differences.

In the somatic lineage, the body itself becomes the object of mindfulness. Through attending to the body as a whole, or to some part or domain of the body, our mind gradually slows down, deepens, and enters a state of peace. Someone familiar with Buddhist meditation might say, "Okay, that is shamatha."

This would be true, but with one most important difference. As we have seen, it is possible to practice shamatha, by attending to the breath at the tip of the nose, for example, and to bring the mind into a relative state of non-thought, seen as stillness, and yet continue to be completely disconnected from the body, from our karma, and from our journey. Again, as noted, it was exactly this type of shamatha that the Buddha learned from his first meditation teachers and found to be leading him in the wrong direction.

The problem with this somatically ungrounded type of shamatha, and the "peace" that it leads to, is that it is not full, complete, genuine peace. Rather, it is a kind of hard, brittle, and cold peace that includes a subtle effort to hold the body at bay. The warmth of the body, and its complex sensory and feeling life—the embodied totality of its experience—are walled off. Enfolded within the hard edge held against the body by this type of shamatha are the classic three poisons in an active, but extremely subtle form: grasping at a "peace" that is easy and uncomplicated; aggression against the abundance, turmoil, and chaos of the body's life; and ignorance of the vast world the body knows and also of the meditator's own ego-driven "spiritual" agenda.

The practice of somatic meditation, on the other hand, does bring us into a state of peace, but it is a profoundly somatic peace—one that is inseparable from deep relaxation—which permeates the body like a deeply satisfying, spreading, golden glow. We feel the peace, not in a primarily mental way, but more in a fully physical way. It is not our mind that is at peace, but rather our body that is deeply peaceful, relaxed, and at extraordinarily deep ease. Shamatha, when practiced in a somatic way, can lead to a deep sense of inner well-being and even bliss.

It is helpful to observe the process through which we arrive at this state of fully grounded and connected relaxation, peace, and well-being. In some respects, this process is quite different from, and far more spontaneous than, the more usual practice of shamatha. Again, take as an example the most common instruction given to shamatha practitioners: to attend to the breath at the tip of the nose. They are often instructed to focus on the breath, factoring out and even ignoring any thoughts, perceptions, and feelings that may arise. The ego ambition of the practitioner to attain this peaceful state is what occupies the focus of intention and drives the practice.

As mentioned, modern people, owing to their habitual disembodiment, already have great difficulty with somatic aspects of sensation, feeling, and emotion. Because of this, perhaps without realizing it, they tend to conceive of the "peace" they are striving for as a state without sensation, feeling, emotion, or even any content at all. When they attend to the breath at the tip of the nose, they are trying to achieve a peace that is disembodied. Sensitive people often find this approach overly aggressive, and rightly so. Many report that it only further increases their sense of disconnection from their sensory and feeling life and further alienates them from any sense of authentic existence. The result is often the feeling of a "hard heart," vacancy, or numbness.

When we practice attention to the whole body, we are instructed to use one of the methods of simple somatic awareness or one of the many body-oriented breathing techniques, such as those described in the Appendix. "Just carry out the practice with an open mind and open heart, but let go of any attempts to achieve anything." We are instructed not to set up any conceptual ideal, such as that of peace or stillness. We are simply attending to the body, with gentleness and curiosity, to see what it brings.

What happens is that the body, through the processes described above, begins to wake up. As it does, we gain a sense of being physically present and grounded in our bodies. We feel we are inhabiting our bodies more and more fully; we begin to include all the experiences of sensation, feeling, and memory that come along with that waking up. In these practices, in a real sense, we are removing the aggression of the ego's conceptual impositions and overlay on the body. We are taking away the heavy lid of preconceptions and agendas under which the body's life had been going on, pushed down, repressed and depressed, rejected and unseen.

Will Johnson comments that uncontrollable discursive thinking is largely the result of energy that is unable to flow freely through the body. Dammed up in the body, it manifests in the pathological form of the compulsive thinking that is the bane of so many modern meditators. Because the energy of the body is denied, it escapes in the only ego-acceptable form it can, as rampant thinking. The more the conscious mind sets itself against the body and its life, the more out of control our thoughts will be. By the same token, though, when we begin to remove the ego blockage, when we surrender our awareness into the body, then the body's natural process begins to unfold in an open and unobstructed way. The body relaxes, our awareness pervades the body, discursive thought naturally and spontaneously subsides, and we enter a state of true, very deep somatic peacefulness and relaxation. We have finally begun to take the body seriously and listen to it, and our body—knowing exactly what is going on— responds by bringing us a very great gift: the joy and bliss of our simple physical existence.

THIRTY-THREE

Are We Willing to See?
Somatic Vipashyana

The profound relaxation that comes through the somatic shamatha work, the sense of physical peace and well-being, is deeply satisfying. Our experience here is so compelling and brings such contentment that we might think, "This is it. This is what these practices are for. What more could one want?"

Powerful as the experience of this fully grounded peace is, though, it is only the first of the two stages of practice mentioned in the previous chapter. Out of the experience of fully relaxed and embodied ease, we find ourself faced with the challenge of looking at what now begins to arise and trying to take it in fully.

Shamatha, the stillness practice, creates an environment, a staging area. It creates a situation in which we will be better able to *see*. And *seeing* is the goal of body work, for it is only through seeing that we are able to change, to experience the fundamental human transformation that we seek. Shamatha is like stilling the agitated surface of a pond, so that it is utterly calm and clear. As we gaze at the surface of the pond, now that its wavelets, its eddies, and its ripples have been stilled, we begin to see—down into its depths—and we begin to observe what wonders are there: fish of all shapes and sizes, tadpoles, turtles, and other beings swimming in it, the plant life growing up from below, and the rugged, colorful bottom itself.

The more we look through the still surface into the depths, the more we realize that our body is inviting us into a process of more and more intimate communication and even communion. As we proceed, we sense that we are engaged in a never-ending process, one that unfolds ever more deeply. First, our body invites us to approach it. Then we are called to make contact. Next, we feel our self drawn to deeper and deeper levels of quietude, harmony, and tranquility. And then, quite spontaneously, we find ourself drawn even deeper to see. Again, shamatha, the cultivation of peace and relaxation, doesn't change us; it is the seeing—vipashyana—that brings the transformation, and that is what we are looking for, why we are here. Seeing is the main point.

But to see in what way? This question cannot be answered in any specific sense. We can say that the body is calling us to see or to know more—more about it, more about our self, more about life and reality. And this is an understanding—not an intellectual understanding, but a preconceptual, stripped-down, somatic sense that comes from being present to what is being shown. It is like the knowing that happens when we wake up in the morning and feel the presence of our beloved lying beside us—it is that simple, immediate, embodied, and direct.

What needs to come upon us from the body cannot be anticipated; it can only be known when it arrives. We feel it arising in our body, and the more deeply we relax, the more we find ourself being visited by somatic emissaries, so to speak, arriving as guests, bringing offerings and gifts of all sorts.

What do they bring? We can say they bring what we did not previously feel or sense or know. This is not something that we did not know in the sense of missing information; they are not adding to our inventory of facts, filling the boxes and cubbyholes already existing in our mind. It is not something lateral or horizontal that they bring, as if they are just amplifying our already known world.

What we did not previously know, which they deliver, is more a way of existing. The body is not interested in our acquiring additional information; it is only interested in our growing into a deeper, more complete, embodied, and authentic way of being. So the knowledge that is brought really involves a shift to a different, now vertical dimension, one that is more inclusive, subtle, and profound.

When this new "somatic information" arrives, the only way we can really meet it is by letting go of the old, releasing our previous life. And this is where the process becomes extremely personal, very challenging, and sometimes quite painful. The more relaxed our body, the more open our awareness; the clearer our vision, the more we are going to see. So the question that faces all of us is this: Are we willing to see what is beginning to arrive, however much it may put us through? Do we have that much longing, confidence, and devotion to our life, to reality, to the unknown that undergirds our existence?

THIRTY-FOUR

Falling Apart

When we engage in somatic shamatha and somatic vipashyana, then, as mentioned, our experience begins to open up in new and often surprising ways. While it is not possible to generalize much about this process, in the somatic lineage, this much is said: in the work, our body doesn't care what our personality may have to go through. This is an ironic way of saying that our ego's agenda is one thing and our body's agenda is another. Our ego is generally bound up in trying to hold everything together. Holding everything together really boils down to holding "me" together by staying disconnected from the body.

Our body, however, has something quite different in mind, so to speak. It invites us to let go of what we are trying to maintain and to drop down into a deeper and fuller way of being. The body has no interest in our keeping things together and, in fact, inherently undermines our attempt to do so. This is why so many people strenuously ignore and tune out their bodies: they are unwilling to surrender their ambition of focusing exclusively on the "me" and its survival. But the body, once we begin to pay attention to it, leads us into a space where we begin to "fall apart," to lose control of our ego project of tightly managing our experience and remaining in a state of ignorance and disconnection. Ego distress naturally accompanies this process; hence, the comment that whatever the conditioned personality may have to go through on the journey is not something that worries the body in the least. And so, as we do the body work, we do indeed begin to fall apart.

Falling apart has been discussed as part of the meditative path by a number of Buddhist teachers, and practitioners are advised to go along with the process and trust it. In most discussions of the topic, however, two things have not been sufficiently emphasized. First, falling apart is a *necessary* part of the journey, not just something that happens to some people. It is an inevitable part of entering through the gate into larger being.

Equally important, *falling apart is a deeply somatic experience.* Let us be clear: What falls apart is not our body, not at all. The only thing that falls apart is our mind or, more specifically, what we typically think about everything, all our concepts of "me" and "the world." It is the self-absorbed, self-congratulatory, or self-mutilating activity of our conceptual process that begins to wobble, totter, shudder, give way, and collapse under the weight of our somatic experience.

But when we fall apart in this way, we notice that the experience is intensely somatic. As our conceptual framework begins to wobble and totter, we feel first slightly uneasy, then queasy, then distressed, and then quite anxious indeed. As it shudders, we feel an increasing dread. As it begins to give way, we experience strong fear. As it collapses, we feel a rush of intense energy that we might associate with panic or terror. One can hardly miss the increasingly somatic nature of this process of falling apart. Uneasiness is felt as a kind of slightly sick feeling; as our falling apart continues, with increasing distress, we feel anxiety and then dread—we may feel like throwing up. While these feelings tend to be localized in the belly, when we begin to experience strong fear, the feeling becomes more extensive—we feel fear through-out our thorax, belly, heart, and throat. Our face may burn and our head throb, and we may feel dizziness or even some vertigo. Then when we feel panic or terror, there is a release of energy that we may experience as rather open and empty, not solid in any physical way yet pervading our whole body. The feeling is very much in our body, yet the solid ground we usually associ-ate with our bodily experience just isn't there. We are finding a very different, much more purely energetic experience of our so-called body.

So, as our mind, or what we think, falls apart, at the same time, *we fall into our body*. But the body we fall into isn't one thing—it is a cascading series of ever-changing, ever-deepening events. We are discovering a lot of things about "physical embodi-ment" that we did not know and perhaps never even imagined.

Falling apart is a troubling experience for all of us, to say the least. We feel our mental superstructure become shaky—trembling, tottering, then plunging into emptiness. When this occurs to people who are disembodied, it is very difficult to stay with the process of falling apart, to follow it through and reap the benefits it offers. If we are primarily in our heads, we will short-circuit the experience and exit into thinking. We will run after strategies of distraction, medication, therapy, work, and so on—anything to try and make sure we don't have the experience again. However, if we are grounded in our physical being, if our awareness is sensed as pervading the body, if in the background of our psychological undoing we feel the body's own sense of peace, well-being, and—dare I say—*security* of a fully embodied existence, then falling apart, while painful, is no big deal.

When we let ourselves fall apart in this way and allow ourselves to fall into our body, we come upon an experience of somatic existence that is quite unique. At this point, the body is like a vast ocean, and our distress at falling apart is like a sudden gust of wind that sweeps down and momentarily churns up a patch or sector, sometimes in big, violent waves, clashing against one another, throwing up cascades of white spray—in a certain sense, a vivid experience, one that can be awe-inspiring, terrifying, and even beautiful, in its own way, but definitely no problem, at least not in any fundamental sense.

So we mustn't be afraid of falling apart. This is just the falling apart of what we think of ourselves and what we assume we need to be. It is only the falling apart of our frozen disembodiment and our self-imposed limitation. So let us realize what a blessing it is when our practice with the body leads us to the point of falling apart. Don't worry, we are not falling into the pit of despondency and despair. We are not falling off the face of reality. In fact, we are falling into reality. We are giving birth, birth to ourselves. And birth is never given without pain and without surrender.

Our ego, our self-apparatus, our disembodied life, is like a suit of armor that is way too small. We are in there, we are being constricted to death, and we are suffocating, drowning in our own psychological and spiritual vomit. Then somebody says, "You know, if you follow the spiritual path, you can get out of this." So we try it out, we practice, and the suit of armor starts falling off. And, of course, then we see what the process is really like—we begin to feel like a raw nerve. We feel very vulnerable. But, on the other hand, we feel the fresh air against our skin, the warmth of the sunlight, the cleansing of the pure rain. We finally begin to feel free.

So yes, we are falling apart and we feel vulnerable, shaky, and maybe even a little crazy. But we are present in our body, in our feelings, like we've never been before. We are starting to wake up and feel our own life fully, after all these years.

THIRTY-FIVE

Tracking Our Emotions

W hen we carry out the body work and begin to experience our self falling apart, we generally find our self feeling strong and sometimes very intense emotions. It is as if the breakup of our previous psychological rigidity and solidity opens up a much more vivid, full, and raw emotional life. This raises the question of the relationship between the body work and the appearance of these emotions and feelings, and how we may work with their new strength and intensity.

Emotions such as passionate yearning, violent rage, desperate loneliness, boundless paranoia, or terrifying fear of annihilation do not just appear in our state of mind out of nowhere. In fact, they are the end result of a process that begins with the primeval openness of our physical body, moves through increasingly differentiated energy to more specific feelings, finally appearing in fully developed form as emotions with more or less explicit links with our story line or ego narrative.

When we become experienced in somatic meditation, we are able to track this process in two different ways. First, as we work with the body, we begin to notice the different levels in the arising of emotion. We can't always look at these directly because, if we do, we actually interrupt the process. But through the work, through sidelong glances that we experience in a kind of random but ongoing way, we gradually develop a topography of the journey our emotions make from the primeval somatic state to their fully developed, most neurotic and ego-bound manifestations.

The other way we learn about where emotions come from and how they come to be is through following the process backward. We can begin with highly charged, intense emotions, and, through our somatic explorations, we can track them backward, through their various developmental stages, to the point of their origins.

In this working-backward process, which the body work makes possible, we want to begin with the highly charged emotions. However, in the beginning, although we may feel strong emotions, we find that they are tangled up with our story line or narrative. "I feel angry because…," "I feel desolate because…," "I feel paranoid because…," and so on. Initially, we need to let go of our narrative preoccupation. We do this through entering into the body. When we do so, while the narrative may dissolve, the emotions do not. At this point, we simply rest in the supercharged atmosphere of our strong emotions, wherever in the body they may be appearing.

There is a common mistake that beginning somatic meditators may make at this point. When they let go of their story line, they may, without realizing it, push away and repress the emotions that are driving it. The trick here is to descend into the body actually looking for the location of the emotions in question. If we stay fully within the body, the story line will drop, and we will be able to abide with the intensity of the emotions.

At some point, the turbulent quality of the emotions we are feeling will begin to settle out, and we will discover a more subtle, continuous feeling underlying the more dramatic displays. Behind anger may be sadness; behind paranoia, fear; behind desolation, hurt feelings. These feeling states are likely to be somatically more generalized than the turbulent emotions. At this point, our task is just to abide in our body with whatever feeling may be going on.

As we continue, an even more subtle level of experience emerges, a general "felt sense"[1] in the body. While it is difficult at this stage to pin down, with any certainty, what we are feeling, we know definitely that "something" is going on. Yet it can only be felt and sensed, not "known" in a more conceptual way. The body will reflect what we have called above a "totality" of experience. It embodies the totality of what the body knows, so it has no specific location within the body. This totality of somatic sense also cannot be named because it is so abundant and so complete that

---

[1]   Philosopher and psychotherapist Eugene Gendlin's term, discussed in interesting ways by John Welwood. *Toward a Psychology of Enlightenment*, (Boston: Shambhala Publications, 2000), see index for references; and David Rome, "Searching for the Truth that Is Far Below the Search," *Shambhala Sun*, (Sept. 2004): 60–63 and 91-93.

any naming would be limiting and artificial. Moreover, what the body knows at this level is implicit, because what we are sensing is folded into, enfolded within, the "something," not yet emergent into the light of our ordinary ego consciousness. The felt sense is a kind of global somatic environment, a totality of just how we are feeling our existence just now. We can't get a conceptual hold on it or pigeonhole it, or else we would lose it; but it is there, emerging, as a particular kind of galaxy of experience.

Beneath this, we may feel a boundary beyond which we cannot pass, at least in terms of having a "something" that is our experience. We sense that boundary initially as fear or even panic. But fear of what? Panic in relation to what? If we abide in that fear or panic, look into it and through it, we may suddenly find ourselves "lost in space," so to speak.

Here, finally, we arrive at our most basic experience of being alive: just the empty, open space of our awareness. When we journey down into the body, to its deepest levels, when we extend our awareness from subtlety to greater subtlety, we eventually arrive at the completely open domain of empty space, our basic body, our basic nature. While this nature is open, spacious awareness without any boundary or limit, nevertheless, it is colored by an energetic demeanor. As the great Dzogchen master Tulku Ugyen put it, this basic, empty awareness is like space suffused by sunlight. It is that subtle. And to arrive there is to arrive at our longed-for destination of full embodiment—it is what our body ultimately is.

THIRTY-SIX

Trusting Our Emotions

The body work calls us to fully and completely *be* with each layer of our experience, whatever is arising within us. This includes the narrative of our "self," progressing through the turbulent emotions, the more subtle feelings, the felt sense, our fear or panic, and our own nothingness. In the work, there can be no rush. Often, we feel that we have to do something about our vivid experience, especially our strong feelings and emotions—and the sooner the better. That, actually, is a large part of our problem. If we feel a tremendous amount of anger or frustration, overwhelming nervousness or fear, terrible emptiness or meaninglessness, we often find our self unable to remain with what is arising. Certainly, when we are not grounded in our body, it is highly unlikely that we will be able to stay with the feelings and emotions that arise.

When we breathe into our body and are fully present, though, we find that the emotions come. When they do come, we go through some kind of process, and then they go, and there is no problem in any of it. How can this be? It can be because we are identifying with a deeper part of our self. We have unplugged our thinking mind for the moment, and then we are there, just in our body, with what is occurring there. We experience the emotions and feelings with no sense of pressure to do anything about them. Of course, when we do this, our conceptual mind is always hovering in the background, our fear tempting us to do something. Frequently, we exit into thinking. So then the practice is to just keep coming back to the body, and feeling what we are feeling.

If we can learn to feel our emotions without rushing, they become the offering that is desperately needing to be expressed in the particular human situation we are just now in, whatever it may be. But we have to take the impulsiveness and the fear out of our expression. We can do that simply by being in our body fully and allowing the emotion to have its life, to move through us to expression in its own time and way.

Often the expression will be the exact opposite of what we might assume is appropriate. For example, if somebody makes us really, really angry and we just allow that anger to burn in us, let it burn without giving in to reactivity, then often quite of its own accord it will turn over, perhaps, into a gesture of kindness that softens everything, or a joke that liberates the situation, or some act of compassion that seems so unexpected and outrageous in the given context that it opens everything up. This kind of expression is not, in any way, strategized, self-conscious, or deliberate. It just arises out of the emptiness of the emotion itself; it surprises us just as much as it does the other person, and brings a sense of open space, freedom, and delight. It can really be quite amazing. As it can be with anger, so with jealousy, paranoia, want, ignorance, fear, hope, or any of the other painful and threatening emotions.

When we remain within the body and are thereby able to remain open enough to allow the process of the emotions to unfold in their own way, we make the startling discovery that the so-called "neurotic emotions" are not inherently neurotic at all. The neurotic emotionality—the self-absorption or twisted reaction that often happens with us—is not a result of the emotions themselves at all, but rather of our attempts to get control of them, to short-circuit their own natural, inborn process, and to prematurely come to closure about them. This discovery, which we make over and over in working with subtle as well as highly charged emotional states, can be experienced as astonishing, moving, and deeply inspiring.

At the beginning of this book, I suggested two possible reasons why modern people often have so much difficulty trusting emotions and working with them in an open way: the particular, highly structured, even rigid expectations of modern life; and a kind of basic paranoia about emotions that emerge from our cultural and religious heritage.

A further, perhaps deeper reason for modern discomfort with emotions is worth mentioning, because it suggests that a shift in our basic understanding can help make emotions more trustworthy and workable, even given our contemporary cultural context and our history.

As we have seen, our modern disembodiment means that people live largely within a conceptual world of their own making, attempting to "handle" experiences by fitting them into the continuous, conceptual narrative of their "I," or ego. As noted, the more disembodied we are, the more strident and compulsive this incessant narrative becomes. In addition, the more disembodied we are, the more isolated and disconnected we are, not just from our emotions, but from a feeling of connection with other people and the larger world. Our disconnection and isolation are reflected in the high degree of personalism (everything is about me, narcissism) and individualism (I am a free agent with no inherent ties or obligations to anyone or anything) found in modern societies. The personalism and individualism that mark modern people is, in other words, a direct function of their disembodiment.

It appears to be true that emotions seem especially overwhelming and frightening for us modern people because of our overly disembodied individualistic and personalistic understanding of them. In other cultures, emotions are often understood within a much larger, less individualistic context. For example, Malidoma Somé speaks of emotions within a different, more transcendent frame of reference. Malidoma says that when someone in his village is taken over by a strong emotion, the entire village attends to that person. The reason is that, for the Dagara people of Malidoma's homeland, strong emotion is never about just one person alone, but rather about the village community itself. In his or her highly charged emotional state, a certain person is understood to be giving birth to something that the entire village needs to know and needs to address. Beyond this, emotion is considered one of the primary ways that the "unseen" or "other" world of the ancestors—the transcendent source of life, well-being, and wisdom—transmits needed, life-giving information to the human community.

Vajrayana Buddhism articulates a similar perspective. When strong emotion erupts within us, it is regarded—in its own nature—as beyond ego and inherently pure. This means that it arises from a realm beyond ego—the buddha nature—it cuts through our ego stability and desire for control, and it invites us to contemplate the wisdom that is contained within it. Hence, in the Vajrayana, practitioners invite the chaos of emotions and attend to them with meditative presence and openness.

When, as modern people tend to do, we regard emotions that we experience as just about us, then their interpersonal and transpersonal implications are denied. We try to "handle" the great power they embody within the frame of our personal self, our individual history, and our individual life plans and ambitions. As Jung has observed, strong emotions carry the transcendent. For an individual to take them too personally is to invite repression and emotional numbness on the one hand, and inflation, illness, or insanity on the other. It is a little like trying to contain the ocean in a tea cup. It just doesn't work and can't work. No wonder that those in modern culture who are particularly sensitive to the emotional dimensions of life often feel marginalized or "crazy," are frequently victimized by culturally sanctioned but inappropriate and damaging medications, and sometimes wind up institutionalized.

THIRTY-SEVEN

Imagination in the Body Work

A s we enter the body with our awareness, as we begin to explore it and engage in dialogue with it, the imagination plays an essential role. This is often noticed by those engaging in the somatic practices—we are constantly trying to visualize parts of our body and imagine our way into various areas, playing "as if" in trying to find certain inner dynamics. This raises some important questions: In using our imagination, are we simply engaging in fantasy? Does it mean that this work is really nothing more than imagination? Or is there something more real going on here? These questions are critical since our responses to them will greatly impact our ability to carry out the somatic work, as well as our confidence in what we discover.

We can arrive at some answers by taking a look at Tibetan yoga, which, in its somatic work, makes extensive use of the imagination. Within this tradition, imagination is called *bhavana,* or "visualization," the act of creating mentally. The Buddhist approach begins with the insight that human beings are continually visualizing, or imagining, everything in their world. The so-called "ordinary reality" of our everyday lives is actually the product of a comprehensive act of imagining or visualizing. When we look at something and recognize it, we are engaging in an elaborate process of receiving sense perceptions, lining them up with already known perceptual categories, identifying them as this rather than that, attaching labels to them, and then setting them within our continuous narrative, including both "self" and "world," our fundamental but misconceived dualizing of our experience.

In order to recognize anything to be some specific thing, we engage in a process of filtering out a tremendous amount of potential perceptual and cognitive information. For example, the "impressionism" of the painter Monet is keyed to the somewhat amorphous blaze of color, the outpouring of visual energy, and the swirling intensities and patterns that are seen in the first instant of looking at a field of flowers. When confronted with this literally overwhelming and disorienting first flash of experience, we literally don't have any mental concept of what we are seeing. Monet paints this first flash. To "make sense" of our visual experience, to domesticate it into a known quantity, without even realizing it, we drastically narrow down our visual experience and line it up with concepts, such as tulips, daffodils, and hyacinths, and red, yellow, and white. And what else is lost to us in this process? The sound and feel of the summer breeze playing across the field? The flowers' wild scents sweeping through us? The shocking depth of the blue sky above? We wouldn't know, for at that point, we think we are looking at a world that, while appealing, falls within known conceptual quantities and is familiar to us. This creates a more or less airtight visualization: we feel we know exactly where we are and what we are looking at.

Thankfully, in life's more intense moments, we are unable to carry through this diminishing and neutralizing process in such a tidy manner. In moments of great emotion, we can look into the face of our beloved and realize, "I have never *really* seen this person before." It is as if we are looking at him or her for the very first time. We might say that our idea of the beloved, which we took to be reality, was the visualization we carried around. But then, at a certain moment, something else crashed through: *the intense reality of the loved one's being, beyond our imagination, manifested itself to us.*

Another example is provided by a friend who was in a jetliner crash in which half the passengers died. Though injured, she survived. She reports that when she escaped from the wreckage and found herself standing in an Iowa cornfield, she realized that she had never before seen the overwhelming reality and beauty of the rich brown earth, the brilliant green of the corn brimming with life, the depth and power of the shimmering blue sky. Her previous, familiar, somewhat humdrum experiences of earth, corn, and sky had been her visualization, but what she saw on that day was something infinitely more real breaking through.

Thus it is that we are always imagining. We imagine that our intimate relationship is a certain way. We imagine what our family, our friends, our job, our financial situation are. Most especially, we continually imagine the person that we take our "self" to be. Sometimes what we are imagining is not particularly challenged by reality. But it also frequently happens that what we have been imagining is suddenly revealed to be rather completely false. Things break through our mental framework that show us quite a different reality, a reality beyond our visualization: a check overdraft reveals that we didn't have the money in our account we thought; a partner whose faithfulness we never questioned turns out to have been involved in an affair for years; we lose a job when we thought things we going well; emotions and behavior on our part make clear that we aren't quite the kind and loving person we had imagined ourselves to be.

It is interesting that, in such situations, we often look back and realize that there had been a considerable amount of information in our environment pointing to the falsity of our visualization, but we just didn't acknowledge it. We often ask ourselves, "Why didn't I let this in? Why didn't I pay attention to what was right before me?" In such situations, we realize after the fact exactly how much we were ignoring what was actually present within our experience, so invested were we in hanging on to our imaginary version. The clichéd phrase "in denial" holds deeper wisdom than we might realize!

We so often find ourselves filtering out what later seems so obvious because that is, in fact, what we human beings are doing all the time. We are always looking for a familiar and coherent world; to find it, we have to ignore a lot. Particularly when we are strongly emotionally invested in things being a certain way, we simply choose not to see many aspects of the actual situation until, of course, things occur that penetrate our ignorance.

We go through life imagining, visualizing, our reality, making it either less or more than it actually is. We might think of this imaginative tendency as creating problems for us. In terms of how our imagination usually functions, it certainly often does. Our discursive thinking, labeling, and pigeonholing of everything acts as a buffer between our self and anything real. When we feel disconnected and cut off from our self, other people, our life, and the world, it is because we have retreated into a purely conceptual world of our own making, where everything is dead and nothing is true. Living in such a conceptualized world makes us very sloppy and inaccurate in relating to people, situations, and—ultimately—our self.

Our problem, though, is not that we imagine our world, but that we believe in and hang on to our imagined version as if it is the real thing. When we look more deeply, we see that the *imagination itself can provide a link between ourselves and reality that stands beyond.* We begin with the fact that, as mentioned, we human beings cannot stay with our naked experience of the world, but create mental pictures of it. We then take these mental pictures to be reality and try to live within them, losing touch with the living, changing nature of our actual life. This is what samsara is, trying to live in mental concepts of things as if they were real.

But because we do try to take our conceptualized versions as real, we set our self up, so to speak. The fact that my visualization isn't entirely accurate at least sets up the possibility of reality breaking through my version and making itself known, showing me the inadequacy of what I have been thinking. Then, in the case of the beloved or my friend standing in the Iowa cornfield, in the breakthrough, we are able to realize reality in and of itself. This reality is just our life—what it is and how it unfolds—but it is a life that had previously been unknown to us because we were lost in our imagination of it, our ideas of what it was. When the visualized or imagined life breaks down, the true reality of it is disclosed. Our small, conceptualized version of the beloved provokes the beloved to protest—"I am not your idea!—and then a breakthrough is possible. Imagination is thus able to provide the link, the connecting point, between my self and reality, and opens the way to seeing things truly and exactly as they are, beyond fantasy and beyond limiting concepts.

But do we have to wait for those very rare, chance, climatic moments in life in order to find the opening through imagination to reality? Buddhist yoga says "no," but rather that we can approach imagination with an understanding that it is no more than conceptual, and also with an openness and even a yearning for what lies beyond. Then we can use imagination, ultimately unreal though it is, as a stepping stone to the reality we seek.

In Buddhist yoga, we deliberately visualize something and use that visualization as a link to the greater reality of what is beyond ego. For example, we might visualize our body as empty yet having various inner manifestations, such as energy, colors, locales of special awareness, bliss, and so on. Initially, we have no actual experience of our body in this way, but are creating a mental picture. Through using our visualization as a stepping stone, though, there comes a moment of breakthrough when we see the emptiness and manifestation of our body without any conceptual or imaginative overlay at all.

The previous examples indicate how our visualization of ordinary sense experience can break down to reveal the reality beyond. It is also true, however, that we can visualize aspects of experience that are much more subtle and less accessible, and, in a similar way, deliberately use our visualizations to open the doors of reality itself. An example from Vajrayana Buddhism may suggest how this can work. In one traditional visualization practice, meditators visualize themselves as Vajrayogini, the adamantine wisdom being, a female representation of our own inner enlightenment. The visualization includes precisely how she looks, how she speaks, and what her mind is like. She is red in color, with one face and two arms, naked, adorned with charnel-ground jewelry, and so on. Her speech is sacred utterance, a Sanskrit mantra traditionally associated with her. And her mind is the mind of enlightenment— empty, clear, and luminous. In a very real sense, the Vajrayogini we have visualized is the imaginary form of our own awakened state, present within but, up to this point, inaccessible. Then, through meditation, we invite the true reality of Vajrayogini—the true reality of our own inner enlightenment which is beyond our imagination—to break through the visualization. The process of meditation itself invites this breakthrough because, in meditation, one opens one's mind more and more fully. Then, at a certain point—though often not before years of practice—the meditator suddenly realizes him- or herself as Vajrayogini, as the enlightened being who is truly empty yet really appearing in the world.

The very same principles apply in the body work. We have a mental image of our body that we carry around with us all the time. At first, we have no direct experience of the body, only an experience of our *thought* of our body, *our mental image or imagination or visualization* of our body. Initially, when we are instructed to place our mind into one area or another of our body, we are directing our mind to a place in our conceptualized or imagined body that actually isn't real.

But then, at a certain point, we begin to glimpse our actual body, quite beyond any and all imagination. Our visualization breaks down, and we are left with a direct experience of our somatic being, without filters or concepts. In this experience, our imagined body simply disappears, and we are left with something quite different. We might find that, rather than being solid, our body seems filled with space; rather than being dull, it might seem brimming over with ever-changing patterns of sparkling, scintillating energy; instead of having a shape that conforms to what we think, it might be felt to have a constantly changing configuration or perhaps no particular shape at all. Moreover, we may find our body continually giving birth to inspiration and even imperatives to engagement with the world. Opening to our "real" body in this way, we are touching our own inner awakening that exists in a pure and unobstructed form within us. At this moment, we are, indeed, touching enlightenment with the body.

So it is that, as we enter each practice in the body work, we do indeed imagine what we are doing. We are visualizing; we are imagining. It is not yet real; we are not yet connected with that which exists beyond our concept. In this way, our imagining or visualizing functions as a necessary stepping stone to the body as it really is. Still, the transition from the imagined body to the real body might take considerable time to begin unfolding and, at the beginning, may occur only in glimpses. Here, as always in the body work, patience is our most important asset.

THIRTY-EIGHT

A Tibetan Yoga Approach to Physical Pain

A s I have said, nothing that arises in our body and in our life happens outside of our journey, of our path, to full realization. Everything that occurs needs to be welcomed with an attitude of acceptance and openness. No matter what happens, *it is imperative that we do not judge it.* Especially when we are going through very difficult and trying circumstances, one cannot repeat to oneself too often, "Do not judge it; do not judge it." Only when we resist the temptation to judge what we are going through can the journey we need to make at this moment continue to unfold, and can we receive the needed development and transformation it may bring.

But what about physical pain? Customarily, I think, the majority of us regard the physical pain that arises from injury, illness, degenerative conditions, difficult life circumstances (such as demanding physical work, hunger, cold, etc.), or simply old age as sidetracks and impediments on the path. Physical pain, whatever its cause, including even the sometimes intense discomfort we feel when sitting on the meditation cushion, is certainly one of the more distressing somatic experiences that we can have.

Tibetan yoga has some very interesting things to say about what physical pain actually is and how we may use it as a stepping stone back into our own embodied fulfillment. Since these are teachings that we can apply even at fairly early stages of learning to meditate with the body, I want to provide a brief description of them here.

The essence of this teaching is that, through descending to the depth in our body that is empty of substance, the open, vacant awareness described earlier, we have a vantage point from which to understand and even experience physical pain that can bring relief, profound learning, and even fulfillment.

By moving down through the layers of our body in the somatic practices, we arrive at a point where our body is an empty, luminous presence. As we continue our practice, we find ourself able to abide there for increasingly extended periods of time. It is from within this unconditioned dimension of our body that we can begin to make a non-ego-based relationship with our relative experience, including physical pain. In this case, it means approaching physical pain as our body itself would see and work with it. When we do so, we are able to discover the way in which physical pain, far from being any kind of problem, actually has the possibility to reveal to us the full possibilities of our somatic being. Tibetan yoga provides three primary instructions to facilitate this process.

According to the first instruction, when physical pain arises, we are instructed to rest deeply within our body. Thus resting, we allow our awareness to enter directly into the pain. This is not the ego looking from its dualistic, self-centered consciousness, but a looking that occurs from within the body itself at the level of its own primeval awareness. In this case, it is not "we" who is looking. Rather, it is we having surrendered our vantage point, and simply letting our body itself "hold" or reflect the physical pain that is arising.

We are allowing the experience of physical pain to register within the deepest level of our body's own awareness, and we check to see what, exactly, it is. If we are willing to let go of our belief that physical pain is "bad"—and this we do by attending very closely to its physical sensations—we may make some interesting discoveries. We may unlock these by asking ourselves some questions: Does physical pain have any substance? Does it have any heart, any essence, that would mark it as "physical pain"? What we may discover is that the thing we thought of as physical pain—which, from within dualistic consciousness itself, seemed so real, so definite, and so problematic—doesn't really have any defining feature or definitive profile at all. It is really empty of anything that would mark it as physical pain. And it is no longer a "problem." If we back up into our dualistic mind again, we discover the very same "physical pain" that has been hounding us. But, within the body's depths, there is nothing identifiable as physical pain—or as anything else either. It is not that the physical sensations have disappeared. What is no longer there is our judgment of them as "bad" and "problematic." But then, strangely, because our labeling of them is gone, the physical sensations themselves appear to be completely different from what we had previously thought.

Lama Thubten Yeshe had a serious and painful heart ailment from which he ultimately died. He used to comment that using this instruction to work with physical pain eliminated all the feeling of "problem" or even of "pain" from the pain itself. He said, "If you do this practice, you won't ever have to go to the doctor to get pain medication." He wasn't saying that one shouldn't be treated for medical conditions, but that, through these practices, one can eliminate the "problem" that pain usually involves, the identity of pain itself that causes us to be so closed down around it and so preoccupied by it.

When His Holiness the Sixteenth Karmapa was dying of cancer in a hospital in Zion, Illinois, his deteriorating physical condition certainly suggested to the attending medical staff that he should be in agonizing and completely incapacitating and absorbing physical pain. Yet, all reports described him as being fully present to others and concerned only about how everyone else was doing. I have often thought that he must have been embodying a high level of mastery of being present to pain, as suggested here, from within the ultimate depths of the body.

Sometimes physical pain is so intense or distressing that, at our current level of practice, we are not able to carry out the first instruction to drop our awareness underneath the pain and view it strictly from the vantage point of the body. If this is the case, then we are offered a second instruction: take the intensity and vividness of the physical pain itself as the object of our meditation. We do this by just putting our awareness right on and into the pain itself. It is as if we are offering our entire being into the fire of the painful sensation. We just plunge into the interior of the pain, into its heart. When we do so, the fire of the pain has the effect of burning through whatever in us is resisting, judging, and trying to separate ourself from the pain as a "problem." We continue going right to the pain and into its depths. As we do so, we find ourself able to abide simply within its intensity. At a certain moment, we can't really feel it as pain anymore: it is just highly charged energy. At that point, there is no person watching the pain from the outside, no one to judge it and separate from it. There is just this manifestation within the body. When this occurs, we can be said to have found our complete and total embodiment, using our physical pain itself as a pathway.

If we find ourself unable to follow the second instruction, then a third instruction is offered: use the pain in a more indirect way to bring us into full embodiment. This third instruction of Tibetan yoga reminds us that, as mentioned earlier, nothing occurs in our life without rhyme or reason. In other words, any relative experience appears with complete timeliness, accuracy, and appropriateness to our immediate karmic situation and its needs. The appearance of physical pain is no exception. When any of us experiences short-term or long-term physical pain, it always comes in appropriate measure to our particular situation. In this sense, it is possible for us to discover it to be a blessing. The arrival of pain cuts through the unique bondage of this moment, liberating us into the body's own freedom and depth. At the moment of freedom, we see just how much expectation we've been having, how much we've been identifying with some relative situation or experience. Being cut through in this way can be experienced as horrific, humorous, frightening, sad, inspiring, and so on. But, in any case, it leaves us with an appreciation of the sacredness of the experience of pain as an incursion of helpful and even liberating wisdom into our life.

Discovering pain as the open emptiness of our body (first instruction) and as its energetic aspect (second instruction) are practices that are initially developed on the meditation cushion. After we have trained in these practices in formal meditation, we can then apply them anytime and anywhere. Discovering physical pain as auspicious coincidence (third instruction) is a practice that can be engaged directly in the post-meditation state simply by looking, again from within the depths of the body, at the impact of the pain on our state of mind and our understanding of our life.

When we approach physical pain through these instructions, we find that, far from being trapped and defeated by it, we are able to work with it in an increasingly open, fearless, and creative way. Our own increasing familiarity and skill in relating with our pain from the very deepest levels of our body can then lead us into and, as Tibetan yoga says, through the process of our own physical death.

THIRTY-NINE

Some Fundamental Shifts

A s the body work continues to unfold, we discover some fundamental shifts in our state of being. The conscious mind, which previously was the engineer of our human existence, moves increasingly into the role of listener and helper. We realize that we're in a relationship with something that holds our life journey. Through the work, we see that the body is continually communicating with us. It communicates initially through tension and release and then through shifts in our emotional life; images come up, feelings, subtle states of mind, memories, thoughts, inspirations, fear, anxiety. There is an entire, tremendously rich interior life of the body, which we feel and experience, but which also somehow remains shrouded in mystery. At a certain point, we aren't entirely sure even how to think about or categorize what we are experiencing—whether it is emotion, energy, or physical sensation—and we begin to suspect that figuring it out is irrelevant and actually detrimental to the voyage of discovery we are making. We are learning different ways of feeling, sensing, and also thinking.

You don't know. And it begins to unfold. You find that you yourself are changing as a person, and you discover a way of being that's much less solid and much less fixed. It's almost as if your life is a river that is running through a forest, and that river is constantly flowing, bubbling, now having one demeanor, now another, one direction, then another. At that point, the so-called "self," that relatively consistent type of person we have always been trying to be, becomes much less important, and there's a willingness on the part of the meditator, or the body contemplator, to allow the self, the conscious sense of self, to dissolve and reform, over and over. At that point, your life really begins to happen in a different way.

As we experience this shift from ego consciousness to somatic awareness, our life and practice begin to open in two interesting ways. For one thing, working with the body in meditation frees our experience of relative reality, liberating the concrete phenomena of our day-to-day lives. When we operate in a disembodied state, we tend to take the experiences of our life as being random, relatively insignificant, and boring. And, of course, we go to great lengths to try to find something interesting or significant in our existence. The more boring and gray everything gets, the more we look to sex or violence or mind-altering substances, or anything, frankly, that can give us some kind of rush—anything to break through the phenomenal boredom and general meaninglessness of our human existence. We may find ourselves thinking, "Next week, I'm going to this great restaurant where maybe I can have a meal I actually enjoy," or "Next month, I'm going on vacation, and maybe then I will be in a place that will genuinely catch my attention and mean something," and so on.

According to the somatic teachings, the problem with our life does not lie in the individual circumstances or occurrences of our day-to-day existence. It's not that they're inherently meaningless and boring; the problem is that we make them meaningless and boring, because we are so disconnected and so invested in maintaining our own sense of "self" that we actually don't relate to anything in a full and direct way. Unwilling to fully live the life that is arriving in our body moment by moment, we find ourself left with no real life at all. In our state of disembodied dissatisfaction, we may think, "I feel like I'm disconnected. Maybe I need to change my job, or change my relationship, maybe, maybe, maybe." But the fact is, as we have seen, that the fullness of our human existence is already happening all the time. In fact, when we work with our body and begin to open up our awareness, when we allow the experience of the body to communicate with our conscious mind and to become known to us in some kind of direct way, we find, in the most mundane details of our life, intensity, meaning, fullness, and fulfillment.

Second, through the somatic work, we begin to discover our body as a vast and multifaceted thing, a veritable expanding universe. The fact is that we have billions of cells in our body. And, as neuroscientist Candace Pert has suggested in her research, it seems possible that each cell is a center of intelligence, awareness, emotion, and experience.[1] Each cell has thousands of receptors capable of different kinds of experience. This is our nature. We are not, again as mentioned, a single, unified entity. We are a universe, each part of which has its own independence, its own status as a living energy, and each of which is interconnected with everything else. We are a galaxy in which each of these things is happening simultaneously. What we see depends on where we look and when we look. At the same time, wherever and whenever we look, we touch the whole, because each part, each cell, is in relation with all the others. The body is thus billions of interconnected events, and the totality, at each moment, is different. The body thus infinitely transcends anything we could ever think about it. Obviously, what we think our body is, or want to think it is, ends up being little more than a shield against the nearly infinite realm of the being of our body.

Through the process of somatic meditation, we begin to discover this vastness that is our own state of being, and the inconceivable abundance, the plenitude of life, that is occurring *as us,* in each moment. And the experience is ever-changing. Sometimes we see empty space. Sometimes we see energy. And sometimes what meets us presents an absolute solidity like the mass before the Big Bang. If we pay attention, it is never the same. But it is always the display of *us,* whatever that may be. It is not very supportive of any concept of a real or continuous "I," that is for certain. In the shift of attention brought about by the

---

1   Candace Pert, *Molecules of Emotion* (New York: Scribner, 1999).

body work, we move from the part of our brain where we do all the thinking, planning, strategizing, and engineering, down into the tremendous, illimitable eventfulness of our actual life.

V
THE BODY AND
BECOMING A PERSON

FORTY

The Body Is the Buddha Nature

The term "buddha nature" is used in Buddhism to refer to our most fundamental nature. It is said that all human beings have buddha nature as the very foundation and core of their human personality. Our buddha nature has three main aspects. First, it is our open and empty awareness itself. In other words, the buddha nature is not intelligence in the sense of "IQ," but rather the ability to see and experience things openly, clearly, and intelligently, entirely without bias. It is our primal intelligence that is always operating in us, whether we are conscious of it or not. In most of us, this primal or primary intelligence is covered over by our compulsive judging and thinking. We do not trust our self, the basic self of our buddha nature, and so we revert to our ideas and our concepts and our reference points about things.

The second quality of the buddha nature is warmth and compassion. When we experience the world from the point of view of the openness of our basic nature, there is a natural warmth toward ourself, other people, and the world. The buddha nature, then, is inherently compassionate. It is only the judging, conceptualizing mind that covers over this warmth and breeds in us unhealthy anger, hostility, and aggression toward others.

The third aspect of the buddha nature is an inner sense of well-being, strength, confidence, and joy in life. The Buddhist teachings say that these are an inherent part of our fundamental person. If we do not experience them as an ongoing feeling about life, it is because, again, our buddha nature is covered over and obscured by our compulsive "egoizing" of everything.

In spite of being covered over in most of us and relatively invisible, the buddha nature is far from being inactive in our life. In fact, it has a directedness to it; it is an irresistible force that is always pushing us to grow and develop spiritually. In fact, as we shall see in this section, *the buddha nature holds the stages of our own unfolding*—of our spiritual maturation—that we must pass through if we are to fulfill our deepest human longing and find the fundamental purpose of our life. The precise directionality of our lives that each of us experiences arises as the momentum of all the unfulfilled karmic debts of our life. In this sense, the buddha nature holds the totality of the process of individuating, of becoming fully and completely who we are.

The buddha nature is, thus, not an objectifiable entity or conceptual reality in any sense. Because who we ultimately are is an open, ongoing, and finally ineffable process, the buddha nature is described as "empty": it does not possess any invariable, definable marks or characteristics. It is, we might say, the darkness or mystery that is continually unfolding as our life.

As mentioned, the buddha nature is behind everything that happens, and needs to happen, on our journey. Whatever happens to us, and within us, is the expression of the buddha nature, pushing us forward in our own unfolding. There is nothing in our life or experience that is outside of it. The buddha nature thus may be referred to as the "totality." As we progress along the path to our own self-discovery, our awakening and realization, our relationship with "our" buddha nature naturally develops and matures, and this relationship is ultimately "engineered" by the buddha nature itself.

Traditional Buddhist texts see other religious designations of "the ultimate" as attempts to point to or posit the buddha nature. Frequently mentioned are Indian concepts such as the *atman,* the innermost self, the *purusha,* the final and ultimate "person," and personifications of reality such as the deities Brahma or Shiva. They would, likewise, see the Judeo-Christian concept of "God" and the Muslim "Allah" as attempts to name the buddha nature. When we look at modern Western thought, there are also parallels. Jung's notion of the "Self," indicating our most fundamental being and embracing the totality, a concept at least partially inspired by Indian thought in the first place, is clearly pointing toward the buddha nature.

It should be clear from the aforementioned, then, that the body itself is the buddha nature. In saying this, we are, of course, not speaking of the body as we normally might conceive of it, or even as we might think of it in increasingly more inclusive and appreciative ways along the path. We are speaking, rather, of the body as we discover it in and through the body work—as the mysterious, open-ended darkness out of which our life is continually emerging, involving personal, interpersonal, and cosmic dimensions.

It is in the body that we meet the buddha nature in its most naked form. By entering ever more deeply into the body and receiving the unending flow of experience that arises when we do, we are in intimate relation with the buddha nature. In the body work, we learn how to let go of the fixed and rigid boundaries of our relatively self-contained, cut-off, isolated "self." In so doing, we place ourself in a position of communication with the buddha nature, our deepest and our ultimate "self."

FORTY-ONE

The Journey Is Our Unfolding Relation with the Buddha Nature

The body, the buddha nature, is called the *alaya*, "the universal unconscious." As the unconscious—that is, everything we are but remain unaware of—the body is the place where we find both the awareness, warmth, and strength mentioned earlier, as well as the directionality that arises from and includes the totality of our karma, our past and present as well as our future possibility.

In the formation of our conscious "self," our "ego" in Buddhist terms, we have walled off the great majority of what we have been, what we are, and what we can be. There are three aspects to this walling off: first, we have established a more or less limited field of awareness; second, this limited awareness is structured and defined by the particular concept or self-image we have of ourselves; and, finally, it is maintained by the managerial aspect of the ego, whereby we act and react to whatever occurs in our never-ending efforts to establish, maintain, and secure our "place in the world."

Our self-concept is actually a bilateral one: it comprises both who I think I am—the subject—and also all the conceptualized objects in my world—who and what I think I am not. In other words, our "self" is actually a mental construct according to which everything we experience is separated into these two interdependent and reinforcing categories of subject and object.

The *subject category* includes what I identify as my own "self," my immediate *personal ego,* and its withdrawal from and reaction against my personal "body," or reality. The object category includes two aspects: first, my concept of everybody else—what we might call the *interpersonal ego*—which is a withdrawal from and reaction against my larger somatic experience of the interpersonal reality; and, second, my conceptual construct of everything in the nonhuman, external world—what we might call the impersonal or cosmic ego, namely, the natural world, animate and inanimate—which is a withdrawal from and reaction against the totality of my somatic experience of the cosmos.

The complex self-concept of "me" is composed of self, others, and world, not as they are in themselves, but as I have pulled back from and reacted against them, enfolded them in my body, and walled them off in my concepts of them. I maintain my belief in the reality of "me" by keeping everything in these subject-object domains enfolded in my body and maintaining my self-concept against it. The marked-off territory of our ego, then, leaves us with a highly restricted field that defines "me" and a vast reservoir, the "universal unconscious," of which we are not currently aware, that is literally unlimited in scope and contents.

The spiritual journey revolves around our developing relationship with the buddha nature. In childhood, our ego develops as the first stage on our path. This involves an inevitable separation from the totality of our being and the carving out of a coherent and relatively controllable "me" in contradistinction to the oceanic expanse of infanthood. At a certain point, usually later in life, the boundaries of the small "self" are experienced as too restricted. We feel we have lost touch with the wellsprings of our own life. The territory of ego begins to be felt as an arid desert in which nothing can flourish or even live. This separation and alienation is felt as a suffering that pervades all of our life, what the Buddha spoke of as the First Noble Truth.

This growing awareness is developmental in nature, rather than a timeless truth about the ego that is now being revealed. In other words, up until this point, the development of the ego has been a healthy thing, a good and necessary expression of our unfolding spirituality. However, as we mature, the precise spiritual demands incumbent upon us undergo a change. At a certain point, the glory of the human ego begins to fade: we find that the suit of clothes it represents is too small for the person we are now needing to become.

At this point, we may turn to a spiritual discipline as a way to develop a healthy and creative relationship with the larger self, the complete person that the buddha nature holds out before us. It is through this developing relationship that the spiritual journey is able to unfold, that we are able to communicate with the unconscious and begin to integrate into our conscious awareness the infinitely vaster field of awareness that it represents.

As we have seen, this integration can only happen by the assimilation of "information," of aspects of our own relative truth, that have been locked up in the darkness of the body as the unconscious. Through integrating this information, our consciousness is educated, so to speak, gradually disabusing itself of what have now become inadequate notions of itself and its world, freeing the energy of awareness that had previously been locked up in the maintenance of its ignorance and delusion, and finding a much more extensive and porous sense of "self" emerging. This is experienced as our coming more and more into our true nature, increasingly becoming the person we need to be and ultimately are.

Within the many modern spiritual paths and techniques that are offered in the service of this most profound and fundamental of all human projects, somatically based meditation stands front and center, uniquely so, I think, as perhaps the most simple, accessible, and efficacious in our modern world. By entering into the body, we temporarily surrender our conscious ego boundaries and open ourselves in a completely direct and naked manner to what our soma may have to communicate, what it may have to say to us just now. Through the body work, the long-sought-after voice of the universal unconscious, the alaya, may be heard. Whatever needs to come through to our conscious self is able to flow freely in an immediate and abundant way.

It is interesting to contrast somatically based meditation with other methods for linking with our ultimate self or person. Traditional religious ritual, of course, can perform this function.

However, it is so often mediated through institutionalized religion and so subjected to concrete interpretation that the necessity for completely personal and unique communication with what is ultimate can be blunted, diverted, or co-opted. In addition, conventional religions tend to locate the truth outside of the devotee, which ultimately leads to his or her disempowerment.

Traditional meditation can be helpful in the individuation process described here, but, as noted, its typically disembodied application in the modern world can yield a disembodied result: we can touch the emptiness of our mind, but, in so doing, find ourself blocked from accessing the ever-expanding field of our relative, conditioned reality—our karmic situation—which is essential for genuine spiritual growth.

Some modern methods are similarly most helpful in the integrative and maturation process, such as conventional psychotherapy or dream interpretation. But these are somewhat indirect methods, as they often do not address the patient's disembodiment and rely on the mediation of a therapist and an accurate reading of dream material. The body work provides a contrast wherein we open ourself directly to the "unconscious" and place ourself in a straight line to receive its transformative information. In this respect, one is reminded of a comment Jung made late in his life: he no longer needed to work with his dreams as much, since the "unconscious" now spoke to him directly. In other words, he received the information of his body directly.

Modern shamanic journeying and soul retrieval can likewise facilitate the integration of contents of the alaya, bringing aspects of our self into conscious awareness in a sometimes dramatic way. This is a specialized technique that is particularly useful when one is deeply "stuck" in one's regular practice. However, it requires another person and is dependent on the skill and maturity of the mediator. It is accompanied by the additional task of "integrating" retrieved material, which can only happen in people willing to face their own habitual patterns and ego-bound relation to experience. As in the case of disembodied meditation, it may be quite difficult to bring about this kind of integration without a deep somatic grounding and without a "view" (the understanding of our basic openness or emptiness) that can accommodate rather than subvert the new information.

Within the many techniques available in the traditional and modern world, somatically based meditation, then, may have a unique role to play. It is accessible to everyone; it involves a direct relation with one's larger self; while benefitting from mentoring, it does not require external mediation, nor is it limited by one's relationship to another person or other external authority; because it is one's own body that is the teacher, the aptness and timeliness of what one receives need not be doubted; and it does not depend on religious belief or affiliation or, in fact, even on identifying oneself as a "religious" or "spiritual" person at all. At the same time, though, the various methods and techniques mentioned previously all have their particular gifts and may be useful to the somatic meditator at various points along the way to enhance or elaborate stages and discoveries on the path.

FORTY-TWO

Ego, the Body, and the Journey

The person gradually disclosed through the body work, the person that we most fundamentally are, is finally incomparable, unique, and without precedent. As we have seen, this person, our complete person, is present in the body as the buddha nature, though in a latent and unconscious way.

Through the body work, we develop our relationship with this larger self. Like any relationship, we need to proceed gradually, step by step. Initially we are introduced; then we begin to get to know this larger self; then we become completely committed to it. Finally—at least theoretically—we attain union with it. Thus it is that our relationship with our deepest personhood develops, over a lifetime, in a process of stages.

Although the person we are in the process of becoming is unique, the stages of that becoming are not. In other words, the unfolding journey toward our own incomparable personhood passes through some common phases. Although these happen differently for each person, nevertheless, they seem to characterize the geography of the journey that is generally recognizable.

The unfolding journey of our personhood, made through the body, is a reflection of the depth and integrity of the body work. The journey is the guarantee, so to speak, that our body work is actual—real and grounded—not just a collection of abstract ideas, wishful thinking, or fantasies. The journey is a reflection of the transformative power of the somatic work. When we do this work in a genuine way, over time, this is what happens.

It is important that we understand the nature of this journey toward realization that we are undertaking. It is not a journey toward some external goal that we will one day obtain. Rather, the whole process is one of stripping away everything that is disingenuous, inauthentic, and false—everything that is not ultimately who we are. It is a process of unmasking, taking off the armor, becoming more and more nakedly ourselves.

We could say that the entire journey is one of becoming more and more genuine as a human being. We are not trying to become someone else or to fulfill some idealized fantasy of who we could be. We are not living up to some high ideal. Rather, we are living down, so to speak, to who we already fundamentally are and always have been. The descent into the darkness of the body is a descent toward ourself in all our fullness and completion, toward our ultimate wholeness.

On this journey, eventually all our attachment and clinging to conditioned identities and fixations must be surrendered. In the beginning, we find ourself letting go of our personal mask, our posturing, the pretense and hypocrisy with which we show a false image of ourself to our intimates, our friends, and the rest of the world, and, of course, to ourself. Much later, we find ourself challenged to surrender more collective identities, such as our identification with our family, friends, age, gender, and racial makeup; our national identity; and even our identity as a "modern" person, with the worldview and basic self-image that being "modern" entails.

What we are letting go of often seems to be "us," who and what we think we are, and it does often feel as if we are falling apart, disintegrating, dying, or even going crazy. At the same time, as we have seen, it is important to realize that this is ultimately not a negative or destructive process. For, in letting go of all our identity fixations, we become able to touch the utter freedom that lies within us and to live our authentic, ineffable life. This brings the most complete fulfillment a human being can ever experience— that of being fully and completely oneself.

Again, as we have seen, in order to maintain our current self-image, we turn away from areas of experience of ourself and of the world that are inconsistent with this image and that represent the great majority of what we sense and feel and go through. It would not be accurate to say that these areas are completely unknown to us—as the psychological concept of the unconscious might suggest. Rather, they exist within our body as experience, but experience in reaction against which we are continually advancing our self-image. This self-image, in its structure and its function, is thus a precise response to what already exists as experience, though on a subliminal, somatic level. In a certain sense, then, we are quite aware of everything that our self-conscious ego refuses to acknowledge, and that is why the self-image can be so effective: it knows exactly what it does not want to acknowledge before it enters into the business of ignoring it. So, in a way, the self-image is a kind of mirror or reactive reflection of these larger areas—of our totality, in fact.

These larger areas, then, exist in the form of experience enfolded in the body. As we have seen, this enfolding is, in some sense, unnatural. All the experience that we receive somatically has a momentum toward awareness; it is the karmic backlog discussed earlier that calls to be discharged. It "wants" to be received within our consciousness; it "wants" to be integrated into it; it "wants" to bring about a self-image that is modified by the experience; and it "wants," by this process, to be discharged of its burden, its purpose. When we resist the information of somatic experience—and it is the very nature of the modern self-image to resist—then a backlog is created and a pressure exists expressing the information that "wants" to break through.

That pressure is experienced as neurosis: the attempt to maintain a view and experience of ourself that is inconsistent with the actual situation, that is in conflict with what our body already knows. We feel the pressure of what wants to break through in the form of various unpleasant and unwanted emotions, such as anxiety, dread, uneasiness, fear, impatience, paranoia, desolation, and so on. The First Noble Truth of suffering means that, simply because we are trying to maintain a sense of self, there is some kind of uneasiness or feeling of things being unsatisfactory or off-kilter all the time. In order to maintain our "self," there is always something we are trying to ignore or deny, and that produces a kind of inescapable suffering, be it mild or intense.

In the previous pages, we have talked about our "unlived experience," our "unlived life," that calls for attention. Why is it that we seem to be so called to live through—completely—everything that has ever occurred to us? We could say that it is an evolutionary exigency: that, for our survival as a species, all experience is valuable; everything that occurs must be received, processed, and integrated, if not now, then later, at some time later in this life when we are ready or, if incarnation is taken into account, in some future birth.

But there seems to be more to it than that. It would appear that there is a force within us—we could call it spiritual—that wants us to be whole. There is a continual pressure of reality against the boundaries of our self-image, at the very least making clear the inadequacy of the self-image, its lack of self-sufficiency and control over its world.

If we heed the call and descend into the body, then we find that information comes through at a rapid rate, information that is literally emerging from the recesses of the body, dissolving, correcting, enlarging, and nourishing our concept of ourself. There is some basic force in our life that wants us to be whole, that will not rest with a self-image that is partial and walls off the rest of us.

Our whole journey is about accommodating more and more of the buddha nature, so that our ego increasingly exists in conscious relation with it, feels devotion for it, and becomes transparent to it. The more we integrate of our larger self, the more stable and open our self-concept becomes. According to Buddhism, there eventually comes a day when the self-concept is barely visible at all, a kind of faint mirage, of no use to ourself whatsoever, but helpful in our relations with those we are trying to help.

The body work provides the way by which this entire process unfolds. The body's aim, as the buddha nature, is always to fill us out, round us out, bring us to our own completion.

FORTY-THREE

The First Stages of the Journey

Once we enter into spiritual practice, we find the path unfolding according to the series of sequential stages referred to in the previous chapter. In this and the next few chapters, we will examine these spiritual developmental stages in some detail. The first stages, discussed in the present chapter, include some kind of profound existential crisis entering our life; the process of understanding this crisis as an essentially spiritual one; the need for our own response to what we have understood; and, finally, committing ourself to a path of transformative spiritual practice.

The journey that unfolds through somatically grounded meditation implies an ego that is functional enough to receive the information arising from the body. We are not talking here about a truly "healthy" ego because few, if anyone, in modern societies can claim to be in this category. Since the journey depends on a "functional-enough ego," it would be accurate to say that the first phase on the path involves the more or less adequate development of such a relative "self." This process begins, obviously, at birth, extending through childhood, adolescence, early adulthood, and beyond.[1] When we enter a spiritual path, if not before, many of us discover that our own sense of self is damaged and dysfunctional in various ways that impede our ability to engage spiritual practice in an effective way. Many of us find ourselves turning to psychotherapy and other methodologies to work on stages of ego development that have been missed or were inadequately completed. It is quite interesting, in fact, that the body work described here seems, in a natural and apt way, to address whatever level of development an individual may be in need of, and to provide avenues of healing.

THE CRISIS

For a long time, perhaps, we are able to exist in the illusion that we can live out our life within the framework of our current ego

---

[1]   This initial, all-important phase of the journey is generally not explicitly discussed in pre-modern Asian Buddhist texts. There are probably a number of related reasons for this. For one thing, because traditional Asian Buddhism tended to focus on the later, upper levels of spiritual development, the developmental stages of the "self" never occupied sustained attention. In addition, the development of a wholesome sense of self may not have been the thorny issue for traditional practitioners that it is in the contemporary modern world. Perhaps these cultures themselves possessed child-rearing perspectives and methods that were sufficiently effective to stand practitioners in adequate stead. It may also be that the problems that did exist were addressed by cultural mechanisms that stood apart from explicit Buddhist tradition. Further, it does appear that people with serious psychological dysfunction tended to be ignored, at least by institutionalized Buddhism, and to be relegated, within their societies, to low and relatively static stations within the social order. Underlying all of this was the emphasis on "non-self" within elite Asian Buddhism and the fact that the maturation of the human personality (as opposed to the "ego") was not generally articulated as a value or focus of the spiritual life.

structure. This illusion is maintained by hope and by wishful thinking that the current unsatisfactoriness of our life is temporary and that by fulfilling our personal ego agendas, suddenly our life will change, our pain will disappear, and everything will be satisfactory.

At a certain point, however, we may begin to sense that the pain, the aridity, and the struggle inherent in attempts to live within the restricted ego domain are not going to go away. We begin to suspect that this is just the way things are and that, if we are going to address the situation with any hope of forward movement, we need to do something other than just to try harder in the same old way.

This dawning realization arrives as something of a crisis. Some crises that we experience in life do not seem terribly serious and do not call for fundamental transformation. They appear as a rupture in the fabric of our existence, but one that seems temporary, something that can be addressed and repaired. This kind of crisis generally leaves no unalterable mark upon us. But there is another kind of crisis that is experienced as much more fundamental and inescapable. This basic, existential crisis often comes with a dramatic personal catastrophe: the end of an important relationship; the collapse of a life's work; cataclysmic upheaval in one's social world; the death of a loved one; the sudden eruption of debilitating feelings, such as intense anxiety or fear, or deep depression; or the onset of chronic or terminal illness.

What sets this fundamental kind of crisis apart is not so much the apparent gravity of the precipitating event, but rather the impact of the event upon us, how we experience it. For Gautama Buddha, for example, it was brought on simply by seeing, one day, a sick man, an old, decrepit man, and a deceased man, commonplace experiences in his culture. But somehow, these ordinary things plunged him into a dark and inescapable despair: seeing that all life ends in old age, disease, and death,[1] he realized that everything he had pinned his hopes on for his own fulfillment was empty and meaningless.

In our own modern life, a crisis becomes an irreversible existential collapse when our basic idea about ourself, our life, and our possible happiness is revealed to be false, without truth, merit, or substantial reality. We feel not only that we have lost any idea of who we are or what is real and unreal, but that the ground has literally fallen out from under our feet.

INTERPRETING THE CRISIS

In the modern context, of course, this kind of ego crisis is often viewed as a pathological development in need of immediate, corrective intervention—whether psychotherapeutic, psychiatric, social, religious, or otherwise.

For Buddhism, though, it is seen as a positive development that, though possessing steep challenges and dangers, is the necessary first step without which a genuine spiritual journey is not possible. In this way, such a crisis is understood itself as an expression of the buddha nature, wherein the actual, stark truth of our human situation comes clearly into focus for the first time. We see that the struggle to attain comfort, security,

---

[1] Conze, *Buddhist Scriptures*, 39–40.

and lasting happiness, which defines the life and activity of our "relative self," is a hopeless task—that relative gains and satisfactions are unable to address the deep longing for fulfillment that all of us feel. This insight is critical to our spiritual unfolding because, as long as we feel that our basic satisfaction *can* be attained through modifications of our life brought about by our conditioned "self" in its current form, the genuine path—aiming at the dethroning of our conditioned "self" as the ultimate arbiter and authority of our existence—cannot be engaged.

An important dialectical relationship exists between this teaching and one's experience of falling apart described previously. When individuals do not possess the view of the inherently limited nature of ego in relation to the deeper self, when they believe their ego perspective is the only possible one, it makes it much more difficult to allow themselves to fall into the kind of hopelessness that must accompany genuine and profound existential crisis and eventual transformation. Over the course of my teaching life, I have met many people suffering the kinds of crisis mentioned previously, including terminal illness, who still feel compelled to hold on to their "relative self" and to the belief that somehow its previous state of affairs will or can or might be restored.

I have pondered why the deeper possible message is not getting through, why the spiritual gate is not seen or entered. Might part of the answer not be this: that such folks have not possessed, within their intellectual repertoire, the notion that such experiences are not necessarily purely negative, but may offer the hope of genuine growth—that there is, so to speak, life beyond ego, or actual death? Perhaps it is that they do not possess, in other words, the *view* of the fundamental reality of the larger self, the view that relative loss may be nothing other than the breakthrough of the greater self, the source of all joy, freedom, and fulfillment. By contrast, those who have been exposed to the non-theistic view of Buddhism or of some other, similar spiritual tradition, seem to have a greater ability to see their breakdown as an at least potentially positive, if still extraordinarily painful, development. Such people seem to be able to allow in the full, desperate impact of what is happening to them and, somehow, to keep their mind and experience open, even within the darkness.

Through the profound existential crisis, the ego has been temporarily weakened, depotentiated in psychological terms. This depotentiation allows the larger, unbiased intelligence of our "true nature" to break through and be heard. Even perceiving our disrupted situation as a fundamental existential crisis with no apparent way out is, in itself, an expression of the buddha nature, of a primordial level of intelligence within us that is no longer distorted by the wishful thinking or self-absorption of the ego.

THE INVITATION

If we have the "view" of the buddha nature—or if we sense the universal goodness of life, which amounts to the same thing—such fundamental existential crises can be experienced as invitations to look into our existence in a fresh way, with new eyes. Once we have recovered from the initial shock of the collapse of our life, we may find our self left with curiosity about what is happening. With everything that we thought or imagined about ourself in a state of disarray and devastation, we may begin to wonder what is left: Now that our dreams have been shattered, who are we actually? Who may we be?

Like the full and unimpeded experience of our own collapse, this curiosity is an expression of our larger self, our buddha nature. To be able to turn and look, with curiosity and even wonder, at our ravaged hopes and dreams implies, again, an intelligence that stands apart from the restricted, ingrown consciousness bounded by the ego. It is our greater self coming toward us.

THE RESPONSE:
COMMITTING OURSELVES TO A PATH

Thus it is that somatic meditation provides us with a way of looking at our life that can not only accommodate the most profound of existential crises, but also help us to have confidence in what is occurring and to discover within ourself an attitude of curiosity toward it. Beyond this, it also offers ways of acting on our curiosity. It provides a detailed set of perspectives, practices, and techniques enabling us to explore our collapse as well as to find out more about it and what it may mean for any future life we may have.

Seeing that we cannot return to our previous status quo, that we cannot make our way back to our ego's prior "business as usual" approach, we see that there is no choice but to go ahead, exploring the landscape of devastation that is our current life, to see what is there. This feeling of choicelessness about our course of action is also an expression of the buddha nature. Knowing we have no alternative, we clearly see that any attempts to turn our gaze in some other, more "hopeful" direction are just expressions of our own fear and hesitation. Again, witness the intelligence of the buddha nature. Understanding it, we determine to take up the practices of the path and proceed onward. Actually, we see that we have no choice but to commit ourself to this voyage of exploration, and that we need only the tools provided by tradition to make the journey.

FORTY-FOUR

Aspects of the Unfolding Process

A s previously discussed, in the first stage of our life journey, our ego or "relative self" emerges within the totality of experience. Of course, for a fetus in utero or a newborn child, we are not talking about experience in quite the way we might usually understand it. Yet, clearly at these early levels there is a registering, an awareness that receives and, in some sense, remembers what is going on. We know this from our own and other people's extraordinarily early memories.

Within our own totality, which is continually arising and being experienced in the body, whatever is deemed incompatible is "enfolded." Of course, to talk about somatic "experience," we are speaking of something that is initially subliminal, sensed but not clearly seen. Moreover, what appears in subliminal experience may come from the "inside," arising as feelings, images, and so on. Equally, it may come from the "outside," as an event, circumstance, or situation, once again calling for our attention and integration.

Whatever arises in and through the body does so, as we have seen, in accordance with the operation of karma. Karma holds our locked-up awareness, the larger buddha nature, of which we are only partially aware. Whatever of our karmic totality has not made its way into conscious awareness abides in the body. At any given time, a certain aspect of that totality begins to press toward consciousness; the totality intends that this come to birth now.

It might not be pressing toward awareness until just now because, before this moment, it was not ready to do so, having been held at some deep level of enfoldment. Again, it may not have appeared in consciousness because, though ready to emerge at a certain moment as a step in our development, we have resisted it and pushed it back into the body. Either way, at a certain point, there is a pressure from the body toward consciousness, to communicate whatever, in the mysterious timing of our existence, is needed or appropriate.

If we resist what is appearing in the body, at the verge of our awareness—and most of us modern people do habitually resist in order to rigidly maintain ourselves—what is trying to arise is pushed back, denied, and again held at bay in the body. There it resides within the shadows of our somatic being, in an ever-increasing residue—as that which our consciousness is in the continual process of ignoring, resisting, and denying.

Residing in the shadows, all those aspects of our totality that are being denied admittance into conscious awareness continue to function in a powerful but unseen way, being reflected in the nature, structure, and activity of our ego.

This process roughly corresponds to the psychological concept of repression, but there are some important differences. For one thing, the activity of the ego in "repressing" experience is seen here as ultimately not negative, but dynamic and creative in function. In our life, the ego emerges out of the unconscious as the field of our conscious awareness, the immediate domain in which our experience can be received and integrated. At the same time, the ego moderates what it takes in, resisting that which it is unready and unable to receive.

There is much intelligence in this. An ego that is too rigid and frozen cannot accommodate the experience that is needed in order for us to grow. But an ego that is simply overwhelmed and pushed aside by experience cannot integrate the needed experience either. Spirituality, it would seem, depends on an ego—a field of consciousness—that can change and grow with the needs of our journey toward wholeness. Thus it is that spirituality is not about "getting rid of" or obliterating the ego, but rather about enabling the ego into a process of openness, increasing experience, death, and rebirth, as it integrates more and more of the buddha nature and itself becomes more aligned with and in service to our own totality. A buddha is not a person who has eliminated or wiped away his or her ego, but someone in whom the ego has integrated so much that there is no longer any room for individual identity at all.

Thus, we can see that neurosis is, in a real sense, an ultimately creative process. By initially resisting our totality, the ego is creating a backlog of "unlived experience." This backlog is felt as an increasing pressure from the body, the "unconscious," the buddha nature. New awareness is called for, and the more the pressure builds, the more struggle on the part of the ego is required to maintain the repression. This is not a situation that can be maintained indefinitely. The pressure mounts and, at a certain point, can no longer be resisted.

This is where the existential crises emerge into one's life. Some people will respond by taking up and following a spiritual path, deliberately seeking a relationship with the source of the pressure, the momentum toward awareness. Others will devote themselves to rear-guard actions, trying to recapture the ego situation they have lost. Either way, the process continues and has its impact. The ego can't win. In the long run, whether through conscious cooperation or by force of the unavoidable, the ego mechanism eventually begins to break down. Whether we like it or not, learning occurs. Buddhism takes a very long view: this process takes innumerable lifetimes, and whatever we may do or suffer in this life—whether we are conscious or unconscious of what is occurring—is part of that ultimately positive, creative process.

There is a second way in which the traditional concept of repression is inadequate in the context of meditating with the body. The idea of repression generally assumes that the objects of repression recede into the "unconscious," where we are unaware of them. In the theory of somatic meditation, as mentioned, we come to see that we are not entirely unconscious of these shadowy aspects, but "sense" them in the body and react to them there. And, as we have seen, they are actually part of our functioning ego itself, as that which it is continually resisting.

Through descending into the darkness of the body, we no longer remain enclosed within the boundaries of consciousness implied by the ego. In this work, we are opening our awareness into the enfolded domains of our experience themselves. When we do so, the messages of the body, the messages of our enfolded or our "unconscious" experience, communicate themselves directly to our awareness. Then, returning to the surface, so to speak, we go through a process of integrating what we have touched into our consciousness, enlarging our self-concept and bounded awareness.

As we have seen, the body itself has its own timetable. Messages come through, information comes through in the nature of insight—we simply see things about ourself and about our world that we had not seen before. Again, this information may be the result of recent repression, or it may simply be utterly new, something that has never before sought to make itself known to us. This information may come in the form of bodily sensations, feelings, images, memories, intuitions, vague, almost imperceptible feeling tones, thoughts, and so on. But in each case, it is the expression of the unfolding process: no longer walled off outside the domain of consciousness, our body begins to deliver information that it has been holding for us and that it needs to deliver now, at this precise moment.

It is important to understand the intent of our basic being, our fundamental self, the buddha nature. It is not quite, as the Jungians might say, that "we" become whole, that "we" attain a completion of personality, or that "we" embody the totality. From the somatic point of view, this kind of language, while helpful up to a certain point, carries forward too much the notion of an "I" that attains wholeness. There is too much the notion of an "I" that survives the process and that is the experiencer of the wholeness.

The somatic lineage proposes a slightly different way of framing the matter: the intention of the buddha nature is for the boundaries to the totality—not *our* totality but *the* totality—to be dissolved. This dissolution, which is accomplished only through a long process of gradual development, is classically said to be for the ultimate benefit of both ourself and others. It benefits ourself because our ultimate and final freedom and fulfillment are only attainable when we recognize that *we are not* and that *only the totality, in and of itself, is.* We could say that we recognize that "we" are nothing other than an expression of the totality itself, except in the final realization, any kind of separate "we" disappears. We—or something— ultimately arrives at wholeness in and of itself. This wholeness is, in and of itself, the nature of awareness. The "end point," then, is wholeness aware of itself. Only here can the journey be felt to have been completed. If there is any sense of ultimate freedom and fulfillment, this is it.

This realization is also for the ultimate benefit of others because the totality, known as the *dharmadhatu,* exists solely as a fount of compassion directed toward suffering beings. When the boundaries walling off the totality dissolve, the full flood of the compassion of reality itself can issue forth, through the incarnated being we are, through our mind, our words, and everything we do. Without human beings performing this role of being utterly nothing in this way, the compassion of the universe is unable to express itself fully and freely. Such is the ultimate benevolence of the human person. Such is the mystery of the human incarnation.

When we are deeply immersed in our body, when the avenues of communication between our body, the buddha nature, and our conscious ego are open, the process of our own unfolding carries forward in a continuous, unabated way. This doesn't mean that there will not be starts, stops, sudden openings, or periods when we feel hopelessly bogged down. But all of these will be part of the actual process itself with which we are deeply and intimately connected.

FORTY-FIVE

A Tibetan View of the Major Stages of Unfolding

E arlier in this section, I said that there are major stages of unfolding that are shared or held in common among those meditators who make the spiritual journey. This raises the question as to what those major stages are and how we may talk about them. A very helpful and, I think, generally applicable formulation of these stages is provided by Tibetan yoga. This tradition describes three *yanas,* or "vehicles," three progressive stages of development: Hinayana, Mahayana, and Vajrayana. *Hinayana* is the "small" or "limited" vehicle; *Mahayana,* the "great" or "expansive" vehicle; and *Vajrayana,* the "adamantine" or "indestructible" vehicle.

It is important to emphasize that these three vehicles do *not* refer to historically existing schools but to stages of the spiritual path and corresponding levels of spiritual maturation as conceived within Tibetan Buddhism. Thus, Hinayana does not, as is sometimes wrongly supposed, refer to Southern or Theravada

Buddhism and Mahayana does not refer to Ch'an, Zen, and Pure Land Buddhism of East Asia. There has, admittedly, been confusion in the past on this important point, because traditional Tibetan teachers have lacked an accurate understanding of Buddhist historical development and have consequently conflated their developmental model with living historical schools—schools of which they had little or no direct knowledge. The "three vehicles" represent stages of spiritual development that potentially apply to any spiritual practitioner, whether they follow the Theravada, Zen, Pure Land, or Tibetan Buddhist path, or some other tradition, including those of the other "high religions" and of the indigenous traditions.

The "three yanas," then, outline the general framework of stages according to which the journey of somatic meditation unfolds. Specifically, when understood from within the framework of embodied meditation practice, Hinayana primarily addresses our own physical body, what we may term the "personal body"; Mahayana speaks of the larger, interpersonal dimension of our somatic being, which we may designate the "interpersonal body"; and Vajrayana speaks about our body in its largest, most universal dimensions, which we may call the "cosmic body."

The summary I offer here follows the one put forth by Chögyam Trungpa Rinpoche.[1] Among accounts of the path in Tibetan Buddhism, Rinpoche's account is unusual for its

---

[1] For example, see Chögyam Trungpa, *Cutting Through Spiritual Materialism* (Boston: Shambhala Publications, 1973).

experiential subtlety and accuracy in relation to the actual unfolding process. One may observe, both in the traditional Tibetan context and among contemporary teachers who represent the traditional point of view, that you can become a Buddhist in quite a conventionally religious way, reading about Buddhism, taking refuge, joining a Buddhist community, and doing a little meditation practice. Here, there is not necessarily any question of a fundamental existential crisis, or of entry into the dharma as a matter of life and death. Nor is there usually the level of meditation practice that is necessary for the authentic journey to unfold to its maximum extent. One of the reasons behind this conventional presentation to Western students may be that these people are typically viewed by Tibetan lamas as "laypeople," for whom a more demanding approach would, within the traditional Tibetan framework, generally be considered inappropriate. Another, closely connected reason may be that Tibetans are simply uncertain— and, I think, with good reason—of what their Western students will do with the teaching they receive, and they often elect the safer, more conservative route.

Chögyam Trungpa's presentation was far more daring and radical. In the early 1970s, he told his early students that he saw them not as ordinary laypeople, but rather as potential "householder yogins," a type of serious practitioner in both ancient India and classical Tibetan Buddhism. These were people who, though often married, having children, and living "in the world," practiced the dharma at the highest level, meditating in the contexts of daily life and in retreat. These practitioners received the most advanced instructions and were sometimes held to have attained complete realization. Some of them, in fact, founded lineages that survive today, including that taught by Chögyam Trungpa.

Rinpoche told us that he wanted to instruct us, not as ordinary laypeople, but as householder yogins, with the full range of the Tibetan meditation dharma, organized according to the "three yanas," including the most advanced Vajrayana teachings. His expectation was that we would meet his generosity with our own openness and willingness to put the teachings we received into practice. Rinpoche expected that the "sitting practice of meditation," as he called it, would be our primary life commitment.

In his presentation of Hinayana, Mahayana, and Vajrayana, Trungpa Rinpoche also used highly experiential language. He made it clear that this was not common in Tibetan tradition but that it was characteristic of those who practiced at the highest, most intense levels—the hermit yogins and the householder yogins. When the journey is, indeed, a matter of one's very existence, what arises must be shared within the circle of teacher and disciples. When you are practicing at a profound level, unprecedented experience flows forth and this needs to be given voice. This is the ultimate meaning of *sangha*.

In this area, Rinpoche was innovative also in certain other respects. For one thing, cultural authorization to articulate one's "practice experience" was often restricted to a minority of the elite, generally tulkus. In addition, one generally talked of practice experience only to one's guru, one's closest teacher. In Rinpoche's case, he talked very openly about his experience with all of us and encouraged us to talk with him and to one another about what was "coming up" in our practice. The following experiential description of the "three yanas," then, follows Trungpa Rinpoche's lead.

Hinayana corresponds to that phase of the journey in which we unfold our "personal body," the body we experience initially as separate from others and from the larger cosmos. In the Hinayana, we realize the inadequacy and, indeed, impossibility of trying to live our life exclusively within the restricted, small self of ego. As a response, we feel inspired to explore our situation openly; to discover a genuine path and commit ourselves to it; and to undertake the practice of meditation. The inspiration at this stage of the journey is to establish ourself in our meditation practice and to open ourself to the discoveries that emerge from that.

The Hinayana phase involves attending to our personal karma, allowing unresolved and—in somatic terms—unlived experience to continually make itself known to us for awareness and integration. This stage is very much confined to a process that seems mainly restricted to us alone, as indeed it must be as the foundation of our journey.

In the Mahayana, we begin to unfold our "interpersonal body," the "body" that expresses itself in the interpersonal dimension, in an immediate and somatically felt connectedness with other people. As we unfold our interpersonal body, we begin to find emerging within ourself a profound and abiding inspiration to help others. We discover ourself deeply touched by the suffering of others and feel an irresistible urge to extend ourself to be with them and share their pain, to relieve their torment, and to consider how we might share with them whatever is sane and beneficial in us and our experience.

Later still in our development, our unfolding begins to include the larger world itself and to take on an increasingly more extensive scope. In the Vajrayana, we thus unfold a level of our own somatic being that is cosmic in its dimensions. We become aware that there is a pattern to the way the world works, the way relative truth operates. This is a pattern that exists beyond the realm of concept or ego, beyond the realm of our personal or even interpersonal karma. Rather, it is a realm that includes them all. This largest reality is also one that can and must be directly and personally experienced. We begin to find, in our own experience, what traditional religions have meant when they talk about deities, forces, and energies as expressions of a sacred, cosmic order.

These three phases build upon one another. Thus, the Hinayana stage of working with our ever-unfolding personal karma is the basis of our spiritual journey throughout life. As our unfolding becomes more subtle, we begin to engage the interpersonal aspect, "the interpersonal body." This, again, now becomes an ongoing part of our work and our journey. On the basis of these two, at a certain point, our unfolding becomes even more subtle, and we find ourself relating to the larger, "the cosmic body." From this point onward, we are practicing Hinayana, Mahayana, and Vajrayana simultaneously: working on ourself, helping others, and finding connection with the "self-existing *mandala* (pattern) of reality," as it is called.

These general categories are extremely helpful in providing an overview of the most basic stages of the journey. However, they are very general and give us only the most fundamental transition points along the way. Questions still remain as to what more, and more specific, might be said about the stages of the journey.

FORTY-SIX

The Body as Guide on the Journey

C learly, there are many stages and levels to this journey. Initially, the body may be leading us toward a more stable, healthy, wholesome sense of self, helping us fill out and complete developmental stages that have been missed along the way. As we continue, we may sense our clinging to our self-concept softening and admitting greater relaxation and our self-image becoming more open, porous, and flexible. Further along still, we may find ourself holding our self-concept more loosely and even experience periods of time when it is not functioning much at all. At this time, we may discover our experience of reality, of the information delivered by our body, flowing in a quite free, open, unrestricted way. Each of these general levels of maturation has its own challenge provided, as always, by the body, for the body is the one that calls into question our current image of ourself, however we may be holding it, and invites us to go further. Even though these levels unfold in a graduated and stage-by-stage fashion, even beginning practitioners may have glimpses of stages far ahead of their immediate level of experience and understanding.

At each stage, whether near the beginning, in the middle of the journey, or near the end, there is always the challenge of letting go, surrendering, and giving in to the dissolution of our current self-concept. And there is always the challenge of rebirth of our self-concept. It is important to realize that coming to rebirth holds its own kind of pain. Death and letting go, painful though they are, land us in a space that is open and filled with ease. But then, we find ourself needing to "come back," so to speak, to reappear. The movement from non-existence back to existence as a "self," even if it is a porus and flexible one, can be felt as extraordinarily painful for the restriction it involves. This will be the case until we are well advanced on the journey, where the "self" that re-arises from the ashes is felt to be quite insubstantial and unreal, little more than a transparent expression of the emptiness from which it is born.

In all of this, the body is a kind, gentle, and most compassionate guide and mentor. In contrast to the rather frightening and off-putting notions of spiritual practice as getting rid of our "self" altogether, the body guides us to let go of our current idea of who we are—yes, to suffer the pain and loss of the letting go and the dissolution, but then to find ourself reborn, this time with another, more inclusive, more realistic, far more generous (to both ourself and others) sense of self. In this way, the path is incremental, but it is continuous and the journey goes on and on and on.

It must be incremental, because—although we may have moments of glimpsing reality itself—our ability to experience, to mediate to others, and finally to dissolve into the totality itself can only develop incrementally. As we have seen, through the surfacing of more and more of our "unconscious," the unlived experience stored in our body, our awareness opens, deepens, and becomes increasingly vast and inclusive. Concomitant with this, our ego, in its progressive rebirth, comes into increasing harmony with the endless worlds beyond, more easily open and receptive to the totality of reality, of the buddha nature, its intentions for us and its movement toward us. Eventually, our "self-concept" is nothing but the totality itself, beyond any and all conceptualizing. At this point, as mentioned, the "ego" has grown so vast and has included so much that it no longer stands in opposition to anything. At this point, it has become everything and is therefore nothing.

In one sense, the notion of being utterly without any "self" is an end point that is perhaps never reached, a far-off goal that keeps us heading in the right direction and guides us along the way. In another sense, though, each time the information delivered by the body is truly heard, we suffer an ego death, and in the moment of dissolution, we have a glimpse of the utter nonexistence of "me."

FORTY-SEVEN

Encountering the Shadow

Modern therapeutic psychology makes frequent reference to the "shadow," the assemblage of qualities and attributes that are being denied entrance into our awareness because they are, at present, too inconsistent with the self-concept we are trying to maintain. The notion of the shadow, first made popular by Jung, points to "our 'other side,' our 'dark brother,' who is an invisible part of our psychic totality . . . It is a part of the individual, a split-off portion of his being." It holds the "unlived" parts of ourself, "qualities the ego does not need or cannot use."[1] The shadow develops along with the ego: the more the ego gains in shape, definition and stability, the more consolidated the shadow becomes. In people's lives and especially in therapy, the shadow makes itself known

---

[1] Jolande Jacobi, *The Psychology of C.G. Jung* (New Haven: Yale University Press, 1973), 109.

through manifestations of the inner life, such as illnesses, emotional upheavals, memories, visions, and dreams, and also of the outer life, through people and situations, especially those to which we have intense emotional reactions.

This concept of the shadow is helpful in understanding the spiritual unfolding that occurs through meditating with the body, but it does need to be redefined, generalized, and also broadened. Within the perspective of Tibetan yoga, as we have seen, everything that is not ready to be received by our conscious mind at this time, everything that is denied admittance to our consciousness, abides in darkness. As we have seen, the totality of the darkness exists in the body in an enfolded state: the conscious mind not being ready to receive the information it holds, it abides in a highly condensed, impacted state in our body, out of sight. There it waits, impending, until the moment in the spiritual journey arrives when—as karmic fruition, out of the darkness—it approaches our consciousness to be received, experienced, and integrated with our conscious awareness.

The term "shadow" is commonly used to refer to everything that is not the ego, the totality of the "not-I" world that the ego holds at bay. While using the term in the same way in this book to refer to the totality of the "not-I," it will be useful to divide this "shadow" into two parts. First are those aspects of our shadow that lie in complete darkness and are not ready to approach consciousness for admission. They are the illimitable inhabitants of the *alaya*, those aspects of our unlived experience whose moment of karmic fruition has not arrived and may not arrive for years or lifetimes.

Second, are those aspects of our "shadow" that do not lie in complete darkness, but reside in a kind of shadowy half-dark between the inaccessible darkness and the full light of our consciousness. These "shadowy" aspects are beginning to approach consciousness. They are those parts of our unlived experience whose time has come to appear as karmic fruition requiring our response. As these contents approach our consciousness, we often sense them—sometimes days, weeks, or even months ahead of time. When we are engaged in our somatic practice, we may discover a brooding, impending quality in our body, a feeling that something is about to emerge from the half-dark. It is no longer in the completely unknown darkness, but what it is can not yet be discerned—it lies in the shadowy no-man's land, again, between the black depths of the alaya and our consciousness.

This can be a mainly somatic experience—a kind of sense of something coming—and it can also arrive in the more specific form of feelings felt in the body, such as anxiety, foreboding, anticipation, excitement, and even dread or terror. In addition, it sometimes announces itself through dreams, comments others make that strike us strangely, even small events in our life that seem to carry some out-of-proportion weight.

In contrast to the deep darkness, what lies in the shadows always has a quality of directionality toward consciousness—it wants to be known now and integrated with conscious awareness. As we have seen, this is a reflection of the natural operation of the buddha nature, of the maturation process by which we humans are called to fulfill our inborn fate or destiny. The accumulation of unlived experience is, as we have seen, part of our process as humans, part of the operation of the buddha nature. But the willingness of our buddha nature to tolerate—to "put up with"—experience that remains unlived is only temporary. Unlived experience, by its very nature, is always awaiting the moment when it can be lived through, deliver itself into awareness, and fulfill its own destiny within human existence.

Whether or not anything significant is about to appear, we always sense the subtle pressure of the directionality of the shadow toward consciousness *in the form of our own resistance.* This may be felt internally as physical tension, pain, or emotional distress, or externally in our slight hostility, impatience, or fear in relation to events in our life. However, because the information of the shadow is always threatening in one way or another to our conscious status quo, because by its nature it "does not go along" with what we want to think of ourself and the world, or want to accomplish, we ignore and push away its information as much as possible, focusing our attention in other directions. And what we aren't willing to look at, we convince ourself we don't see.

But, of course, in order to advance on our spiritual journey, we need what the shadow holds. It is interesting that, in a way, while we resist the information contained in the shadow, there is something in us that longs for it at the same time. There is something in us that longs for the half-light and the darkness of the shadowlands, longs for the mystery and the unknown reaches of our being. This "something" is our awareness; just as unlived experience wants to be received and lived, at the same time, our own awareness wants the same thing. It wants to receive that life fully.

We have seen the way in which parts of our larger awareness become tied up and preoccupied with keeping the unwanted contents of the body, the shadow, the *alaya*, at bay. Tied up in this way and suffering the resultant restriction, awareness itself wants to liberate itself into its own boundless, unconditioned state. Many people come to meditation because they feel a compelling need to open and free themselves, whatever may be the cost to their ego.

And many meditators, especially those drawn to Vajrayana, feel an overwhelming thirst toward experience, not simply to find openness in their minds, but to taste and touch the relative phenomena of their lives in a completely naked, unconditioned, and boundless way. This overpowering thirst to experience anything and everything fully, with no barriers but with absolute nakedness, is an expression of awareness seeking its own completion. There is an intelligent hunger within awareness itself, a passionate knowing, that only by fully engaging relative experience and uniting with it, may it come to its own final fulfillment. This thirst is, finally, a thirst to meet, befriend, and unite, not just with what lies in shadow, but with the totality of the darkness that stands behind. What hungers and thirsts in this way is nothing other than the body itself, the buddha nature.

Within the perspectives of Tibetan yoga, the "shadow" is multilayered and potentially all-inclusive. It can include, as the

Jungians emphasize, negative qualities that contradict the positive qualities of our self with which we most strongly identify. But the shadow can also manifest aspects that are further afield, that may have little or no apparent relation to the person we think we are. Beyond that, the shadow can include layers and dimensions of experience that stand outside of basic cultural expectations of what is possible or what reality is like. Finally, it can bring depths and subtleties of experience that lie outside of any kind of recognizable human experience at all: incredibly, there is even a shadow side to our human assumption that time and space are real.

FORTY-EIGHT

The Personal Body

It is interesting how the process of intimate communication, communion, and union with the vast realm in shadow unfolds in a gradual, progressive, almost systematic manner, from surface to depth and from depth to greater depth. By way of suggesting this process, this and the next few chapters consider the layers of the shadow mentioned previously, those corresponding to the Tibetan "three yanas" description of the unfolding process, which include the "personal body," "the interpersonal body," and the "cosmic body."

As we enter the body work, typically we first meet those aspects of ourself that lie in shadow because they are in immediate contradiction to our current self-image. As we consider this first phase, it should be kept in mind that it provides the ongoing foundation of our work. In this sense, we will be engaged with this level of our shadow from this point onward into the indefinite future. This is because, until attaining full realization—whatever and whenever that may be—we will always tend to personalize everything that happens to us, to try to create individual psychological territory, a renewed self-concept, out of whatever happens in our life, including the occurrences and insights of our somatic spiritual work. This being the case, as we continue with our body-centered meditation, we are always going to be confronted with the ways in which we are trying to withdraw from the ever-evolving nature of our existence and to freeze the current situation as a bulwark against the natural cycles of life, death, and rebirth. None of this is any problem or mistake; it is just part of the creative process of our journey. At the same time, though, we always need to identify these freezing patterns—as indeed we will be forced to do by the body—let go of them, and allow ourself to move on.

This first phase of our work, then, is meeting those aspects of ourself that are in immediate contradiction to qualities with which we have composed our current self-image. This first phase itself unfolds in steps. In the initial step—which is itself, again, ongoing—we become aware of the most superficial and obvious inaccuracies of our fabricated self-concept. This is our social persona, those aspects of our self-image that are simply reflections of what we think others want us to be, the social mask that we put on for the world. To the extent we have come to think that we are the same as the social mask, the body work confronts us with painfully contrary information. As we begin relaxing the most surface layers of tension, we begin to see all kinds of things about ourself that do not conform to the mask. We may notice that, while we present ourselves as thoroughly competent, there are parts of us that are lazy, sloppy, and irresponsible. Again, if we are trying to keep up an image of a loving and committed parent, we may begin to uncover a deep layer of resentment, anger, and mistrust, and fantasies of escape from our children. Whatever our mask, we begin to see that we are actually both less and more.

As we progress in the body work, we find ourself noticing further aspects of ourself—in the form of qualities, characteristics, feelings, and even thoughts—that are more disturbing: aspects that we may find quite unacceptable and even shocking and morally reprehensible. This deeper dimension of our personal shadow is no longer simply in contradiction with the perceived expectations of our social sphere; it runs counter to what we think is right, good, and necessary for us to be in order to be acceptable to ourself, even on the most minimal level.

For example, we may think of ourself as fair and impartial toward other people and then see that we are actually constantly playing favorites based on our own personal hunger and neurotic needs. We may think of ourself as kind and compassionate, then find that we are actually irritated with people much of the time. We may regard ourself as nonjudgmental, but then observe that, on a subtle level, we are constantly judging people and everything they do. We may feel that we are quite an open person, but then see that we are always wanting something from others and that that incessant, unconscious demand actually underlies our "openness." Again, we may think of ourself as quite present, but then notice a deeper layer where we are actually continually tuning out and turning away from situations.

Even beyond this, the financially struggling accountant may see how very easy—and tempting—the prospect is of embezzling money from his company. The courteous driver, when cut off by a rude and reckless one, sees the very realistic possibility of becoming a murderer. The loving husband finds, one day, he actually doesn't care about his partner at all. The well-behaved suburbanite discovers insane jealousy and rageful fantasies in relation to next-door neighbors. It isn't just the others who have criminal and psychopathic tendencies. It's all in us and it's all real.

And so it goes, on and on and on. As we continue with our somatic exploration, these things, formerly in shadow, reveal that what we have been thinking about ourself is partial and extremely one-sided. As the work becomes part of our ongoing life, we begin to find that every time we try to think something about ourself—"I am this way"—we immediately see that this other, opposite thing is also true, at the very same time.

For example, perhaps we are a teacher —always, we think, willing to see our shortcomings. Suppose we just taught a class that we think was good, clear, helpful for the students. Perhaps we are not so crass as to actually think the thought "Wow, I am a good teacher." But we may be dwelling in a more subtle version of the same thing, resting in a kind of pleasant, slightly dulled-out self-satisfaction. Perhaps we receive some "positive feedback," which just reinforces our smugness.

Present to our body and making itself known through our somatic work, immediately the shadow counterpoint and correction begins to flow to us and through us. We suddenly recall a terrible talk we gave a few months ago. "I certainly am capable of that, at any time." Then we begin remembering other muddy, aggressive, demanding, or needy lectures we have given. Next we receive a note from a student saying how "off," confusing, and disturbing he or she thought our presentation was. All of this may then reveal how much we want to think something good about ourself, how we are trying to wring confirmation, solidity, security, and pleasure out of this situation. This kind of information may be irritating, sickening, or disturbing, but it is always informative and always deflating. What is being deflated is any type of substantial self-concept that we are in the process of trying to form. And, always, it lands us back in the body, with our totality.

It is interesting that the deflating information continually arising from our somatic awareness is not always "negative," at least not in the way that we usually think. We may, at a certain time, be invested in thinking negative things about ourself, in feeling dejected, discouraged, and depressed. We may be feeling very sorry for ourself indeed and be quite creative in working all our experience into this "negative" self-concept. At such times, there is always this other thing nagging us, information that is saying something quite different. This could be simply knowing on some level that, in fact, we are not as bad as we are trying to think. It might be recollections of our positive capacities and gifts, genuine inspirations that keep trying to surface, or perhaps other people willing and able to suggest ways to work in and through our morass. Such experiences may be met with irritation, denial, or anger, but they serve, once again, to call into question what we are trying to think about ourself, the self-concept we are trying to consolidate and maintain.

Of course, in our search for some kind of solid, consistent self-image, we might take the contrary information that led to our deflation and try to turn it into a reference point of some kind. If our initial fixation was on our positive qualities, then we could flip over our thinking into self-hatred: "See, I really am no good; I really am a complete fraud and have always been one." If our initial fixation was on our negative qualities, we could take the contrary information of the body and begin to develop a grandiose version of ourself: "I am really great after all; the negative things were never true." But to enter into this kind of thinking is, once again, to disconnect and abandon the body, exiting into the thinking process. Once the demise of whatever we were thinking has occurred and landed us back in the body, our job and task, the discipline of the practice, is to remain where we have landed, in the emptiness and plenitude of our somatic being, just feeling and sensing how it is for us just then.

Thus, the more deeply grounded we are in our body, the more every attempt to secure our idea of ourself is met with contrary information. We are living in a situation of continual ego buildup and breakdown, formation and dissolving, all happening rapidly and without cessation. With this kind of thing going on all the time, we find ourself unable to arrive at a self-concept that is static, substantial, ongoing, or consistent. When our ego concept is constantly being challenged, eroded and dissolved, we find that we aren't anything that we can think for any length of time at all.

Rather, we are just all these things, all these thoughts and contradictory qualities and experiences, which are rushing toward us and changing in an unending succession. Feeling that we are nothing definite, solid, or continuous often leads to a feeling that we are nothing identifiable at all. In this way, our intimate dialogue with the shadowy aspects of our being keeps landing us back in the very big space of our own inner silence, the primordial stillness and openness of our own body.

We continue with our somatic meditation, quite aware that—at least from the ego's standpoint—there is something decidedly suicidal in the process. The more we practice, the deeper we go, and the less able we are to form a self-concept that is static and continuous. At the same time, we find that the practice itself reveals that there is no need for us to react to this inability with the dejection, depression, or despair that may be more habitual to ourself and others. Of course, we *can* react with such feelings; but we also see that there is another choice: rather than fall back into abject depression or into scrambling for conceptual ground—which are, after all, just further attempts to regain ego territory—we can step forward into the light. Such dissolving of the ego concept can lead us directly to the freedom we seek, if we can just stay in our body and with the somatic process.

As we continue in ever-deepening relation with the body, we notice that something basic is changing in us. On one level, of course, each somatic exploration yields deeper relaxation, more direct connection, and a more intimate dialogue with the shadows. But on another level, we begin to see that our basic relationship with the darkness has shifted in some fundamental way. We see that we are now operating differently as a person. We seem to be living in a kind of no-man's land, a borderland between the light and the darkness. Our ego now seems to have moved into the role of mediator, continually looking into the shadows for what is life-giving, and willingly—and even cheerfully and with humor—mediating and mentoring that to consciousness.

Now living much closer to the domain of the body and its precincts, falling into its mystery as needed, we find ourself strangely unconcerned that we have lost the solid sense of self that we used to identify with life itself. In fact, we are no longer striving to locate ourself with a "self-concept" as such; instead, we seem to be identifying with what we might call a "self-process," the continual formation, dissolution, and rebirth of our idea of who we are. We are finding that, through the body work, we are becoming not just a different person, but a different *kind* of person, much closer to what we have always wanted to be.

FORTY-NINE

The Next Layer: The Interpersonal Body

As we have accumulated much experience and have come to more sophisticated ideas about our body, still, in the encounter with our somatic "other," we have to continuously let go even of these. Each successive journey into the darkness of our body reveals that it is truly "other," always more than anything we have been thinking. In fact, over time, we begin to suspect that our body may not have any limits at all, that its very nature is continually to lead us through and through, and beyond any and all definitions and limiting conceptions.

At a certain point, we realize that even the idea of "our" body is somehow questionable. There is something haunting us, some nearly imperceptible, yet unavoidable, sense of inadequacy in our feeling of strict personal "ownership" of our body. There is something in the shadows that wants to be communicated about our assumption of separation from others. We are meeting the shadow that calls into question our body as strictly personal domain and personal territory. This shadow is nothing less than the bodies of others.

The fact is, the more we descend into our body, the more we uncover a very vast and expanding interpersonal world of connections with other people. It is not that, becoming more somatically and emotionally present and aware, we form new connections with others. Rather, the more somatically and emotionally subtle we become, the more we discover connections with others that have already been there, perhaps "forever," presenting themselves as fully formed, in their existence pre-dating any discovery of our own.

We discover, then, that to have a body is already to be in intimate and extensive connection to others. As we explore this developing awareness, we find that our "body"—far from being restricted to "me"—is actually, in some strange way, inclusive of the other embodied ones, the other people in the world. We discover that our own body is, at a more subtle level, actually an interpersonal body—our embodiment, this body of ours, has, inherently, a vast, perhaps unlimited interpersonal dimension.

We can see this in the way that the more embodied we are, the more aware we are of other people. When we are dwelling largely in our concepts, when we are disconnected from our body, other people appear in our life as objects. We really do experience them as separate and have little feeling for their life, their being, as a subject. Abiding in our mind, we treat them with the same casual disregard and disdain with which we treat our own person. They fall prey to the same predatory behavior that we unleash on our own physical and psychological selves.

The closer and more easily present we are to the darkness of our body, however, the more we sense and experience others as inseparable from ourself. When we meet another who is afraid, we find that fear already resonating in us. Someone else's depression speaks within us as a heavy, leaden hopelessness. Somebody's paranoia fills us suddenly with a kind of lurking threat. Another's over-brimming happiness may likewise be felt within as a kind of somatic gladness, filling our senses blissfully. The more we know of our body, then, the more we find that our own embodiment actually includes others and the more easily we are able to be in them and as them. We see that the idea of any clear separation does not apply.

Our interconnectedness with others can also manifest in a less direct way, as a delayed reaction. Sometimes when we are with someone else and ask them how they are feeling, they may claim and believe that they are not feeling anything in particular. But then, afterward, we are literally hit with a wave of feeling, such as anger, despair, self-hatred, or unbearable loneliness, that we know is not ours, in a personal sense. If we are sensitive, we realize that we are experiencing the unacknowledged feelings of the other. This kind of experience is possible for any of us at any time but is perhaps most common among therapists, body workers, and other health professionals. We feel what the other is feeling because, ultimately, there is no hard-and-fast boundary between us. It is almost as if, because they were unable to admit the shadow of their own feeling into consciousness, the emotional charge built up to the point where it had to break through somewhere, and it broke through in us. It found expression through us. Our own openness to their denied experience, strangely, may help them feel much better, without their even knowing precisely why. But they may say, "I felt seen; I felt heard; I felt held." Little may they realize how somatic and how connected our knowing of them was.

Particularly if we are healers, the ability to dwell at the level of the interpersonal body can be extraordinarily beneficial for our patients. Consider, for example, someone with recurrent bronchitis who has come to her healer for help. She and her healer perhaps both suspect—because, in alternative healing lore, grief is often said to be held in the chest—that her chronic bronchial problems are connected with inadequate love from her mother in early childhood and subsequent grief. But how to find healing?

Her healer may begin by simply placing her hand on her patient's chest. At first, she feels nothing. But then, extending her awareness into her hand and then further beyond herself, into the thoracic cavity of her patient, she can feel, very clearly, the tightness, the congestion, and precisely where the brachia are irritated and swollen. She just rests in this experience. In the course of twenty or thirty minutes, her patient may report that she feels a kind of relief, as if something cool and soothing is developing in her chest.

Then, or in a subsequent healing session, the healer will extend her awareness further, to a more subtle level, and feel a terrible fatigue in the chest of her patient, so complete and so crushing that she herself cannot imagine even the effort of turning over in bed. The healer senses a weakness, a lack of strength, a deep vulnerability. Going further, she comes upon an oceanic sadness and, deeper still, terrible fear, the trembling and shaking of a small child who is not connected, in her heart, with the deeper wellsprings of love, confidence, and ease that, by all genetics and all biology, should have been given, been mediated, by her mother.

The healer's process is simply to feel. Importantly, though, she is not feeling someone separate and disconnected from her. She is not feeling a person at all. Rather, her own awareness is with the other and within the other, because of her (the healer's) own embodiment, more clearly than the other's own awareness of herself. It is as if the healer's own state of being is the congestion, the tightness, the irritation, as if her own feeling is the terrible fatigue, sadness, and fear. In a sense, she has realized the other as herself; she has realized herself as the other. There is no separation. She dwells fully and completely within the experience of the other person. There is nothing else.

Simply in experiencing the physical and emotional being of the other person, the healer is activating the most powerful kind of healing there could ever be. The healer is resting within her own sense of connection to and continual nourishment from the depths of her own body, with openness, relaxation, and trust. From within this, she is able to connect with the "illness" of the other. At the same time, the other—perhaps without knowing it at first—is opening to the "health" of the healer and thereby being connected with that all-healing source of the body's greatest depths. Is it the healer's depth she is experiencing or her own? At this point, from the viewpoint of either person, there is no difference, which means that the "patient" is now finding linkage in the deepest way.

The patient's body is now connected with the underlying love—theoretically available in herself but never developed because of her mother's inability to mediate this to her—that she experienced insufficiently as a small child. Through repeated sessions, without a word necessarily being spoken, for the patient, everything can rearrange itself in a new way. This is true for the healer also, for she has been through the illness of the patient, experiencing it completely as her own and, with her patient, has mysteriously resolved for herself whatever of her own personal karma was waiting there for her.

Our discovery of the interpersonal dimensions of our own body, then, is helpful to others not because we are having a different experience from them or having an alternative reality to offer. It is helpful, rather, because we can allow ourself to enter the other's most intimate, threatening, intense feelings, to be there, but perhaps more clearly and fully, and with more confidence than the other can just now manage. In effect, we are opening to them our connectedness to our own somatic depth, to the unconditional health and well-being of our deepest somatic stratum. Through our opening, our somatic connectedness then becomes their connectedness to that same depth and reality in themselves, which henceforth becomes more and more available to them. As always with the body work—and this is one of the body's great lessons—we most help precisely by not *doing* anything, but just by being. Of course, we can be that way with others only because we are able to be that way with ourself—at the level of the interpersonal body, there is no difference. Once we are able to abide deeply within our own body, then being with the other is really nothing additional and nothing extra. In being with them, we are really just being at a deeper level with our own body, which, at this deeper, more subtle level, already includes them.

FIFTY

Layers of the Interpersonal Body

Our discovery of the interpersonal subtleties of our body enables us to be with others in a new way. Whenever we meet another person, whether a stranger, an acquaintance, or our most intimate partner, there is always the shock of their otherness. There is always the temptation to try to manage them by fitting them into our mental inventory, to intimidate or cajole them into hiding their otherness, or to find some shared mental or emotional ground, even if it is not true to either of us. In us, there is always the temptation to externalize and try to ward off, tame, domesticate—to destroy—the potential threat of otherness. Interpersonal relationships, in these ways, always offer the possibility of mutual conspiracy, mutual deception, and a lack of integrity.

When we are easy in the body work, though, we are in a position to welcome the edge of fear that here, as always, alerts us to an "other." We find in that fear an invitation to return to the darkness of the body, to its open, undetermined way of being, so that we may see—or, rather, be shown—how it is and how it can be with this other person.

In any relationship, there is always some shared ground, but there is also much difference, much that is not and perhaps never can be mutually known or held in common. The body work brings us to the profound insight that all of this is eminently workable, all of it is humorous, hopeless, and delightful, all at once. There is nothing wrong with any of it, either with us or with others, whatever the areas of intimate sharing and whatever the unfathomable chasms that separate.

We have so many experiences with other people, and, in our habitual way, we think them in need of some kind of fixing, some alteration or adjustment. When we reside in our somatic being as the interpersonal body, however, we see that the way others are is exactly as it should be; it is part of an unfolding journey of the relationship that can only begin precisely where we and the other are, exactly at this moment.

When we abide within the body, we are no longer imprisoned by the unconscious demand that relationships "work out." In fact, we can find much relief and joy in coming to the realization that no relationships ever work out in any real or lasting way. Otherness can never be finally overcome. Having come to this conclusion, and really accepting it, we can be humorously surprised by an experience of tremendous openness and intimacy just where we least expected it. We can realize, laughing at ourself, that the only reason we were previously unable to experience this relationship as "working out" is because we carried around the idea that it should. Having let that go, then, what we had both hoped and longed for—which was hanging us up in a frozen waste of unfulfillment—was able to happen in a very natural and spontaneous way.

The work with our "personal" body shows us just how to work with our "interpersonal" body. Just as in our personal somatic explorations, so too in the interpersonal sphere, we have to let go completely of what we think in order to connect. In relationships as in our immediate personal body, as long as we are hanging on to some idea or expectation of how things should or could be, we are not going to find the avenue of connection. In this way, our training in personal body work ends up being, at exactly the same time, training for how to be in relationship, in the interpersonal body.

Just as we enter the darkness of our physical body, so too we need to be able to enter the darkness of the interpersonal body. Each relationship has its surfaces. Like the surface of our physical body, the outermost layer of relationships is a conceptual overlay of ideas, assumptions, and preconceptions about what and who this person is, how they should be for us, and even what it means for us to interact with them. Beneath this surface of the "interpersonal ego," the depths and subtleties of our actual relationship lie enfolded.

In working with the interpersonal body, we need to move through this impacted surface, let it go, and descend into the unknown, unfathomable space to discover what this relationship is and needs to be. We do that, again, by descending into the darkness of our own body. When we go deeply enough, we run into the darkness of the interpersonal body. In meeting and integrating the shadow of our interpersonal body with our consciousness, we are discovering more and moving further toward who we ultimately are.

FIFTY-ONE

How Other People Help Us Meet Our Shadow

I n the present section, we are exploring the three layers of our ego—the personal ego, the interpersonal ego, and the cosmic ego, all restricted and reactive conceptual overlays respectively of our own person, other people, and the cosmos. Through our disconnection and withdrawal from our somatic experience into our conceptualizing mind, in order to obtain a tidy, controllable, and secure version of reality, we thus wall off the vast majority of our experience of ourself, other people, and the immense universe beyond. All this walled-off experience is trapped in our body in darkness, where it awaits our willingness to experience and integrate it.

Thus it is that, as our somatic awareness develops, the shadow of our greater being rushes toward us, inviting communication, intimacy, and union. A special domain of Buddhist psychology, that of Yogacara, considers the way in which "external" encounters with other people can powerfully incarnate the appearance of our shadow, our unlived life, and make it available to our experience. As a fitting conclusion to this discussion of the unfolding of the interpersonal body, let us consider how our increasing openness and sensitivity to others enables our interactions with them to powerfully make our shadow available to us for encounter, acknowledgment, and integration.

According to the Yogacara school, when we have any experience of the external world, and particularly of other people, we are meeting our own shadow, our own enfolded body. This is not to say that the external world that we encounter is nothing but our experience. No, there is certainly an external world independent of our experience. But what we *see* in that world, what we *notice*, and *what it means to us* are a direct reflection of our own unresolved karma.

A simple example will illustrate this point. Suppose we are at a social gathering with, say, twenty people in the room. At a certain point, a woman walks into the room and calls out, "Hello, everyone." Everyone turns to look. But no two of these twenty people see the woman in the same way. In fact, in some sense, there are twenty different women being experienced at this moment. For one, she is an intriguing stranger; for a second, a date who has just arrived, provoking hope and fear; for a third, a daughter or a sister; for a fourth, an ex-wife whose mindless extroversion has once again provoked fury; for a fifth, the preschool teacher of one's child; and so on. Each person in the room will not only see this person differently in these obvious ways, but will respond differently to her gender, her age, her appearance, her racial group, and so on. What each person sees will embody his or her feelings, preconceptions, and judgments—likes and dislikes, hopes and fears. What is significant, though, is that what they choose to focus on in the other person is a reflection of their own self-concept, their own ego in the largest sense, as this stands against what lies beyond. What they see in the other person are aspects of themselves—my date, my "ex-wife," etc.—that they think really are this other person, rather than a projection of their own situation. In seeing the woman, each person thinks, "She is really like this; she is really this way." In other words, the woman embodies aspects of each person's own awareness, but no one sees it. They think their impressions have really come from "out there," that what they see exists objectively and independently of themselves. But though unrecognized, it is their personal karmic fruition, their unlived experience, that is arising in the form of "the other" at the moment of her entry.

The same thing applies with inanimate objects. If twenty people look at the same oak tree, they will see something different depending on the place from which they are viewing it, their station in life (a woodcutter might see potential firewood; a young boy, something to climb; a homeowner, something that might fall on his house in a storm; a graphic artist, something to depict; and so on). In addition, each person's experience will be conditioned by all of his or her previous experiences of trees and especially of oak trees. Again, what arises for us as the fruition of past karmic causes and conditions is not the abstract, generic experience of a tree, but the specific, finally individual and unique experience of this tree at this moment. The tree holds our own purchase on reality, our own ego concept, but we don't see this; we think, without realizing it, that this is really how this tree is.

When we first encounter a person or a tree, our experience is enfolded. In other words, we see them as an external object, "not us." So far, the information that this precise karmic ripening has presented to us lies shrouded in mystery, in darkness. So far, it is inaccessible. Seeing the other as separate, our self-concept remains intact. In order to meet the shadow that this encounter brings to us, we need to realize that it is "our dark brother" coming to reclaim his relation to us, bringing information we need in order to grow. But how do we come to this realization and reclaim that part of ourself that the other is holding?

An example taken from dream interpretation may serve as a good analogy to help us understand this process. Suppose a person with some familiarity with dream work dreams of a dark, aggressive, raging figure who is chasing her. In the dream, she is afraid for her life and runs, seeking to escape. Upon waking, initially, the dream and its dream figure seem quite other to how she experiences herself. However, once awake, she takes the attitude that this dark figure may be a part of herself, some unwanted or unacknowledged quality, that she may be fleeing—a part that is, nevertheless, seeking to be met and received by her, and integrated with her conscious viewpoint. She realizes that the dream is the agent of her larger self seeking her out.

She takes the timing of this dream seriously: it has come up at this point because this aspect of her unknown self requires admittance, just now. She will then pay close attention to her conscious experience, to see if she can find there moments of aggression and threat manifesting themselves, perhaps on a subtle level, that she is moving away from, but which are insistently appearing and reappearing, "seeking admittance." The more she notices that "this is also me," the more the intention of the dream will be honored and fulfilled, and the more her conscious standpoint, her self-concept, will undergo transformation. She may well find in herself, and as herself, the dark power of anger, wrath, and rage, and may come to understand that these are intelligent and apt—and even necessary—responses to certain kinds of external situations. She will have to let go of her former self-image as an unfailingly "nice" person, but she will gain a much fuller sense of self, for now that this aspect of her shadow has been integrated, these qualities will henceforth be available to her in her life as a woman in the modern world.

It is exactly the same when we meet external situations and occurrences with others. Suppose we meet someone who provokes an intensely negative reaction. Suppose that we take immediate advantage of the gift of this meeting by proposing to ourself that "this person is an aspect of myself. On some level, I have these abhorrent qualities. On some level, I am this person." Strangely enough, if we are willing to do this, we may very quickly notice in ourself—through remembering events, noticing emotions, recalling things others have said to us—that we, in fact, possess these very same qualities. While we may not necessarily exhibit them to ourself or others, we can see clearly that they are there beneath the surface, that we have the potential to exhibit them at any time, and that, circumstances being different, we might well act in an even more unpleasant, irritating manner than the person we are contemplating. In this way, we "unfold" the previously enfolded and impacted encounter that provoked such a negative reaction. Through the encounter, we are able to meet and join with an aspect of our previously unacknowledged person.

We meet our shadow, not only in those people who provoke strong negative reactions, but in those for whom we have positive feelings, as well. When we react with very positive feelings, we are similarly encountering aspects of our enfolded self. When we fall in love, we are meeting an aspect of our deeper self that is calling for integration. Likewise, when we work with a greatly respected teacher in school or a spiritual mentor who moves us deeply, we are coming face-to-face with aspects of our enfolded self. We have an opportunity slowly and over time to integrate the split-off part of ourself through the relationship itself. But we can take much more direct and immediate advantage of the situation by realizing that this encounter is bringing the shadow right to our doorstep. By looking directly within, by receiving the relationship without manipulation and even without comment, by simply looking to see where this "other" dwells, we can discover missing qualities in ourself, thus incorporating the shadow aspect in a direct and immediate way.

While the most readily understandable examples of meeting our shadow in the external world are obviously the dramatic ones, it is important to realize that, according to the Yogacara, literally every meeting is an expression of our unresolved karma. There are so many meetings in life that bring us face-to-face with what is unfamiliar: if we are male, the very different way a woman we know may go about things; if we tend primarily toward the thinking function, the approach of people who rely on feeling, sensation, or intuition to know and move through the world; if we are middle-aged, the seemingly alien worlds of tiny babies, young children, adolescents, young adults, and the very old; if we tend to be mainstream, the ways of being of people living at the margins, criminals, the insane, people embodying different races and nationalities, and people in situations of terrible poverty, social ostracism, or disease.

In each such encounter, the person emerges from the shadows, into the light of our experience, as an expression of our ripening karma, bringing with him- or herself some part of ourself that we need just now. In each encounter, we are meeting just that aspect of ourself that is clamoring to be received, experienced, and integrated with our conscious awareness just at this moment. How do we do this? As with our personal body, so with others, our interpersonal body: we do not withdraw from the immediacy and somatic intensity of their presence; we do not judge or come to conclusions about them on any level. Instead, we receive the totality of what they embody, what they are.

Each encounter, each situation, however minor and insignificant it may seem, thus holds an aspect of our person in need of being unfolded, of being received and integrated. It is always the unrecognized aspects of our larger self that are coming, seeking us out at this moment. This is precisely what is meant in the Vajrayana when it is said that, in meeting the other openly and without barrier, we are meeting our larger self. When we look in our partner's eyes, it is the larger self—our body, in the larger sense, as the body of reality—that is looking back. Every experience of life is an expression of wisdom, of our deeper nature calling us to recognize it and see it as who we truly are.

FIFTY-TWO

Integrating Further Depths of the Shadow

I n exploring our somatic being, as we have seen, we learn more and more how to abide in the shadows of the body, amidst all its openness, its uncertainty, its mysteries, and its abundance of life. As our journey progresses, it is always a question of how much, how fully, we can allow ourselves to *be*. As we move beyond the need to have a rigid, consistent, continuous self-concept, we find our self more and more willing to allow our body to constantly call into question and disrupt our prevailing idea of who we are, and to give birth to a more open, porous, and flexible way of being. As we experience this ongoing process of death and rebirth, we find that our ability to accommodate who and what we are gradually increases. Where does this capacity to accommodate ourself in greater and greater measure come from? Clearly, it comes primarily from our evolving relationship with our body, from our ability to live on a more somatic, rather than a primarily conceptual, level.

For example, at any point in our life, we are a certain age with a specific idea of who we are, a specific self-identity. As we experience our body ever more deeply, we to realize that, in fact, this is only a small fragment of who we are. We discover that we are capable of being, at any moment, any of the persons we have ever been, through all the ages and all the experiences that we have ever lived through. In a real sense, they are all in us.

In a previous chapter, I recounted my own experience of finding myself as a baby in his crib, unattended, crying with hopelessness and despair, filled with immeasurable rage at a mother who would not come. In my somatic embodiment, I was not remembering that small child's experience—I was being it. For a period of time, I *was* that tiny, abandoned child who had lost all hope, and I was nothing else. In fact, as the small child had been, I was nothing other than the feelings of despair and rage.

It is the same with all the other ages and all the other beings we have ever been, along with all their experiences. Through our dreams, through feeling and emotional states that come suddenly upon us, and through the people we meet and situations we find ourself in, we discover not our current self, but an other—a person from a different time and place: an encounter with our parents in our childhood; meetings with friends and acquaintances we have not thought of in decades; awkward, intense anxiety of puberty; feeling the strange, heady, first intoxication of passion; a first moment of love for our newborn child; unbearable longing for a lost friend. Each of these embody, in some way, some person who we've been—baby, child, adolescent, young adult, new parent, etc. This is not a person corresponding to our current, somewhat removed memory, not with this intensity of feeling, this depth of pain, this all-consuming longing, this wild passion or joy. Or is this the self we were but just could not fully be until right now? Is it all other ages and selves we have ever been but could never fully be, which have been enfolded in our body until now, when we can finally live them fully and include them in our journey toward wholeness?

One of the most interesting layers of unfolding that occurs for modern somatic practitioners involves areas of experience that stand outside of basic cultural expectations of what is real or possible. I am speaking here particularly of experiences that point to orders of reality that are sometimes dramatically different from the ones we usually inhabit as modern people. These might include encounters with the "natural world" that reveal supernatural dimensions; finding oneself in certain places that literally seem not of this world, but of another, sacred dimension; perceptions of a present but generally "unseen world," that finds expression in the cosmologies and pantheons of the world's religious traditions; having experiences of "magic" or "synchronicity" for which the "scientific worldview" has no explanation; or meeting animals that are more than animals and people that are more than people.

The important point is that such experiences are not examples of dissociation, nor are they expressions of random fantasy or hallucination. They are, the body work shows us, already present at a very subtle level in our body, in our perceptions, in our somatic experience. There, they have been enfolded, repressed into the body, because our conscious, cultural orientation cannot accommodate them, not only denying that such things exist, but also denigrating and ostracizing anyone who reports experiencing them. Such realities make up a very large part of the unacknowledged shadow of contemporary culture, and, as we shall presently see, when we engage the body at its most subtle level, we meet them face-to-face.

FIFTY-THREE

The Cosmic Body I:
Transcending the Scientific Worldview

A s experienced by the body, the external world—the cosmos in the largest sense—is inherently a sacred and magical realm. This cosmos is, moreover, not separate from the body, but is rather the body's vast, extensive form.

Many people remember early childhood perceptions of the world as a mysterious and magical place, quite different from later experience and far more meaningful. We may recall, for example, the timeless quality of the breeze whispering through pines by the sea; a brilliant blue sky that held the utter peace of a hot summer day; approaching thunderstorms bringing some kind of unknown, powerful abundance of life; a strangely shaped tree in our yard that seemed charged with a frightening, august presence; certain places in the woods that seemed filled with a kind of non-ordinary reality; or an old grandfather clock whose steady, rhythmic ticking held some ancient truth of comfort, security, and love.

It is customary in modern culture to think of such experiences as "not really how the world is," as "childish," fanciful projections onto the world that need to be outgrown in adulthood. The "grown-up" way of perceiving the world as lifeless and meaningless is held to be more mature, more accurate, and truer to life. The popular idea of the "scientific" universe as simply the manifestation of dead matter interacting according to certain "laws" is held by most people to be definitive.

Some of us may take an interest in past or present indigenous religious traditions of the world, such as those in Australia, Africa, or North or South America. What is striking about these religions, of course, is that they often articulate an experience of the world as mysterious and filled with meaning—an experience that has much in common with our own earliest perceptions. In those cultural traditions, certain animals may be experienced as non-ordinary beings bringing truth and reality to humans. Certain other aspects of nonhuman nature, such as trees, rocks, mountains, rivers, and bodies of water may be perceived as sacred presences with intelligence and intention toward humans. In the indigenous "earth-based" religions, communication with these presences is considered necessary to the ongoing project of becoming fully human and experiencing a life worth living.

It is interesting that nineteenth- and early twentieth-century anthropology typically discounted such perceptions as reflecting an immature state of human evolution. In explicit references to Western childhood experiences, it was often held that such indigenous ways of seeing the world were reflections of the "childhood of the human race," the result of misunderstanding coming about through either erroneous conceptual thinking or dire emotional need. Since modern science had revealed the real world to be devoid of meaning, the experience of the "primitives," as they were called, could be outgrown once and for all.

During the past three quarters of a century, though, the question of what constitutes our most basic way of perceiving the world has been taken up again in some new and refreshing ways. Historians, philosophers, practitioners of the arts, psychologists, anthropologists, deep ecologists, phenomenologists, and others have been asking how, most fundamentally, we experience our world as human beings. What is it that marks our most basic human manner of perception? Some very interesting responses to this question have begun to emerge.

When we are able to be aware of our most basic level of perception, we find that it does not at all conform to the small, limited, desacralized "scientific" world that most people assume to be "the way it really is." In fact, our innate perceptual experience has no boundaries or limits at all: each perception has a kind of mysterious, boundless quality. Suppose we call to mind a particular tree that stands near where we live. When we do, a mental image of that tree immediately arises, perhaps including general shape, size, trunk and branches, the way it stands in the ground, its color, and its overall appearance. This mental image, then, has identifiable and recognizable features. However, our actual experience of that tree when we look at it from the viewpoint of our most fundamental level of awareness, from the depth of our body, is very different. It doesn't have any of the features that we usually think of as belonging to it. It is a far more uncertain, powerful, and meaningful presence. This is how, at the most fundamental perceptual level, it actually reveals itself to human experience.

When we see the tree in the dead way, we have distanced and removed ourself from our own primary somatic experience of it. We have withdrawn from our perception at the basic level of the body and retreated into our concepts. When we see the world in this dead, denatured way, it is really our own thoughts that we are experiencing, not the world as it initially and most fundamentally gives itself to us.

Within the somatic perspectives being developed here, what has happened is that we have enfolded our actual experience of the world into the cosmic layer of our bodies, our *alaya*, covering it over with our "cosmic ego," the solid, conceptualized image of the universe that we carry around with us as modern people. We have set the wall of our ego against our more primal perceptions as a kind of denial, which, like all aspects of the self-concept, requires ongoing reconsolidation and maintenance.

It is quite interesting that the "scientific" manner of experiencing the world is not affirmative: it is arrived at by excluding a huge range of innate, experiential information (intuition, feeling, a sense of connectedness, the abundance of sensation, the immediate recognition of the value of the other, etc.) and by saying what the world is not—it is not *really* given to us in our feeling life, our intuitive impressions, our actual experiences; it is not powerful; it is not mysterious; it is not magical; it possesses no inherent meaning. What our world *really* is, is the abstract picture arrived at by the specialists.

Initially, of course, such an abstraction doesn't conform to anybody's actual experience. But the valuation of the abstraction over what is actually seen and felt does send a strong message: "Your earliest and most basic perceptions of reality are not to be trusted; you cannot trust your experience. What you are taught by 'modern culture' to think about reality takes precedence."' Much of the burden of conventional preschool and primary education is to train people out of their preexisting way of sensing the world and into the meaningless, conceptual version established by the popular idea of "the scientific community" as the real one. Through this process, of course, we eventually become almost completely unaware of the non-conceptual stratum of the world and come to believe that our denatured and deadened concept is the actual reality, the *only* reality. We may continue to maintain contact with the (now) underworld of magic through dreams and through the work of visual artists, poets, and musicians; but rarely do we really consider that the world we find in these ways might be the real one.

FIFTY-FOUR

The Cosmic Body II: The Earth as Our Body

As we progress in exploring the body, there comes a point when it is apparent that our experience of the "external world" is undergoing a shift. We sense that what is out there is actually much bigger and also much more mysterious and open-ended than we had previously thought. The ordinary world of mundane perception gradually dissolves into an increasingly vast and expanding universe, a cosmos of unimaginable proportions bordering on infinity.

When this experience occurs in the course of the body work, it does not come as a complete surprise. From the very beginning in working with the body, there have been moments when we had glimpses and even extended periods when we touched a universe that is very different from the more habitual one that we are used to.

Over the course of meditating with the body, the focal length and configuration of our awareness have been undergoing an alteration. Rather than being preoccupied almost entirely with the world outside or tangled up inside in our thoughts or emotional states, we sense a space within ourself that is open and very vast, a kind of backdrop to all our experience. In the course of the body work, we have come upon this space in specific places that act as portals, such as the lower belly, the heart, the back of the palate, the top of the spine where the sphenoid and the atlas meet, the back of the head, and sometimes occasionally even the entire body bounded by our skin. Meeting and looking through, or dropping through, these portals, we have suddenly found ourself in space without conditions or limits and, perhaps, we have been able to explore a little of the boundlessness we have found there.

This illimitable space that we discover in the various locales in our body—or perhaps through various locales—already has cosmic dimensions. It presents itself not only as without any limits, but also—experientially—as not having any "location" at all, including that of our body. This very specific experience leaves us with the questions "Is this space inside our body? Is it outside? Where is it? What is it?"

At a fairly early stage of training in meditating with the body, the cosmic dimension of the body is touched: we deliberately begin to open our awareness beyond the limits of the apparently physical and personal body. Through the group of Earth Breathing practices (an example is given in the Appendix), we extend our awareness downward, below the surface of the ground we may be sitting or lying on. Initially, we meet our own concepts of what is under us. But through repeated practice, we discover that we can, abruptly, "look" down into the earth—and that what we find is open space. Beyond this, we can actually drop our entire awareness into the space of the earth under us.

The exploration is gradual. Initially, we drop down just a foot under us, then two feet, and so on, down to ten feet. Then we go down 100 feet, 1000, 2000, 5000 feet, then a mile, two miles, ten miles, and beyond. As we become more familiar with these vistas, we find ourself able to enter the earth under us and fall as rapidly as we wish, with no apparent limit. On the way down, so to speak, our experience changes; the deeper we go, the more primordial the feeling of the space that we find.

What we learn through this Earth Breathing technique is that while we may *think* of the earth as a solid mass of dense matter, the actual experience we have when we extend our awareness downward is entirely different. The earth is space, but it is a certain kind of space: it is empty but, at the same time, inviting, warm, and with the feeling of peace and equanimity. And it is incredibly grounding. Strange as it seems, the deeper we go down into the space of the earth, the more open the universe seems to be and, at the same time, the more grounded we feel. None of this is anything that we might have anticipated. When we arise from our meditation, we find ourself there on the earth in a very simple and ordinary way; but, strangely, while in one way the feel of the earth under us is solid and supporting, in another way—which doesn't contradict this feeling and, in fact, expresses it—the earth is unconditionally open, spacious, and accommodating.

This feeling evolves in interesting ways. Initially, we simply find that the earth under us is space. But then a feeling tone begins to become evident—the warmth, peace, and equanimity just mentioned. As our experience becomes more subtle, we feel a call from the depths under us: it is as if we are being called back, called down to something incredibly important, to that which we have, in some way, been missing all our life. As we continue, along with the longing, we discover a growing feeling of contentment and security, as if we are approaching some kind of primal resting place.

Continuing downward to deeper and more and more subtle levels, we find our experience becoming more and more primordial. Moreover, we begin to notice that the earth's primordiality is inseparable from our own. The deeper we drop into the earth, the closer we feel we are coming to who we really are. In discovering the being of the earth, we are discovering the full depth of our own body, our own self. We are, in fact, approaching the place of our origin, or perhaps of *the* origin, the deepest wellspring of being from which we and everything else are continually emerging.

FIFTY-FIVE

The Cosmic Body III:
The Initiatory Process

The deepest, most hidden and inaccessible layer of enfold-ment for modern people—and perhaps all people—is the cosmic layer of our body. This enfoldment is maintained by the continual reinforcement of our limited, habitual ways of per-ceiving the extra-human universe that we live in. In this part of our self-concept, we conventionalize and attempt to make familiar what we may call the cosmic dimension—a dimension that is completely present to somatic experience yet, at the same time, utterly beyond human convention and inherently unknowable in any definitive sense. The various religions and philosophies of humankind, insofar as they are relatively static and rigid pictures of how things are on the cosmic scale, represent such attempts to regularize and conven-tionalize. And, of course, the modern, popular "scientific" picture of the universe is a particularly extreme way of doing this.

There is something critical, though, that distinguishes most traditional religions, and particularly the indigenous ones, from the modern scientific worldview, as popularly understood: in contrast to the scientific one, indigenous approaches tend to be open-ended and facilitate communication with the living reality that lies behind and beyond the conventional picture. This open-endedness and ability to communicate with cosmic reality is brought about through initiation ceremonies.

It is the tendency of children everywhere to take the concepts of reality expressed by their elders as reality itself. In indigenous initiation, the adolescent is shown that the conventional view he or she has learned and come to take for granted is ultimately not real. The purpose of indigenous initiation ceremonies is, then, just this: to bring young people into their own contact with this living reality; only then do they understand the point and purpose of their spiritual traditions and the truth behind the cultural façade. Only then can they themselves find nourishment and sustenance from the living cosmos and thus become creative and mature adults in their society.

This suggests the huge psychological and spiritual price paid by the loss of authentic initiation ceremonies in modern culture: having separated ourselves from the "superstitions" of the archaic world of indigenous culture, we find ourselves living in a strictly dead, denatured, and conceptualized world, one completely divested of living spiritual reality. In that way, our development is impeded, we are cut off from the wellsprings of life, and we find ourselves trapped in the inflexibility, aridity, and disconnection that, in many premodern societies, are seen as the pre-adolescent mentality. Over the years, many indigenous spiritual teachers from different traditions have told me basically the same thing: that it is this lack of genuine initiation into the living cosmos that is the single and most fundamental cause of the rampant increase of psychological sickness in modern people—the basic reason why so many of us, emotionally, never get out of childhood.

This perhaps helps us understand why the body work is critically important—and so fascinating—in the modern context: once we have reached the cosmic level in our own somatic practice and maturation, we find ourself engaged, in a natural and spontaneous way, in a process that approximates the archaic initiation of indigenous societies. It is almost as if the need for the kind of initiation described earlier is implicit within us, on a genetic level, and when we are open to it and have a method for engaging it, it begins to unfold very powerfully.

More specifically, at a certain point in the body explorations, in an organic way, the "natural world" part of our self-concept, our "cosmic ego," begins to break down. The enfoldment of our experience of the cosmos as a living reality begins to open and unfold. This unfolding takes its root in the experience of the body as, ultimately, the primordial space of the earth itself. In arriving at this perception of "ourself," we have become aware of a level of our own personhood that is inseparable from the larger cosmos. It is interesting that in moments when we discover ourself as the boundlessness of the earth under us, we cannot really say that there is any longer any distinction between what is seen and who is looking. At that moment, we are the earth; we are the awareness of the earth aware of itself.

This standpoint, so to speak, of an experience of the earth beyond subject and object opens the way for the unfolding of a different way of being in and with the rest of the cosmos. Initially, we may begin to feel something very strong calling us—calling, calling, calling continually: a mountain we have seen, a glacier, a particular valley, an open vista, a certain hillside or place in the forest, a tree, a river, a lake. We start to sense—although we cannot quite believe it—that the mountain, for example, is alive, aware, and strongly inviting us, pulling us in its direction. There is something about it that is drawing us to it in the most compelling way. We may dream about it at night and feel its call during the day. What we feel is entirely somatic: our hearts are on fire and its call is resonating throughout our bodies. Such is the depth of somatic life, of *feeling* life, that is now becoming our way of being.

We have learned from our body work that such calls are not to be disregarded. The whole process of working with the personal, individual body has shown us that the body, beyond our own ideas and agendas, beckons and invites us in certain ways. Our own journey unfolds to the extent that we heed these calls, irrespective of how unexpected, strange, or threatening they may seem. As our work of unfolding extends to the interpersonal body, we find the same calls and the same need to heed them and surrender to them.

It is the exactly the same process with our more extensive "body," the body of the cosmos. We understand that we must heed the call that our heart hears, no matter how it does or does not fit into any ideas we have. In the case of our mountain, we must let in its insistent and incessant and compelling pull. Letting the call in will mean, most likely, spending time in the precincts of the "sacred other" that has become such a living and even commanding presence for us.

In doing so, we are making an important offering. This offering is all the greater, given that, especially for us modern people, heeding such a call is often in such complete contradiction to anything that we or anybody else conceives reality to be. In doing so, we are affirming the immediate somatic experience of our body and our heart; we are placing it above whatever we may think. We are letting go of our rigid hold on our restricted, impacted "cosmic" self-concept. We are opening to the cosmic body, the cosmic reality, that lies beyond.

When we are willing to take this leap out of our mind, out of our cultural conventions, the cosmos responds by showing itself in new, ever more primal ways. In relation to our mountain, for example, we begin to discover that it is, indeed, a presence, a towering, living force—not just an intelligence, but immensely powerful, immaculate awareness itself—how can one say it?—so much more potent and all-pervasive and pure than what we have known of our own awareness up to this point. In knowing the mountain as a subject, in opening to its wild, incredibly deep, primal energy, we may find ourself swept clean of any vestiges of ourself. In meeting the mountain, we meet ourself in an entirely new way; we find out, at a much greater depth and reality, ourself discovering the truth of who we are.

The journey of cosmic unfolding may occur in relation to one phenomenon, as in the case of the mountain, or it may occur through a succession of "meetings" with different "others." In either case, over time, we find that the entire range of our perceptions of the world is undergoing a shift. We realize that it is not just this mountain or this tree that is alive. Rather, the entire cosmos, as it shows itself to us in each moment, is alive—each river, each hillside, each cloud, each starlit sky, each glimpse we have of the moon, is abundant with its own unique and individual being, the living reality, that it is showing us at just this moment.

We see especially that the idea of any perceptual object being the same from one moment to the next is simply not true to life. We can *think* that the experience of this mountain, this tree, this vista, is the same over time only because we haven't looked closely enough; or maybe because we haven't looked at all. Mesmerized by our own thoughts of how things are, we have not bothered to attend to what we actually perceive and experience things to be. When we do, we see that each moment—even with the same rock, day after day, year after year—has its own unique being, its own living reality, and its own "message" to us at that moment.

But what kind of message could a rock have? When we open our perceptions to a tree, a rock, or a mountain, or to anything else, there is a kind of weightiness, a gravity, an intensity of presence, an abundance of meaning, a "beingness" in what we experience. The rock is so there, so immovable, yet so still and peaceful. So heavy, so much itself, yet also, when we open our awareness into it, so open, not bounded, utterly spacious and free.

We find ourself so deeply touched and affected by how this rock has given itself so completely to us in this moment. We realize that our relationship with this rock, at just this moment, is completely and utterly personal. What is being communicated, what we are receiving, is so completely and exactly what we are thirsting for, just now, though we didn't see it until this moment. The rock is literally bringing us our very life. Moreover, in meeting this other, this living being of the world, we find revealed to us some primal depth of ourself. What is communicated to us touches the very depths of our being and changes us.

Being touched by the world in this way and to this depth, moment by moment, there is a gradual dissolution of the "cosmic ego" aspect of our self-concept. This process, we discover, fantastically accelerates our journey of self-discovery, of finding out about and becoming who we ultimately are. As so many of the indigenous, earth-based spiritualities express it so well, "This world holds our very life."

FIFTY-SIX

The Cosmic Body IV:
Until the Very End of Being

The experiences of our life that open up through increasing embodiment, and particularly our experiences of the nonhuman, natural world, are not metaphors referring to something outside of themselves; rather, they are immediate, direct, primary realities. Such experiences of the natural world are also not peripheral to our spiritual unfolding; at a certain point, they become absolutely central to it. And, finally, they are not about something else, something separate from us; they are ultimately about us; they are unlocking us, who we most fundamentally are. *In some deep and always mysterious way, the living cosmos is us; who we are, at our deepest levels, is it.*

In our modern world, most of us think of our "embodiment" as being strictly concerned with our immediate physical bodies. Most people approach somatic work with the impression that the scope and limit of this work is defined by the circumscription of their skin. Work at this level is, of course, profound, powerful, and transformative. But the point I want to emphasize here is this: as we progress more and more deeply into our physical body, as long as we don't hold back, we find ourself voyagers, not only into it, but through it into vaster and vaster realms of being. We discover first that, at a deeper, more embodied level, our true body is actually an interpersonal body, and finally, that it is nothing less than the cosmos itself. And, something that cannot be said too often: this is not a matter of theory, but of direct, personal experience.

When the sun sets, as dusk deepens further and further into darkest night, if we are open to it, we will find ourself making a journey from the known quantities of the daylight world into the much larger, mysterious, fecund presence of the unknown darkness, with all it holds for us. When we open our heart to the mountain before us, if we are willing to let go into it, we discover the profundity, imperturbability, and strength of our own heart. But it is not personal: we discover that our heart is the mountain, the mountain is our heart. When we round a corner of a trail in the woods and come suddenly upon a stag, standing uphill, fierce, proud, and fearless, we are meeting invincible courage and dissolving into it. And when we surrender to ravens playing in the wind above a mountain crag, we enter into the utter joy and freedom of being itself. It is truly this way: at those moments, there is no separation, none whatsoever.

It is not that such experiences reflect what we already know of our heart, our courage, or our joy. Instead, it is as if—through the depth of our perception of the natural world—we are discovering a new depth, a never-before-seen primordiality to our own state of being. It is also not that we are finding an extension of our already existing body. Rather, such experiences break apart anything we have previously thought about our body, even at the interpersonal level, and reveal our embodiment to be of a truly unimaginable, universal scope. Such is the unfolding of our cosmic body. This unfolding, then, represents entry into a new, fabulously primal level of our own embodiment. It is a very real and, I think, very, very old initiation. It is—as are all true initiations—a unique, joyful, fiercely and decisively transformative stage on our journey.

We have seen how the interior of our physical body unfolds first as more open than we had suspected, then as the space of our own awareness itself. In our further unfolding, again as we saw, we discover that this "interior space" is not limited to our body at all, but is to be found "outside" of us, as a cosmic reality, in the earth beneath us; in this unfolding of our cosmic body, we discover an increasing boundlessness to our own awareness. In other words, the presence and reality of the earth is not a limitation to our awareness as we might have thought but, quite to the contrary, an extension and further expression of it. In the somatic unfolding, the next stage is to find this limitless space and primal presence, not only in the earth beneath, but all around us, in every direction and to the limits of what is.

Such discoveries, when we first come upon them and every time thereafter, are more than surprising; they are extraordinarily astonishing and astounding. At the same time, we feel we have finally and fully met ourself: "This is who I truly am. How could there be anything more, anywhere under the sun or anywhere else in the universe, than what is right here, right now?"

And yet, there is more: there is the further unfolding of the journey itself. For, as we have seen, as long as our relative world remains to any degree enfolded, our awareness, however boundless it may seem at present, is still limited. It has not reached its fullest unfolded extent because, until the very end of being, there remains further to go, more to unfold.

At this stage in our journey, we have largely unfolded our immediate physical body, and we have begun opening our interpersonal body. Now, we find ourself in the process of addressing our cosmic enfoldment directly. With each experience of the external world, we are invited—in fact, we find ourself compellingly called—into its unlimited, universal depths. As we do so, the unfolding process continues and our awareness is further freed. Each fresh encounter with the world is thus a further discovery, a further opening, a further letting go into the boundlessness of what is.

Have you ever been present to a raindrop falling on a window sill, watched its great globule tumbling into sight, splashing on the sill, spreading out in slow motion, and exploding into a thousand specks of light? Have you ever gazed into a campfire, suddenly finding yourself within it, discovering your own state of being as nothing other than the raging inferno, burning, burning, burning, fueled by all it meets? Have you contemplated a lake and then suddenly found yourself lost in its endlessly wet and watery world? Have you ever looked at a strangely shaped boulder on a trail and found its clear, uncompromising, ancient awareness holding you? Have you glanced up into a great tree only to meet an ancient presence looking back at you with immense understanding and care? Have you ever, one day, looked up at the sky and realized with a sudden, electric shock that courses through your body, that you are meeting a vast shimmering awareness, incredibly alive, that is watching you, utterly seeing you through and through, holding you within its boundless love? Such perceptions are not hallucinations, concocted experiences, or drug-induced states. They are natural and spontaneous perceptions of the world when awareness is open, free, and fully grounded in the body. They are nothing other than our most fundamental human birthright.

What is important about such experiences is that, through them, we are undergoing the deep initiation into who we ultimately are. Now that longing that so many modern people feel for naked, unbounded experience of the natural world makes sense. We long, sometimes so intensely, because we are longing for our own fullest embodiment, our own ultimate being: we *are* the earth; we *are* the water, the fire, the air, the space. The mountain *is* our heart; the running streams, our blood; our mind, the limitless sky; our thoughts, the small passing clouds. Ultimately, we are nothing other than these. And so we come upon our own deepest being, our own most primal self. We arrive at the astounding realization that, finally, we are the cosmos, and it is a process of discovery: as we journey through life, we are literally finding ourself, at deeper and deeper levels, in everything we meet.

The cosmic order of experience is possible for any of us at any time, whether we are in the wilderness or in rural or urban environments. Insofar as there is a perceivable world, the cosmic dimension is ever available. When we see the city streets wet and steaming in the summer sunshine after a sudden downpour, we may find ourself touching eternity. The scream of sirens in the night tells of the care and love that bind us all. The tension, anxiety, and stress on the human faces we pass on a crowded street reveal the universal tenderness and pain of the human person. We may even find in the city itself a living, breathing, transcendent presence underlying, animating, and holding it all.

The preceding helps us understand the full meaning of the Buddhist teaching on egolessness: we see that our "ego," the tiny self-concept we have constructed as "me," is a dream without reality, and, in this realization, far from recognizing our fundamental state of being as nothing, we grow into the recognition that it is everything. Unlocking our unconditioned awareness further and further through the "relative" experiences first of our immediate body, then of our interpersonal body, and finally of the cosmos itself, we discover that we are not, and never have been, anything but the totality, and that our human body and our human life are nothing more than a means for the recognition of this and for sharing it with others. All of this we gain once we enter the gateway of the body fully and completely.

This discovery of our final and ultimate state of being has many, many important implications for potential impact, not only on our individual and collective lives as human beings, but also on the global crisis we all now face. For example, the foregoing suggests that the basis of contemporary deep ecology can be nothing other than such full somatic awakening and awareness. It is not good enough—because it is too indirect and ineffectual—to know only intellectually that we are inseparable from the world around us and that each creature and each natural reality has its own reason for being and its own place in the cosmic order. Rather, we must experience how, at the deepest level, our being is actually the being of the world. There is ultimately no separation; at the deepest level, we are all this life, all this reality. This kind of immediate, direct, and intimate experiential knowledge may make people crazy in relation to prevailing conventional values and mores, but it makes them sane when seen from the largest viewpoint of humanity and its possible future on this earth.

FIFTY-SEVEN

Who Am I?

At the very core of our human person is a single question: "Who am I?" Somehow, throughout all of our life, we are haunted by this question. "Who am I? What is the meaning of my human existence? Why am I here and what am I to do with my life?"

No matter how much the struggle to survive may take up our attention, no matter how compelling our day-to-day challenges and circumstances, irrespective of the intensity of our mundane hopes and fears, this question is always there, sometimes in the background, sometimes in the foreground.

Of course, religions, philosophies, and psychologies all propose answers to this question. Yet, few of us seem to feel completely satisfied by answers that are merely conceptual or intellectual or that are provided by others, be they people, institutions, or larger cultures. At least for many modern people, the answers proposed by some individual or some tradition, no matter how logically coherent or sophisticated, feel insufficient and inadequate, and we are left with our question.

Human beings seek a direct, tangible experience of who they ultimately are. Without this direct experience, we feel like a person dying of thirst in the middle of a desert, just hearing about water. Most of us long, from the depths of our being, to actually drink in the fresh, life-giving water of our deepest nature, experiencing the full depth of our personhood and knowing, in a direct and non-conceptual way, who we ultimately are. When we work deeply with the body, as we have seen, we make a series of discoveries that bear directly on this question, "Who am I?"

The first and most important discovery is that the "unknown" is the very center of our somatic being and the core of our personality. This center of the "unknown"—which we experience directly in the body through the Earth Breathing and other somatic exercises—is open, empty space. As discussed, it is a field of awareness that is simply clear and unobstructed. As we are able to surrender more and more fully into it, again as we have seen, we discover that this ultimate space of the body has no boundaries or limits and, in fact, is absent of any reference points at all. In touching it, we experience a moment of being utterly lost: we completely lose any sense of "self," even of anyone watching. At the moment of "meeting," as mentioned, there is quite literally no one observing and nothing being observed.

This is truly the *unknown*—not as a concept, but as a direct experience—precisely because it cannot be known in any kind of dualistic way. In other words, we cannot stand back and observe it as a perceiving, thinking, and judging subject, because when we do step back, it is gone. Only in the moment of touching this state of being in our body, of touching enlightenment—for that is ultimately what it is—is there the true knowing of our fundamental nature: simply awareness knowing itself.

Although we experience this primordial state of our body as completely sufficient and beyond any kind of causality, nevertheless, it is not passive, disconnected, inert, or without implications for our relative lives, our karmic situations and engagements.

For one thing, we notice that this state of being, which is so utterly "beyond" or transcendent, nevertheless has an immediate and powerful impact on our usual ego activity—the incessant conceptual activity of thinking, judging, hoping and fearing. When we touch our basic nature, in that moment, all our fearful, reactive, restrictive conceptual posturing ceases. In that moment of knowing, the vast sky of our own basic being is, so to speak, clear of clouds or atmospheric phenomena of any kind. The experience of this most primal stratum of our own nature cuts through all discursive activity, on the spot, completely eliminating it.

This basic, somatic nature of ours—the emptiness or unknown—also has another kind of impact: it gives birth. In other words, the more we can touch and abide within the endless, unconditioned space—the utter peace—of our true body, the more we find a kind of upsurge arising from within it. This upsurge comes in the form of energy of all sorts—flashes of perception, insights, sharpness, inspirations, sudden emotions such as sadness, compassion, tenderness, and so on.

We experience what arises in this fashion in a certain kind of way: what surges up does not have the usual feeling of restriction or limitation, nor does it carry the mark of claustrophobia or taint that comes with ego-centered perceptions, ideas, and strategies. Rather, to our direct experience, the phenomena arising from the depths of our body feel free of taint or contamination. They feel real, they feel true, and their calling card is purity and integrity.

Moreover, what arises comes with an inbuilt injunction, even an imperative: experiencing it, we feel an overriding need to express or to act according to the upsurges, the egoless insights and inspirations, the selfless warmth and compassion, born out of the unknown. When we generate some idea or project from the hope and fear of ego, we always have an expectation driving us and an assessment to make: "Should I do this or should I not? Will I experience more of what I want by doing this, or am I likely to experience more difficulties?" We sense the taint of ego and, working very much from ego designs and ambition, we have to evaluate and judge everything.

However, when an insight or an inspiration arises directly from the depth of our soma, it bypasses the entire mechanism of ego's constant hesitation and strategizing, its continual weighing of hope against fear. What arises from our primal nature presents itself in an utterly compelling way. Perhaps we are called upon simply to take in an insight or a perception, letting it change our way of seeing things, or perhaps we will find ourself called upon to express what has arisen or even to act upon it. As often as not—perhaps, in a way, always—we experience what arises as the "call" as uncomfortable, inconvenient, or even threatening to our ego stance and status. In this context, I think frequently of the prophets of ancient Israel and what the great unknown, Yahweh, required of them. And I call to mind the example of Jesus and his agony in Gethsemane, just prior to his crucifixion, when he realized what was being asked of him. He may have been culturally and religiously Jewish and he may be considered the founder of Christianity, but his willingness to heed the call coming from the deepest places no matter what the cost expresses and ennobles something profoundly and universally human.

When we do the body work, we realize in a most direct, immediate, and tangible way, the answer to the question "Who am I?" We discover that who "I" am is an open, ever-unknown, and ever-unfolding situation. Who I am is, ultimately, the great mystery at the very core of my being, as well as what arises out of that and what I have to do about it. Since what arises from our basic nature is always unanticipated and surprising, it is always without precedent. All of this is the great unknown and its natural, spontaneous expression.

When we inhabit our body fully, then, we realize that the answer to our question can never be reduced to a fixed and enduring concept or idea. There is no definitive answer that can ever be given to the question "Who am I?" Or, to put it another way, one *can* speak of definitive answers, but only as the somatic fullness and finality of each moment. Such an answer is valid only for the moment in which it arises; then it dissolves in the face of the next moment of our unimpeded, unfolding experience, which, in its turn, provides a momentary answer to the question "Who am I?" Such answers are nothing less or more than the basic mystery of our being, in its emptiness and its expression. We are what we are in each unique moment of our life—and there is nothing else.

When we live out of the body as our basic nature, our life is always occurring beyond ourself, beyond the limit of what we can grasp or understand: of all the mysteries of the universe, the greatest one is the mystery of our own being—not because we cannot experience its ultimate truth, but because we can.

We might ask, how can we speak of this deeply somatic way of experiencing our life as an "answer" to the question "Who am I?" It is an answer because the experience of it carries certain marks of its own ultimacy. For one thing, we experience it as self-validating: it appears as true, real, and incontrovertible, just as when we stand outside in a downpour, there isn't much question in our mind that it is raining. In addition, our experience of ourself in this way brings a sense of freedom, truth, and understanding. Further, we observe that this "answer" is utterly other-centered: it yields an unending tenderness, compassion, and selfless action for all that live and suffer, for all that is. And, finally, it fills us and fulfills us utterly. We see that nothing more has ever been needed or wanted. Everything is and always has been right here.

When we experience ourself in this way, we feel that all our questions have been answered, not only about ourself but about all other things as well. In this, no external validation is needed; the increasing sense of spontaneous creativity, of caring about others, and the openness and flexibility that our life increasingly manifests suggests the basic integrity of what is occurring.

Throughout this process, of course, the body work is the key, the "path to immortality," if you will. By enabling us to descend beneath the confusion and noisy tumult of our compulsive and competitive discursiveness, it puts us in touch with the empty ground of our being. It gives us a method to stay close to what is born from that "groundless ground." And it offers a sense of somatic confidence from which we can hold, express, or act in harmony with what stands beyond time.

The preceding suggests, then, that the ultimate goal of "meditating with the body" is the ability to be entirely who we are, in all our emptiness and what is born from it. This goal involves the complete liberation and fulfillment of ourself and unreserved and resourceful compassion for the world, for its suffering beings, and for all that is. This exalted goal, like that of any spiritual discipline, is an end point that is probably never fully attainable, at least not in this life, and so the journey toward it continues in a kind of endless way. Nevertheless, at whatever our stage of maturation, it hangs like a distant star in our sky—and sometimes not so very distant at all—guiding us and helping us sail a steady course.

CONCLUSION

FIFTY-EIGHT

Becoming Who We Are

T he term "dharma" refers to the deepest truths and realities of human experience. These truths and realities are hardly dead and lifeless, nor are they static. In fact, they are the very essence of brimming and abundant life itself, ever-new, ever-changing, ever leading to new vistas of being. As we have seen, for us humans, such unfolding truths and realities always come with a call and an imperative. Buddhism, as a tradition, exists to provide access to that abundant life which is reality itself, to show us how to uncover it in ourselves and how to live it fully.

Sometimes modern people misunderstand Buddhism's focus on the individual human journey as well as its injunction to people to find out who they are and to seek their own ultimate fulfillment. With our Western suspicions of meditation, of looking within—and, frankly, our fear of being alone—not infrequently, we tend to reject the inward looking of Buddhism as somehow disconnected from the social context and disloyal to it.

If Buddhism were a static tradition with an unchanging inter-pretation of what people are and of how they need to engage their world, such suspicions would have some merit. But Buddhism is nothing other than a set of practices to open up the mysteries of the human heart and the deepest realities of our human experi-ence as those exist, uniquely in us, right at this moment. And, as we have seen, the human heart is not personal: the more we fathom our own hearts, the more we find there the being of others and, beyond that, the very heart of the world itself.

It is undeniable that others and the larger world, so belea-guered at this moment in history, need everything that we have to give. But what to give is the problem. It seems finally clear that we cannot find out what to do simply by thinking about it. We need to gain our inspiration and our direction from much deeper sources. But what are they and where are they to be found?

At least according to Buddhism, those resources lie fully ready at hand; they lie in the depths of our own bodies and our own hearts, in the secret precincts of our own lives. Rather than think-ing endlessly about what might work and trying this and trying that, in a kind of trial-and-error method, perhaps we should try looking into the depths. If we do, I suggest that we will find not what we as individuals think; rather, we will come face-to-face with what the other suffering beings need, and we will uncover what the natural world itself knows is wanted and required for life on this planet to continue. But the ego must be dethroned, its arrogance must be dismantled, and we must begin, before it is too late, to listen to the ensuing silence. All of this is about becoming who we are in the deepest sense and about surrendering to what creation is asking of us and needing from us just now.

The particular ability of modern people to hear and heed the call of dharma, to become fully who they are for the benefit of all, may be unique in the history of Buddhism. To understand this, let us recall that, over time, Buddhism has found itself in the custody of some very conservative cultures, ones in which the change, creativity, and individuality that were occasionally able to emerge from intensive practice were often unwelcome. More often than we may want to think, "the dharma" has been identified with the traditionalist status quo of Asian agrarian cultures and assimilated to their patriarchal, conformist, and collectivist ways of thinking.

At the same time, as we have seen, Buddhism is an inherently radical tradition. Through referring deeply to human experience as the final spiritual authority and through its willingness to call into question accepted norms and values, Buddhism—at least in its more meditative forms—has always been somewhat at odds with the cultures in which it has flourished. And, particularly in its meditative lineages, it has always given birth to a few heroic souls who followed the path to its end and did realize the kind of incomparable life first proclaimed by the Buddha. Thus, the lineage of authentic spirituality has been kept alive.

What is different in the modern setting is that the "lonely journey" can no longer be for a tiny minority. Now, because of the collapse of traditional cultures and the rampant proliferation of the "non-culture" of consumerism and materialism, modern spiritual seekers find themselves in a cul-de-sac. They can no longer fall back on the tried-and-true amalgamations of culture and religion that have existed for thousands of years, because they no longer have a culture of their own that can amalgamate. Nor can they simply adopt the versions of spirituality of other cultures because such traditional approaches too often strike modern people as unthinking, rigid, and closed-minded. The freshness of experience modern people seek, and the affirmation of the sacredness of their own selves and world, too often just aren't there.

Thus it is that there seems to be no other choice for most of us except to enter into the heroic quest for what is deepest and most true in ourselves, our lives, and our world. It would seem that we find ourselves with no other alternative but to recover our full embodiment and our full, individuated personhood. To do so, we will need to abandon, once and for all, discursive thinking—disembodiment—as our primary way of orienting ourselves in the world. Perhaps we *can* do this because our disembodiment has reached such insane proportions, such an extreme and experientially unacceptable state, that we will feel literally compelled and even forced, as our only alternative, to engage a world where we are living out of the full, unique embodiment that is possible for us.

And we are going to have to express ourselves. In many of the traditional Asian Buddhist cultures, individual expression was severely restricted and regulated. Increasing numbers of serious Western practitioners have reported the difficulty of getting their Asian teachers to talk openly about themselves, their lives, or their experience. Within Asian Buddhism, apparently, speaking in such a way is considered rude, impolite, egotistical, and even anti-dharmic.

It is not difficult to see why people's expression of personal experience could be seen as threatening within the strong social and religious conservatism of traditional, conformist cultures. As Georges Bataille, the French philosopher, has pointed out, the affirmation of individual human experience as of supreme and unique value (sui generis) is automatically destabilizing of any kind of conservatism, including that of cultural standardization, institutionalized religious authority, or social control. When a person speaks out of the depths of his experience, he is, in effect, saying, "This unique experience of mine is important. It is sacred. It is worth speaking. What I am expressing has significance for our collective life." To speak of individual experience is to affirm the category of the unique and individual. It is, implicitly at least, to call into question the assumption that the ultimate authority is found somewhere outside, in the collective.

But we live in different times and, precisely because of their intensity just now, we—each and all of us following this path—must be willing to speak of our experience, to speak our hearts. We must speak openly about our practice and our lives, without hesitation and without excusing or justifying ourselves—where we have become lost, how we have been terrorized and tormented, our tragedies, how our journey has unfolded, what we have discovered, our hopes and fears—all of it. By doing so—and it is already happening—I believe that a new Buddhist culture—perhaps I should better say a "meditative culture" or even a "human culture"—will be possible. But rather than being based on values extrinsic to Buddhism or other, similar meditative approaches, it will be able to emerge from the collective experience of practitioners themselves, irrespective of traditions or lineages. And it will include many others who are entering their lives with the same kind of profundity and abandon. It will signal a new value—that of the sacredness of experience itself—which is to affirm the sacredness of the individual in all his or her incomparable reality—as the possible center and the heart of a kind of social order or global community.

There is a final point, which, though perhaps implicit in the foregoing, needs to be made explicit. From the viewpoint of Buddhism, individuality is not an ego thing. Sometimes we hear traditional Asian teachers tell us that the realization of individuality and the expression of individual creativity are egotistical, an expression of samsara. But I sense that such claims are more likely reflecting Asian cultural values than being anything inherent to Buddhism itself.

In my view, not only in the West now but worldwide, holding back and trying to assimilate to conventional values—including Buddhist ones—hasn't worked, isn't going to work, and is clearly going in the wrong direction. I feel that practitioners everywhere are waking up to the same realization—that developing and expressing one's own individuality and creativity is actually what the planet needs and what reality is calling for. We as practitioners know this because when we meditate, when we enter the wilds of the unborn mind, we run into our deepest selves—not as a given, but as a challenge and a mission—and fulfilling this mission is the imperative that is being laid on us.

As I was reflecting on these things, I came across a writer named Edward Edinger, a Jungian analyst, who observes that the task of realizing our individuality as modern people, and perhaps ultimately as humans, is a transcendental task. It has been given to us by the universe. It is our job and it is what we have to do. In his terms, this task is our fate; it is our destiny—and not just of a few of us, but of more and more people throughout the world.

This, perhaps, points us in an intriguing direction: that our unique and ultimately individual self is, at the same time, an entirely impersonal event in the universe, proceeding from and reflecting throughout, in its grand design and its details, a transcendent source, a transcendent intention, and a transcendent activity. Perhaps, especially in this day and age, this is what the dharma is at its most profound—and why our own complete embodiment has become such a necessity. Perhaps we are nothing more than custodians of this unique life and are being called to our full embodiment to inhabit, to experience, and to communicate it fully, not as a personal thing at all, but as a moment in the unfolding of being itself.

APPENDIX

A Glimpse of the Body Work

The actual practice of the body work discussed in this book is best learned and practiced with a trained and experienced instructor. Words on a page can give a general idea about the work, but 80 percent of one's learning comes from the feel created in "live" teaching situations. Nevertheless, in order to give some practical context for the preceding pages, I would like to say a few things about the actual practices of the somatic process of meditating with the body.

Since the body work is simply making a deeper relationship with our own body, and since the protocols unlock a universally gentle, natural, and gradual process, the work itself is extraordinarily safe. In fact, it is less intrusive then anything else one can do to open up one's psychological and spiritual life. Many of these practices are already being used by psychiatrists, psychotherapists, and other psychological healers. Reports so far indicate that the work can be most helpful not only to those of us in the definitional range of "normality," but also to those experiencing considerable psychological distress and turmoil. In these latter cases, though, working with a psychologically trained health professional seems to produce the best and most lasting results.

Some people ask, "What is the relationship of this somatic training to regular meditation practice?" The best answer is, I think, that the somatic work *is* meditation at its best. It is true that, if we are already meditating, when we begin learning the somatic exercises, it seems as if we are doing something different. It feels different from our regular meditation practice most likely because our regular practice is so disembodied. After we have worked with the somatic protocols long enough to assimilate them at a deep level and find our way to an intimate and open relationship to the body—and this doesn't take very long—then any time we go into our bodies, we are meditating, and any time we meditate, we do so in an embodied way. To meditate, at that point, is to meditate with the body. They are one and the same.

During the time period when we are learning and carrying out the meditating with the body practices, there are several different ways we can use them. First, we can practice the somatic protocols on their own. They *are* meditation in and of themselves, and a very deep and transformative kind at that. Especially when we are first learning the practices, I would suggest spending about forty minutes on a given protocol. I would also recommend that practitioners begin and end each forty minute session with five or ten minutes of silent, formless meditation.

This helps us prepare for the work and then feel and assimilate its results at the end.

Second, if we are already meditators, at whatever level, and we have a regular practice we wish to carry out, we can begin each meditation session by practicing one of the basic somatic exercises. If we have an hour for meditation, I would suggest at least fifteen minutes of somatic work. If we want to meditate for two hours, we might begin with perhaps twenty to twenty-five minutes of body work. When we do this, the meditation will proceed in a much more open way.

Third, we can use the somatic practices if we are sick, suffering from an injury, or are particularly emotionally upset. This "special application" of the practices can be very powerful in bringing awareness and healing to our situation. People with long-term and even terminal illnesses, degenerative conditions, or serious injuries can find much solace, relief, and occasionally even a measure of healing from the work. Sometimes it can bring success even when all other efforts have failed.

In the corpus of somatic meditations and contemplations, there are seven basic practices. These include (1) basic postures, sitting and lying, as well as the dynamics they unlock; (2) the ten-points practice; (3) threefold breathing; (4) earth descent/breathing; (5) cellular breathing; (6) lower belly breathing; and (7) internal meditation on the subtle body. Each of these practices is carried out in a lying down and a sitting up position, making a total of fourteen. Each of these fourteen has perhaps five or six variations, adding up to around one hundred somatic protocols. These variations address mainly the intention of the practice—whether we are using the practice mainly to relax, to learn more about inner patterns of tension, to connect with the earth, to look into the inner spatial aspect of the body, to open to the space of awareness outside, to see what happens when we do the practice with no intentional focus at all, and so on. Theoretically, though, on any given day, a teacher—and the experienced practitioner—may go in any one of myriad directions with a particular protocol, depending on the atmosphere, energy, level, and specific needs of the occasion. So, really, the possibilities of individually distinctive protocols are endless. In any case, there certainly can be no question—nor is there any need—of describing very many of these in this Appendix. My thought is to pick a few of the more basic ones so that readers can gain a general idea of what is involved in the body work.

Readers may wonder why we carry out each practice in a lying down and also a sitting up posture. All the ways we hold ourselves activate specific levels, kinds, and qualities of awareness. When we lie down, we assume the posture of the infant, supine and relaxed, but open, awake, and alert—and intensely ready to learn. By contrast, adults generally don't lie down in such a relaxed mode unless they are going to rest or go to sleep. The rest of the time, they are "upright" and tense, with their all their adult agendas, ambitions, and paranoias in full activation.

When we lie down in the manner of an infant, we are able to access the infant's state of openness and unconditional readiness. When we carry out the protocols in a lying down manner, we are able to explore them very, very fully. The protocols all involve relaxation and letting go as their beginning point and their ground. This process is most easily and fully accessed in the lying down mode. When we lie down, we can move through the relaxation and the letting go to discover the full range of possibilities for learning about our body and developing our awareness. Having really experienced what it is like to be somatically fully present, relaxed, awake, and aware in the lying down mode, we can then sit back up in our more adult mode. Now that our adult self is reactivated through the upright posture, we become much more aware of how we depart from the open state that is possible for us—discovered in the lying down mode—and literally tense, freeze, and eventually numb out. Moving back and forth—from lying to sitting, and back to lying down, and then sitting up again—we gradually learn how to be in our adult mode of posture and perhaps even engagement, while remaining within the lying down possibilities of openness, alertness, and unconditional awareness.

Practitioners can engage the somatic work at whatever level they like. At one end of the spectrum, they can purchase the *Meditating with the Body* program from Sounds True, or download these practices from soundstrue.com, learn some of the basic practices, and actually make a great deal of progress on their own. Some of my students who are Meditating with the Body trainers teach introductory and mid-level weekends, as I also do. Even in a short time, people can learn much, take home what they have learned, and, again, make a great deal of progress on their own.

At some point, though, practitioners begin to feel some longing for deeper and more ongoing somatic training. In response to this need, our foundation Dharma Ocean offers a five-month intensive training course that I teach every year. The program begins and ends with a five-day intensive residential retreat in April and September at our center in Crestone, Colorado; in between is a five-month at-home study course in which students have a guided somatic meditation to do each day, a lecture to listen to and assimilate each week or two, readings, and a work book to follow. They also have regular calls with a Meditating with the Body trainer and phone meetings with a small group of their fellow students. The program is intensive and supportive; I find that by the end, even those who have never meditated before possess much understanding and deep experience of these practices, and leave with the tools to carry their own meditative and spiritual work forward in a good way.

Graduates of this basic Meditating with the Body program are eligible to attend our annual week-long Advanced Meditating with the Body intensive that explores a different area of more advanced somatic practice each year. For those who wish to go even further, I teach an advanced program in Vajrayana Buddhism which is a meditative tradition only fully accessed through the body: the whole point in Vajrayana is, as mentioned earlier, to "redeem matter," to realize the sacredness of this body, this life, and this earth. As some readers may have guessed, the view underlying the body work, from its simplest and most basic forms, is the view of Vajrayana Buddhism.

THE BASIC LYING-DOWN POSTURE

Begin by lying on your back on the floor or ground—a comfortable surface (firm, but not too hard)—with your knees up, your feet flat on the floor, and a yoga strap tied just above the knees. The strap should be tied tight enough so the knees are just touching or almost touching. We're creating a triangle between the knees, the feet, and the floor, so that you can relax your thighs, lower back, and pelvic area. Your feet should be comfortably spread apart so that you feel stable and can fully relax. You may also want something supporting your head, such as a folded towel, a sweater, or a small pillow, to raise it slightly.

Cross your hands at or over your lower belly with the left hand under the right hand, little fingers down toward the pubic bone, thumbs up toward the navel. This gathers your energy and awareness toward the core of the body. Feel the earth under you and let your body sink down as if into the earth. The more you can allow yourself to feel supported by the earth, the more fully you will be able to relax.

Check the comfort of your position. You want to be really relaxed, so your body's not being strained in any particular way. You should be holding yourself so you can completely relax the muscles in the lower back and the inner thighs and so there's no effort of holding at all. You're really relaxed: the triangle of your knees, two feet, and the floor should be very restful for you. Then, put your awareness in your body, and just let yourself continue to relax.

Soon after you begin doing these practices, you'll notice that any time you lie down in this way, in the same position with the intention to do body work, the body responds very quickly. This is the one time in our life when our body actually becomes the focus of attention. We're not using the body for something else. We're simply making a relationship with it as it is. It's the only occasion when we ever do this, including in our sleep. The body begins to respond, to relax, to develop a sense of well-being, even in just taking this position. So just take a few minutes, and let your body completely relax.

As you're just lying there, you'll notice that your body begins to let go. A muscle here, a muscle there, a tendon here, a joint there: it begins to release the tension in various places. It's a very living situation. You might think, "Why am I here? There's not much happening." That's not true at all. As long as you're attentive and you put your awareness into your body, there's a very dynamic, very lively process of relaxation that the body goes through. But you have to be present. You have to be in your body. You have to be intentionally and deliberately feeling your body for this to work.

TEN-POINTS PRACTICE

[Note: this practice is described in considerable detail to suggest the level of attentiveness, precision, and subtlety with which the body work is carried out. The other practices discussed below are described in more abbreviated fashion.]

A. Ten-Points Practice, Lying Down

We're going to begin by doing a practice known as the ten-points practice. This is something that we'll use almost all the time as a preliminary to the other practices. In a sense, all the body work is contained in this one practice. The ten-points are the two feet, the two sides of the buttocks, the mid-back, the two shoulder blades, the two elbows, and the head. This practice enables us to learn how to come into our body; to begin to awaken sensation in its various parts and regions; to begin uncovering tension, relaxing and letting it go; and, through releasing downward, to develop a sense of depth and grounding in relation to the earth under us.

Take the lying posture described above, and just feel the earth under you. Let your body settle. You're going to begin with the feet. Just put your attention into your feet. Try to feel the sensations, both the external sensations—the pressure of socks, the temperature of the room—and the internal sensations—the tightness, the sense of mass of your feet. Just feel that.

Next, begin relaxing the feet. The basic principle of body work is that tension maintains itself when we're not aware of it. As soon as we put our attention into a certain area, then we can begin to relax that area. We develop the capability of letting go of that tension. When we really feel it, we can begin to let it go. That doesn't mean that it disappears all at once, but it begins to melt.

When we are first learning this practice, we work in some detail. Start with just the big toe. Put attention into the big toe. See if you can feel the sensations connected with the big toe on both feet. You're going to work in parallel fashion, doing both sides of the body at once. Can you feel the tip of your big toe? Can you feel the top of your big toe? Its tip and its sides? The underside? The center of its mass? Feel the tension in the big toe, put your awareness right into it, and begin to let it melt or dissolve.

Where or how does it melt? It melts down into the earth. Throughout this ten-points practice, we're feeling a particular part of our body and letting go of the tension, letting the tension travel down into the earth. There is a release of energy downward.

As you feel the tension, you may notice there is a kind of softening that begins to occur. It can happen in the toe itself or in the adjacent area. You're feeling your big toe, and maybe the softening is back where the toe joins the foot. It may be just a slight softening at first. The more your attention goes in, the more the melting process can occur. How long should you stay with the big toe, working with it? Stay with the big toe—and each subsequent toe, part of the foot, and other area of your body—until you feel that you are sensing something and making a connection with this part of your body.

Now go to the second toe on both feet. Feel it, feel its mass and density, feel the tension—and begin to release. Then feel the middle toe. Feel the sensations, a little bit of tightness. Release. Relax.

Even if it seems that you can hardly feel your toes at all, even with good attention, just put your awareness there with strong intention. That's the important point: your intention as well as your attention must be there. In time, the toes will begin to wake up. Don't be concerned if you can't completely follow the practice at first. It will unfold for you really quite quickly over the first few weeks of practice.

Next, move to the fourth toe. Try to feel the fourth toe in as much detail as you can: the tip of the toe, the nail (yes, your awareness can include "inert" parts of your body), what's under the nail, the mass of the toe, where the fourth toe joins into the foot. There's tension in every single muscle group, down to tiny, even miniscule, places. Our whole body is actually riddled with the tension of ego. Ego is a process of somatic holding on. This is something that's well known in Zen tradition. Holding on is an ego process. Letting go is a somatic process. When we let go of our ego, we let go of our body. When we hold on to our ego, we hold on to our body. So in working with the body, we're actually getting at the very roots of the ego process. We let the tension melt, and at the same time, we're letting our constricted awareness melt and open.

In the process of releasing, make sure that you are releasing downward, through the soles of the feet, emptying the tension into the boundless space of the earth beneath. The downward release is critical to actually being able to let go fully and make a connection with the earth beneath us, our larger "body." Trying to release upward somehow doesn't work—it is too mental and doesn't really include the body. If you try to release upward, you will lose your body in the process and find yourself more tense and somatically disconnected. Releasing sideways also doesn't work, because that is basically like sending your "stuff" into the interpersonal network, toward others. Our fundamental feeling about others won't permit full letting go. The earth, the place of all origins and the place to which we ultimately return, is the right and fitting space to which we can truly let go, to experience the sense of being received and loved when we do.

Come to the baby toe. Work with this in the same way. Now you're feeling all five toes. Feel them, and let them begin to melt. Now, come to the ball of the foot. See if you can feel the tension around the ball of the foot. Now come back up into the interior of the foot, the bottom of the foot, the lower part of your foot away from the toes, and then the inside of the ball of the foot. There's a lot of holding around that. See if you can feel it, and begin to relax. Then go into the outside of the foot, just behind the baby toe.

Now we come to the arch of the foot. Start at the surface of the arch, and then let your awareness trace the tension back into the interior of the foot behind the arch. This is typically very tight, with a brittle, vulnerable kind of tension—very taut, rigid tension. Then come to the instep and the interior of the foot. Feel the tension; just simply feeling it, it begins to melt. You have the sense of letting go, of letting the tension very gradually begin to dissolve. Then come to the ankle bones on the inside, the ankle bones on the outside, the Achilles tendon. Work with each area until you sense something there and feel you are making a relationship with it. Your awareness may be very marginal at first.

Again, tension is traveling down. Now you're feeling your whole feet and letting the ongoing melting, dissolving, relaxing, letting-go process unfold. The energy is traveling down. It's like a continual current of energy down into the earth. See if you can feel that.

In this practice, we are spending a lot of time with the feet, and there are some important reasons for this. For one thing, as Chinese medicine makes clear, energetically, the foot is directly and powerfully connected with every other part of the body. All the major meridians can be accessed through the feet. Second, we focus on the feet because we are developing a level of intention, attention, and awareness that, once cultivated in our work with the feet, will enable us to move more quickly, with precision, depth, and subtlety, throughout the rest of the body.

As you practice with the feet, notice that the rest of your body is starting to respond as well. When you work in any part of the body, and particularly the feet, the whole body is affected. So if you find a call to release in your lower back, or your shoulders, your hips, or your midback—no problem. Feel the invitation of the body to release, accept it, and let go.

Next, the ankles. Now you're relaxing the feet and the ankles. Then you'll move to the lower calf muscles, energy traveling down through the feet. Soon your whole leg can begin relaxing. Include the shin bone—the bones hold tension just as much as the other parts. It can be quite surprising for beginning practitioners exactly how aware one can become of tension in the bones. Relax the muscle on the outside of the shin bone as well.

Now the whole lower leg. Feel the tension in the lower leg and the feet, and release down into the earth. It's as if you're just letting go, abandoning, releasing, relinquishing your grip on the body. Let your feet sink into the earth. Your whole lower leg, your ankle, your feet are dissolving into the earth. Release all the tension—feel how exhausting the maintanence of tension is. Tension—it's so exhausting to have an ego, and to have to constantly hang on. Now you're invited and given permission to release that.

Come to the buttocks on either side. Feel them contacting the earth. Let the whole pelvis relax and release, and shed its burden of tension down through the buttocks into the earth. Pay particular attention to the inner thighs, up high where the femur joins into the hip sockets on either side. On the inside of the upper thighs is the bottom part of the psoas muscle, often a place where we can feel a lot of tension and holding. The psoas muscle is the longest muscle in the body, and it's a very important muscle because it's what joins the upper and lower halves of the body. The ultimate source of the ego is in the psoas. So in working with the psoas, we're working with the whole process of grasping and fixation. As it attaches in the upper part of the inside of the thighs, the psoas runs over the pubic bone, back through the pelvic cavity, and attaches on the lumbar spine and the bottom vertebra of the thoracic spine. It is very central to the process of releasing tension. Usually you can feel it mainly on the inside of the upper thighs. Feel the tension there, and begin to invite the psoas to release and relax. In sitting practice, a tight psoas is often responsible for a lot of our physical discomfort, especially in the lower back and the hips.

Right now, you're working on the psoas with direct awareness, feeling the tension, releasing. Feel the outside of the hips; again, release, relax. And now the energy is traveling down through the buttocks into the earth. Move your awareness into the pelvic girdle and the bones that make up the pelvis; move it especially into the pubic bone. See if you can feel the internal skeletal structure of your pelvis, at least to some extent. The front part of the hips, the hip bones themselves, the pubic bone, the tailbone: you're just going to work on the bones for a little while here, feeling and releasing downward.

Now move your attention to your knees and the full length of your thighs. The direction is down through the pelvic cavity, through the buttocks, into the earth. We are working with the two buttocks, but you will notice that the sacrum and the tail bone are also points of contact with the earth underneath. You've done the two feet, used them as a point of contact with the earth, and now you're going to use the two buttocks. The energy is sliding down the front of the thighs and the back of the thighs through the buttocks into the earth. It is also sliding down through the femur, down into the hip socket, down through the buttocks into the earth.

As you do this, imagine that your buttocks and your whole pelvis are dissolving and melting downward. See if you can feel your pubic bone, hip sockets, the outside of your hips, your sacrum, your tailbone. Come into the genital region, the perineum, and the anal area. Explore each with close attention; find the tension, and release, relax downward. Especially in the perenium, the area between the genitals and anal area, right between your sitz bones, there is a great deal of energy and tension. Even if your perineum was damaged because of an episiotomy, the inner energetic perineum is intact. It's the outer body that has all kinds of problems, but the inner body doesn't. It's whole. The more we tap into the inner body, the more the outer body becomes whole as well.

Pay special attention to the anal region and the interior of the lower belly. You're just relaxing, releasing tension so it can go down through the buttocks. There's a sense of a huge burden being released when we do this work, which is the burden of our ego. We have this job of trying to maintain ourselves through hanging on to our body, freezing our body so that we don't feel. That's how the ego survives, strangely enough. You're relaxing, releasing, letting go of that continual effort.

Just feel how, at first, you hold in the pelvic cavity and then, second, you release. It's like dropping off to sleep, in the sense of that kind of letting go, except that you remain aware. Your awareness doesn't disappear.

Now we come to the midback. Release from the front of the chest down through the midback, opposite the bottom of the breastbone. If you can't quite feel the tension in the midback, come up to the front of your chest at about the level of your heart and allow the tension there—which is usually more accessible—to flow down through the midback into the earth. Take some time with this.

Next come to the shoulder blades. Feel the shoulder blades touching the earth. Feel all the tension behind the shoulder blades, up into the shoulder joints, and up into the upper back. Just try to put your awareness there, feel the tension, and then release. You have to feel the tension first; you don't release right away. You take a moment, you feel the tension, you feel yourself holding on, then you release. Again, explore this a little.

Move into the elbows, pulling energy from the fingertips, down the hands and wrists, the lower arm down through the elbows, into the earth. From the shoulders, the upper arms, down to the elbows, sink, relax, release ever more deeply. Completely let go. You don't have to hang on in this position. Really let go.

Now try to feel altogether the nine points you've been working with: two feet, energy traveling down, two buttocks, midback, two elbows, two shoulder blades, energy flowing down through all of them. Your whole body is releasing, relaxing, letting go.

As you're lying here, you're simply going to feel your body. In the earliest Buddhist tradition, one of the main subjects of mindfulness practice is not the breath, but is actually the entire body. So this is going to be what you'll pay attention to. You're going to have your attention from the neck down, in your body. Just be aware. Just be mindful of all the sensations of the body. If the mind begins to wander, just come back to your body. Do this for a few minutes. You're in the body. You don't have a head controlling things, observing—that head is gone. You just have a body, and that's where your awareness is.

And then, finally, go into the head. Beginning with the face, imagine that the skin and flesh of your face is dissolving, down through the skull into the earth. Just completely relax the face. Relax the eyebrows. Relax the eyes, the eye sockets. Relax the nose, the cheekbones, the upper jaw, the lower jaw. Completely let go. Let everything drain down through the skull into the earth. Completely relax. The skull itself. The ears. Let all the tension you find flow down through the back of the head and into the earth.

Now put your attention on your whole body, all at once, feeling the ten-points altogether. The whole body is completely relaxing, completely releasing. You're letting go of any fatigue, any burden, any tension, any cares, any thoughts. Everything is flowing down into the earth. You can scan your body, see where the difficult parts may be. For many people, under the shoulder blades is really tough. It's a very adult kind of problem that the upright position creates. You could focus on that. Feel the tension underneath the shoulder blades, then release.

You can go right to the edge of going to sleep in this practice; that's not a bad thing to do, as long as you can stay aware. It's a different kind of awareness. It's much more penumbral, a much more shadowy kind of awareness than you're likely accustomed to.

Feel your body. Feel your whole body. Feel what's going on in it, and release. Just imagine yourself sinking into the earth, dissolving into the earth.

At this point, you're just aware. You're not thinking—you're just letting all the thoughts and all the physical tension dissolve.

Now that you've gone through the other areas, check back in on your inner thighs where the psoas is attached. See if you can see some holding there that you'd like to release. When you go into the upper inner thighs, it's really the thigh bone you're looking at. That's where the psoas tension is. It's right up against the thigh bone, the upper fifth of the thigh bone.

So you're constantly scanning your body, you're looking for tension now, and releasing. Through the feet, the buttocks, midback, elbows, shoulder blades, head. And you can let your awareness roam back and forth through your body, looking for points of tension. When you find them, really let them become uncomfortable, feel them become a little too intense, and then you can enter into them with your awareness. You can begin to take responsibility for the tension there. And release.

This concludes the ten-points practice, lying down. Take a few moments and, when you feel ready, you can sit back up in your meditation posture. Now you can either continue with your regular meditation practice, do the ten-points practice sitting up, or enter one of the other somatic practices. I'll assume, for this discussion, that you are going to do the sitting up ten-points practice.

B. Ten-Points Practice, Sitting Up

Now you're going to go through the same basic process, but in a sitting up posture. The sitting up practice is a little different from the lying down version, but the principles and the process are the same.

Your feet and buttocks are touching the earth, possibly also your knees. You're going to let your energy dissolve downward, taking all the tension with it. You're feeling the earth under you really quite strongly, and allowing the tension of your body to dissolve into the earth underneath. There's a steady stream of energy downward. This time, you're going to start with the crown of the head. It's as if someone is pouring warm, golden, blissful oil over your head. That oil is flowing down over your skull, through your skull, over your face, down the back of your neck, shoulders, through the body, gradually working its way down to your buttocks, your knees, and your feet. Take some time with this process, perhaps ten minutes or so, letting the oil flow over and through you.

Just do this, feeling the release of tension, and particularly tension in the shoulders. Let all the energy of the body, all the tension, flow down to the places where you're touching the earth, into the earth. Relaxing completely, completely letting go.

Stay in your body, keep finding places where you're holding, and relax them. Let the energy flow down. There's a constant sort of wash downward, through your buttocks, through your perineum, through the knees if they're touching the floor, through your feet. It's a steady flow down; you're relaxing, relaxing, letting go, melting, releasing, energy flowing down into the earth. It's almost as if your buttocks are melting into the earth.

Try to really stay with your body. This is what you're mindful of: the body. It's a constant process of release and downward flow. As you're paying attention to your body, you might notice that your posture will call to you off and on for slight adjustments. Try to listen to your body and see what might be needed. Your body actually tells you. As you learn how to listen to your body, over time you'll find the posture that you need.

When you have finished, you can simply sit in the openness and blissful relaxation of the body or, if you wish, return to a more formal meditation technique.

EARTH DESCENT/BREATHING

A. Earth Descent/Breathing, Lying Down

In order to carry out the earth descent/earth breathing, begin, again, by assuming the lying down posture. In order to enter the earth practice, now do a very abbreviated form of the ten-points practice (five to ten minutes).

Now you're going to connect with the earth under you. You do this by letting your body sink down into the earth. It's not going to be your physical body, of course, because your physical body remains on the surface. But you're going to visualize your awareness extending down from your ten points—two feet, two buttocks, midback, two elbows, the two shoulder blades, the head.

As you relax and release through those ten points, your awareness is going to travel down into the earth. So the process of relaxation and of letting go of the tension, as we do in the ten-points practice, actually becomes a vehicle for us to descend into the earth. Awareness is not restricted to the body, as many of you know. We can send our awareness beyond our body in many different ways. Not only in Buddhism, but in modern experimental research (such as scientific researcher Russell Targ's research into "distance viewing"), it is clear that our awareness is not confined to the physical envelope of our body.

You begin on the in-breath, going in and being in the body as a whole; on the out-breath, you're going to descend down about a foot into the earth. Just let your awareness drop. It's as if it just falls down of its own accord. On the out-breath, you're letting go. It's as if it's your final breath. On the out-breath, you let go, and as you let go, your awareness drops. In-breath, be in the body, out-breath, let go and drop into the earth about a foot.

Then, on another out-breath, drop two feet. Then three feet. And then ten feet. In-breath, you're in the body; out-breath, you just drop down ten feet.

Then on the out-breath dropping down ten feet, this time, you can just stay there. When you breathe in there, ten feet down, don't come back up. Just let your awareness abide beneath you about ten feet.

Then, go down twenty feet and stay there.

On each out-breath, go down a little bit further. On the in-breath, you're not going to come back up, but just stay where you are. On the out-breath, go down further. So, out-breath, twenty feet. Hang out there. Out-breath, thirty feet. Out-breath, forty feet. Out-breath, one hundred feet. Out-breath, two hundred feet. Notice what your awareness is like when you're down two hundred feet. Notice its qualities. It may be just open and empty, and maybe dark. But look and see what it's like for yourself. You're moving into the darkness. The darkness holds the totality. It's your darkness, your totality.

Then drop one thousand feet. Then a mile. Then just explore around you. Let your awareness drop just as if you tossed a stone off the edge of a cliff. Your awareness just drops down a mile. It just drops. See what that space is like when you're down there.

The deeper your awareness goes into the earth, the more you relax and the less wound up you are with the gripping on the body on the surface that goes with the ego.

Work with this. In the beginning, it's not easy. It's unfamiliar. But there's always a sense on the out-breath of just relaxing and letting your awareness drop.

If you find yourself thinking and centralizing back up in the body, just let go again. Let your awareness drop. Don't worry too much about the distance; just let your awareness drop into the darkness and try to stay with it, hang out there. You can keep on with the process of descent, on and on and on. You can do it for ten minutes or for half an hour or more. As you become more familiar with the process and more skilled, you will find it more and more interesting.

This is the earth we are dropping into, this is the *experience* of the earth, as opposed to what we think. We have all these ideas, but this, when we drop our awareness down, this is what we find. Open, empty, peaceful, dark, and somehow warm and reassuring, perhaps surprisingly so. We might not think that space could be warm and reassuring, but the space of the earth is. Everything is accepted. Everything is accommodated here. Out-breath, just drop down into it.

After exploring this for a while, perhaps the ten to forty minutes suggested above, take a moment or two to gather yourself. When you feel ready, you can sit back up. As you're sitting back up, try to stay connected with the big space under you.

B. Earth Descent/Breathing, Sitting Up

Now you're going to carry the earth practice into the sitting up position. We begin this by feeling the perineum. Your perineum, as mentioned earlier, is located right between your sitz bones, in between the genitals and the anal area. In many people, there's strangely quite a lot of tension there. There's a kind of holding back in the perineum, which is a holding back from the earth. The disconnected, pathological ego doesn't want to be connected with the earth, because once we connect with the earth, everything starts opening up.

You need to identify this holding back or this tightness in the perineum. Just see if you can do that. As you identify what's there, see if you can relax. See if you can feel that your sitz bones are actually sinking down on your cushion. Relaxing the perineum means relaxing the anal area and also the genital area. There's a lot of holding there for all of us, whatever your gender or sexual orientation may be, whatever your fear of just letting go, of letting ourselves sink nakedly, connecting to the earth. See if you can find the tension and then relax it.

You have to keep coming back to the body. What you notice is that when you're there, you relax, and then you think of something, and all of a sudden it's tight again. It's a process. You have to really be in the perineum, and you have to stay there. Every time you start to freeze and pull back, you have to release and open.

The next step is to begin the breathing. You're going to breathe from underneath you up into the perineum, feeling and visualizing bringing your breath through the perineum from under you. You're going to reach down ever more deeply into the earth. You're going to drop your attention down, and breathe from that place. So, try dropping your attention, your awareness, about a foot under you, then breathing up from that place. Your attention is a foot under you, but you have a feeling of breathing your breath from that place beneath the perineum where your attention is staying. You're bringing it up, breathing the earth energy up. And as you breathe, the perineum and the sitz bones relax further and descend toward the earth.

Now you go down two feet, breathing up from a point two feet under you. You're opening a channel from the earth two feet under you up into the body, through the perineum. Then three feet, and five feet, and ten feet.

Do this for a couple minutes. Your attention now is about ten feet under you, and you're breathing up from that point. Bring up, breathe up the energy of the earth in through the perineum. You're leaving your attention about ten feet under you, but there's a general sense of breathing up through the perineum from that point about ten feet under.

Now go down fifteen feet. Your attention is fifteen feet down under you: that's where your main locus is as you're breathing up into the perineum. Now, just see if you can go down one hundred feet, and breathe up from that point.

You'll notice that to do this requires a constant dialogue with your body. You're constantly feeling tension that needs to be released. You may have to adjust your posture throughout this, because the more deeply you're connected to the earth, the more your body will communicate what needs to happen on the surface. Be fluid, be flexible. Just try to relax completely.

As you do this—as, indeed, with the other somatic practices—you may find strong emotions surfacing, emotions of

sadness, grief, or distress, or, equally, emotions of relief, gladness, or even joy. There is no problem with these emotions
rising to the surface. There is no problem with us bursting into
tears or into laughter when we are alone or when we are in a
room practicing with others. When I teach the Meditating with
the Body programs, in a group of fifty or sixty people, there is
almost always an undercurrent of tears from one or more of us.
It is a sign that the practice is actually opening us up beyond
and beneath our habitual limits.

Just be one hundred feet down, breathing up. Let your awareness be open, and surrender into the space.

The conversation continues between your body and your
awareness in the earth under you. You're working with it, you're
present, you pop back up to the surface in discursive thinking,
then again you drop down. The body needs to relax further.
You open, then you start coming to the surface and shutting
down, then you open again and drop. Working with the earth
in this way is a very dynamic process. There's constant, constant
adjustment and working with it: opening, shutting down, catch-
ing yourself, opening, dropping down, breathing up from that
point below.

After doing this for a while, until you feel satisfied or completed
for now, just sit for a minute without doing anything, making no
effort at all. See how your body feels and how your mind feels. Just
notice. Use no technique at all. Then, remaining connected with
the depth and openness of the earth, just keep sitting in that way,
or return to a more structured meditation technique.

THREE-FOLD BREATHING

A. Threefold Breathing, Lying Down

This practice is done in the same lying down position described earlier. If you like, once again, you can do an abbreviated ten-points practice, lying down, to prepare yourself for the threefold breathing.

With your hands folded as in the lying posture, bring your attention into the lower belly, between the perineum and the navel, and breathe into the space of this region. On the in-breath, allow the cavity of the lower belly to expand, imagining that it is a balloon that fills up; on the out-breath, let the balloon collapse. Notice if you feel any tension or constriction around this open cavity. If you do, relax the tension and let it go. Then come up to the front of the lower belly and see if you can relax the front abdominal muscles. Notice if you are carrying tension in the sinews of your inner thighs and in the area around the anus. Just feeling the tension in part of your body invites whatever release. On the in-breath, notice the tension, and on the out-breath, try to completely release. Explore this whole region, including in your exploration your perineum, your sacrum, your pelvis, your hip joints, and the front, back, and sides of your lower belly. On the in-breath, identify areas of tension, and on the out-breath, invite those areas to release and let go. Feel the entire inner space of the lower belly. Do this for a few minutes.

Now bring your hands up to the mid-chest and cross them left under right at the base of the junction of the lower ribs, over the xyphoid process, the bottom tip of the sternum. Feel the space between the breastbone and the back of the spine and breathe into this cavity. Imagine that there is empty space in this area, and that you are drawing breath into this open cavity at the midchest. On the in-breath, the cavity in the midchest fills with *prana*, your inner breath or life force, and opens up, and on the out-breath, release and relax. Again, you can visualize that you are filling a balloon in the midchest, letting it collapse on the out-breath.

The more space we create in the body, the more the tension in the body begins to make itself known. As you breathe into the cavity at the midchest, notice if you feel any tension in your back (especially in the rope-like tendons that extend on either side of the spine), in your shoulder blades, and in your lower ribs. On the in-breath, fill the cavity at the midchest. At the full culmination of the in-breath, notice the tension surrounding the inner space and feel the fatigue of the muscles, tendons, and bones. On the out-breath, release and let go completely. Check to make sure that you are filling the entire cavity at the midchest with breath, filling the entire midregion, including your sides, the back of the ribs, and the back of the spine. With the in-breath, feel the space expanding outward at the midchest in every direction, and with the out-breath, completely relax. Explore this for a few minutes.

Next, come up to the collarbones, placing your fingers on the collarbones or the fingertips on the outside of the collarbones. Begin to breathe into this region. You are bringing the breath up under the collarbones and trying to lift them up, toward your head, with the in-breath. Notice if you feel any tension, particularly in the arms, hands, fingers, wrists, shoulders, and upper back. On the in-breath, notice any tension, and on the out-breath, relax. See if you can discover the open space right between the collarbones, just below the throat, that creates the empty region of the upper chest. Fill this empty region of the upper chest with prana on the in-breath, and then relax completely on the out-breath. Again, you can use the balloon visualization to help you tune into the filling and emptying of the upper chest.

To finish, return your hands to your lower belly and place them there as in the basic lying down posture. Now briefly work with all three areas of the empty space we have discovered in this practice, beginning with the lower belly, then the midchest, and then the upper chest. You can do this by beginning the breath in the perineum, filling up through the midchest, and completing the in-breath at the collar bones. Do this gently for a few minutes. Then relax your hands by placing them either by your side or on the lower belly, and lie still without any particular technique. Feel the quality of space in your body and rest your attention on that quality of spaciousness and peace.

B. Threefold Breathing, Sitting Up

Once you have become familiar with the threefold breathing practice lying down, you can begin to do the practice sitting up. As with the other body work practices, this is a way of bringing the practice more into the waking, "adult" world, in which we are more engaged with the world around us than we are when lying down. As with the other somatic practices, the sitting up version of the threefold breathing is usually entered from some brief practice of the lying down threefold exercise.

This particular application of the sitting up threefold breathing process emphasizes linking each of the areas with one another, using the breath. Other applications of the same practice put more stress on simply exploring each area in relative independence from the others or on how focusing our awareness of the three regions impacts the way we are able to take our meditation posture.

At the conclusion of the threefold breathing in a lying down position, return your attention to the lower belly and take a few breaths into the perineum, opening and relaxing the perineal muscle. Now sit up on your meditation cushion in a relaxed posture, legs crossed, with hands resting lightly in your lap or on your knees. Try having your eyes either a bit open or wide open (in order to work with both outer and inner awareness).

Continue to breathe in through the perineum, checking your alignment to make sure you are not too far forward or too far back. Bring the breath up through the perineum into the interior of the perineal muscle and into the area around the anus and the sitz bones. Let this area relax, and feel yourself sinking down and connecting with the earth. Now bring the breath into the lower belly, into a point midway between the navel and the perineum that is also midway between the left and right side of the body and midway between the front and the back of the body. Bring your breath in from all directions and breathe directly into this central point in the lower belly. Be sure to breathe in through your perineum as well as through the sides of the body. Breathe into this central point and let the interior of the lower belly fill. Notice the sensations throughout your body as you breathe into the lower belly. Investigate if your belly is open or restricted. If you notice any tension in the lower belly, explore this area and adjust your posture a bit forward or backward or a bit to the left or right to see if this creates greater relaxation and openness.

Next, breathe into the midchest just behind the xyphoid process at the base of your sternum. Allow the breath to fill the sphere of the midchest and allow yourself to relax completely on the out-breath. On the in-breath, fill the midchest completely; on the out-breath, relax and open the back, front, left, and right of the midchest.

Then, come up to the area of the collarbones, the area of the upper chest, and breathe into the space between the collarbones. On the in-breath, imagine a balloon is filling up in your upper chest, and on the out-breath release any tension you discover.

Now go back to the lower belly and take three long, slow breaths into the lower belly. Bring the space and awareness you have generated in the lower belly into the midchest and take three long, slow breaths into the midchest. Then bring the awareness and openness of the midchest and lower belly into the upper chest and breathe three long, slow breaths into the region of the upper chest. Then move back down to the midchest with three long, slow breaths and then back to the lower belly with three long, slow breaths.

See if you can bring the breath up through the perineum and fill the entire interior of the lower belly, then the midchest, and then the upper chest. Keep some of your attention on the perineum and some of your attention on the breath, filling up the whole body up to the collarbones. All three regions of the body should be drinking the water of life, the breath that is flowing upward from the perineum. Finally, let the breath flow all the way up to the back of the skull. Remember to keep a portion of your attention on the perineum, which is the entryway for the breath. This will give you a sense of being rooted and grounded as you bring the breath all the way up through the three regions of the body and up to the back of the skull. On the in-breath, bring the energy up, and on the out-breath, let the breath go out while being attentive to the five places we are working with (the perineum, the lower belly, the midchest, the upper chest, and the back of the skull).

Continue to breathe in through your perineum, bringing the breath all the way up to the back of the skull. Notice your mind and the quality of your breathing. Observe the larger environment or feeling of your mind and body in which this practice is occurring. Finally, let go of any technique whatsoever, and look at your mind and notice how it is. Sit in this manner for a few minutes to feel and assimilate the benefits of this practice.

CELLULAR BREATHING

A. Cellular Breathing, Lying Down

Take the basic lying down posture and do a short, ten-points practice.

Now we are going to slightly change your posture to do the cellular breathing exercise. Rather than putting your feet on the floor with your knees up, stretch out your legs, without the yoga strap, and put your meditation cushion or another pillow underneath your knees and lower legs. You can position this cushion as high as you like—whatever is most comfortable. You're just draping your legs over the cushion, in most cases making your knees a little closer to the ground than in the basic lying down posture. Your feet may not touch the ground, which is fine, or you might be able to stretch them out farther, resting them on the floor. Basically, we want to be completely, totally relaxed, not having to hold the legs up at all, and we are going to need the greater leg extension to do the exercise. If the knees are bent too much, it is harder to do, so we are bending them less this way. They can be slightly bent, but not bent too much.

Take a minute and work with your posture, work with your placement on the floor, and make sure you are really comfortable. Through the other practices, you have developed the ability to focus your breath, which is a very powerful tool. In this exercise, you are going to use that ability in a different way. You are going to start breathing into specific parts of your body, working your way up from the toes all the way to the top of the head. Taking them bit by bit, the basic idea is whatever part you have breathed into is included in the next part, so by the end of the practice, you are breathing into the body as a whole. Again, you start with the big toe, breathing into it, bringing the breath in, and gradually work your way up. So, when you are breathing into your knees, you are still breathing into your big toe, your feet, and your legs. Everything you have worked with up to that point is included.

Now to remind you a bit of the view, as is discussed earlier in the book. When we bring our breath consciously into different parts of our body, there is the physical part, in this case pulling the breath in through the pores of the skin. But at a deeper level, there is the inner breath, by which we are bringing the life energy into that particular part of our body. This brings awareness with it, and invites the unfolding and the delivery of the karma in each part of our body. Karma simply means the next step in the unfolding process of our being, as encoded in us, in the body. It is part of who we are physically, even though we are not aware of it. We are inviting that unfolding process; the encoded next step of our human life is invited to display itself. That is what the breathing does in each part of the body. It creates a situation of openness and unfolding and encourages the process of unfolding, the unfolding of our life. The important point here is that this unfolding is already implicit in every cell of our body. We are a very specific organism on the planet, and in the very cells of our body is what we need to be, what we need to become, in order to fulfill our human destiny or our fate. We are working with our destiny when we do this breathing, in the most specific and concrete way we can ever imagine. But don't be scared—this shouldn't seem too heavy. Just relax and enjoy the process of opening up our sense perceptions in these areas. The body will take care of the rest.

So, begin by breathing into your big toe, just working on this for a little bit of time. What you are trying to do is to bring the breath in through the toe, through the pores, and begin to feel the sensations in the big toe. The two big toes are probably not going to feel the same. And, again, don't be distressed. You are breathing in, and you might not be surprised to find some pain there. That's fine. You can feel your toenail—it is sort of hard and dense—and then you can feel the flesh under your toenail. Feel the tip of your toe. You're just breathing in and feeling the texture. Feel the interior of the big toe, the bones, and the joints that may well be sore. The big toe takes a huge amount of stress and very often is achey, yet we are often not aware of it because we are too busy thinking to really pay attention to this extremely important part of our body. Breathe into it. Bring life to it. You are bringing life, you are bringing feeling into your big toe.

So, this is very similar to the progression of the ten-points practice, but with two important differences. First, we are intensely breathing in through each part of our body, each pore, not focusing simply on attention and relaxation. This breathing greatly heightens the process. Second, as mentioned, as we move from one part of the body to the next, we keep breathing into the part we have already been breathing into. So the total area of the body being breathed into increases and accumulates in that way.

Bring the breath all the way to where the big toe joins the foot, but no further. Just come up to that point. And then go to the toe next to the big toe and follow the same process. What you'll notice as you breathe into the big toe and the second toe, because we are now including both, is a process of relaxation. The big toe is actually very tense. You can relax it. The second toe is also very tense. Relax. And as you relax the big toe and the second toe, you'll notice that sometimes the energy of other parts of the leg will actually start to flow down, and that's fine. Then bringing in the third toe, which may be a little harder to feel. Just keep breathing into it until you start to feel it. Then include the fourth toe, adding it to the others as you breathe in through all of them. Finally, add the baby toe. So, now you are breathing in all five toes, all five at once.

Feel how very sensitive the toes are, and how awake they are. There is so much intelligence there. Just feel that. Now, you can come up into the ball of the foot, on the inside. This is a joint that obviously receives a tremendous amount of stress, and may be very tense. Try to relax it. Feel the energy. Feel the tension. Feel the soreness. Next, breathe into the middle part of the foot, right behind the middle toe. You are bringing the breath in, in a very deliberate and focused way. Begin breathing into the outside of the foot. Remember, you are adding each part to all the previous parts we've been breathing into, so now we are including all five toes and the bottom of the foot. Next, breathe in right behind the toes, on the inside and the outside. You are really bringing the breath up into the interior of the foot, looking for tension, and relaxing. Next, you come up into the arch of the foot, moving up the bottom of the foot.

Notice that as you are working with the feet, your whole body is going to make some minor adjustments in its alignment. It's very interesting—just keep an eye on that. You'll especially notice it in your pelvis and your legs. As you go along, you will find that some microrealignment is going to want to happen there. Welcome it.

Next, breathe up into the heel, so that you are now in the bottom of the foot, breathing up though the bottom, the sole of the foot, into the foot. Through the toes, the front arch, and heel, breathe up into the interior of the foot. Come up to the ankle bone on the inside of the foot. Breathe up through the arch into the ankle bone on the inside. And notice how that might very well effect the alignment of your hips, your psoas, your lower back. Then you'll breathe up the outside of the foot into the ankle bones on the outside and the Achilles tendon.

Now you are breathing into the entire foot up through the toes, the heel, the middle arch, the front of the foot, and through all the skin, all the pores, on either side, up into the ankle. The foot, now as a whole, is a living, breathing, intelligent entity on both sides. Keep noticing the legs and hips as you do this and how they might want to readjust slightly as you move along.

Continue, breathing up into the calf muscle through the foot, on both legs. Next, breathe into the shin bone, then up through the muscle on the outside of the shin bone, the outside of the leg, also in through the pores.

Bring the breath, then, all the way from the toes, the entire foot, the lower leg, up into the knee joint. Also breath in through the pores of the skin in the knee, front and back. Stay focused. Be present, and just feel the nature of the knee joint, the muscles, the tendons, the vulnerability of the knee. The knee is energetically very open in a certain way. If you have pain, just breathe into the pain. Breathe in it and through it. Let it be.

Next, come up into the front of the thigh, the back of the thigh, the sides, come all the way up to the hips, so you are breathing through the entire foot, the entire lower leg on both sides, the knees, and then the front of the thigh, bringing the energy up into the hip joint. You are bringing the breath up from the places you have already worked on, and are also breathing in through all the pores of that particular area.

At this point, you are applying a lot of exertion, a lot of attention, but at the same time you are relaxing into deeper and deeper levels in your body. Your attention is rather taut or rapt, but your body is increasingly relaxed.

The more energy you can bring into this cellular breathing by bringing the breath in, the more these areas will wake up and become alive and vibrant and aware. Move deeply into the hamstrings and up to the buttocks. Add in the sitz bones. Now you are including both legs, beginning from the toes, all the way up. Now, breathe through the sitz bones and into the anal area, the perineum, the genitals, and then up to the pubic bone. Bring the breath all the way up from the toes to the pubic bone and into the hip joints on either side. Then move into the lower belly, and up to the navel, at the same time coming in from the outside, through the pores. Take your time; go step by step through these areas. Fully feel them and awaken them before moving on to the next.

Take a moment at this point to make sure that you are breathing in, sumultaneously, through everything we have covered so far. On the in-breath, the legs, the feet, and the pelvis become alive. They become bright. They open up. They are filled with life, awareness. On the out-breath, relax any tension. You are totally focusing your breath, bringing it into the lower part of your body, and you can really intensify the bringing in of the breath. You are bringing life, awareness, vitality, energy. Just feel that.

Continue on, bringing the breath up to and into the xyphoid process in the front, then up through and into the back. Come up to the collarbones. Come up the back to the shoulder blades. You are bringing the breath, the prana, into your entire body, through all the pores, all the way down to your toes. Add the thumbs, include them in this process; add the first finger, the middle finger, the fourth finger, and the baby finger. Come up into the palms, the back of the hands, the wrists. You're still including the rest of the body. You're folding in these last parts. Come up into the forearms, the entire lower arm, the elbows, the upper arm, and up into the shoulders. So now you are breathing though the entire body, up into the shoulders. Then, gradually, bring your breath a little higher each time, into the lower part of the neck, and the middle part of the neck. Then add the base of the skull; bring the breath into the back of the skull, the jaw, the lower teeth, the tongue, the lips, the upper teeth, your cheekbones, then the flesh of the face, the eyes, the ears, the forehead. Breathe into the scalp and finally the brain.

Now you are breathing through the entire body, through every pore of the entire body, into every portion of its interior, all its bones, muscles, and organs, into all the cells of the body. Just work on that for a few minutes. It isn't easy, but if you stay with it, the energy, attention, and sense of intense vitality will become greater and greater.

As you are breathing through the entire body, notice if there are any places that perhaps seem a little dead or a little resistant to the breath, and you can emphasize those areas a bit. You are still breathing through the entire body, but you are ending up in that particular spot, trying to bring more life to it, more energy, more awareness, more feeling of being awake and sensitive and sentient.

Continue this for another minute or two. Try to make a lot of effort now, maximize your effort and exertion to the utmost, breathing in through every pore of your body, into every single cell of your body, surface and depth, simultaneously.

Then, when you think you can't possibly do any more, you can just let go of the technique and lie quietly. Feel the energy circulating throughout your body. This is the inner breath, the prana, which is your vitality, flowing through your *nadis*, or energy pathways. Your body is now very, very awake, and you can feel an electricity flowing everywhere. Stay with this for several minutes, enjoying it and being completely in the flow. Stay with it until you feel really satisfied. After resting for a few more minutes, you can sit back up. As you do so, continue this sense of the full body, cellular breathing but gently now with a very light touch.

B. Cellular Breathing, Sitting Up

This practice can be done on its own, beginning in a sitting up posture, or as a continuation of the lying down cellular breathing. Basically, you just recapitulate, in your sitting up posture, what we just did lying down. If you just did the lying down practice, you can do the sitting up practice much more briefly, taking perhaps five to seven minutes for the whole thing. If you haven't done the lying down practice first, and you begin in a sitting posture, you might take twenty to thirty or forty minutes for the whole thing. The timing really should depend on your own feeling. Stay with each area until you feel it has really opened up, come awake and alive, before moving on, through every pore of the body, bringing the breath into every cell.

Whether you are lying down or sitting up, here is the challenging part: There are going to be parts of your body that you don't like and you don't want to be aware of. Maybe you think you're too fat, maybe you think you're too thin, maybe you think you don't have a good upper body. Maybe you are afraid of your heart or afraid of your stomach or afraid of your liver. Whatever it may be, bring the breath in through every pore of the body into every cell of the body, and pay particular attention to the parts of your body from which you might want to shy away.

Bring your breath in in a very loving way. It can be loving, nurturing, tender. If you have an injury or a disease, it is very appropriate to breathe into that, but continue to bring the breath through the whole body and then into that place, so that you are in a way setting up a situation in which the whole body is nourishing and bringing vitality and healing to that particular distressed part.

It is like having some children that you are peaceful around and others who always put you on edge and drive you crazy: at a certain point you have to pass beyond judgment, and your love has to be open and impartial toward all of them. This is what you're doing. This is also an opportunity to correct your alignment in your sitting posture, because in this open state your body is going to notify you of what is going on, if something is slightly out of kilter, and you are welcome to respond to that.

As you continue to breathe in through every pore of the body, into every cell of the body, check your body and see where you are still holding on, where you are not completely relaxed. This is a little more challenging when you are sitting up, because the tendency to tense up is much greater than when you are lying down, but all the same, scan your body and find out where you are not completely relaxed: whether it is your shoulders, your back, or your legs, just work with that. As you do this breathing, see if you can make minor adjustments to bring your body into a greater feeling of ease.

Take an interest with what is going on with your body. It is so filled with life and movement and energy. Continue breathing. When you are sitting up, you can, if you like, emphasize your legs and your buttocks and your perineum. You can bring the energy up through your legs and perineum, up into your body, and let your upper body just sort of float over that very grounded situation. Let your shoulders really hang. Sit and let the energy flowing through your body provide all the uplift needed. You don't have to do a single thing or make any effort in your sitting posture, except to be with the life force flowing through your body.

Index

cellular breathing, 343, 372–383
earth descent/breathing, 307–309,
    325, 343, 361–366
energy and, 71–72
lower belly breathing, 343
threefold breathing, 343, 367–372
Buber, Martin, 39
buddha nature, the, 14, 244–245, 246,
    248–252, 262, 266–267
    the body as, 223–226, 238
    crisis as expression of, 242–243
    definition of, 223–224
    emptiness of, 224–225
    unfolding and, 224, 227–232
Buddha, the, 44-45, 169, 173
    biography of, 167, 168
    body of, 166–173
    Buddhacarita, 167, 168
    dharma of, 6–9
    embodiment and, 44–45
    on the First Noble Truth, 139, 229
    Shakyamuni Buddha, 166
    universalism of, 173
Buddhacarita, 167, 168
Buddhism, 240n1, 333–339
    Asian, 240n1
    authority in, 10–11, 17
    Avatamsaka Sutra, 155
    "birth of the ego", 79
    on the breakdown of the ego, 250
    on the buddha nature, 225
    Ch'an, 6, 9, 255
    Chinese, 6, 9, 255
    crisis and, 20–26, 242–243
    on discomfort, 79
    disembodiment and, 20–26
    Dzogchen tradition, 193
    embodiment in, 44–45
    on experience, 141, 152, 167
    first encounters with, 4
    history of, 166–173
    individuality and, 338–339
    institutionalized, 9, 11–12
    on interconnection, 169–170
    Japanese, 4, 6–9, 255
    karma and, 121–125, 133–134,
        138, 141
    knowledge and, 100–104

Madhyamaka, 155
Mahayana tradition, 13, 155
    meditative traditions, 6–9, 158, 357.
        see also specific traditions
    modern, 21–26
    modern culture and, 333–339
    optimism of, 15–16
    Pure Land, 255
    questioning and, 15
    on *samsara*, 134
    Seon, 6
    Southern, 254–255
    spirituality and, 13–15
    Theravadin tradition, 4, 6, 254–255
    Tibetan, 7–9, 21–27, 102n1,
        121–125
    tradition in, 16–17
    transitions within, 7
    the ultimate challenge of, 13–17
    Vajrayana tradition, 13–14, 199,
        206, 346
    Vipassana movement, 6–7.
        see also Theravadin tradition
    Western practitioners of, 7–8, 9, 21,
        45–48, 256–257, 336–339
    Yogacara, 289–296
    Zen, 4, 6–9, 255, 351
Buddhist psychology, 159, 289–296

C

cause and effect. *see* karma
cells, 219–220
cellular breathing, 343, 372–382
    lying down, 372–380
    sitting up, 380–382
Ch'an Buddhism, 6, 9, 255
chaos, 93–94, 157–165
childhood, 123–124, 301–302, 311,
    312. *see also* infancy; repression
Chinese Buddhism. *see* Ch'an Buddhism
Chinese medicine, 353
Christianity, 32, 34, 41, 136, 225, 329
claustrophobia, 86
clear seeing, 177, 182–185.
    see also vipashyana
"coming to fruition", 133, 134–137,
    146, 151, 155, 265, 266
commitment to the path, 245–246

REGINALD A. RAY, PhD draws on four decades of study and intensive meditation practice within the Tibetan Buddhist tradition to address the unique problems, inspirations, and spiritual imperatives of modern people. He is the founder and Spiritual Director of the Dharma Ocean Foundation, a nonprofit educational organization dedicated to the practice, study, and preservation of the teachings of Chögyam Trungpa Rinpoche and the practice lineage he embodied. The first full-time faculty member and chair of the Buddhist Studies (later Religious Studies) Department at Naropa University, he is the author of *Indestructible Truth, Secret of the Vajra World, Buddhist Saints in India, In the Presence of Masters,* other books, and several popular Sounds True audio programs, including *Your Breathing Body* and *Mahamudra for the Modern World.* Dr. Ray regularly leads residential meditation retreats at Blazing Mountain Retreat Center in Crestone, Colorado. For more information as well as access to free audio talks and guided meditations, please visit dharmaocean.org.

SOUNDS TRUE is a multimedia publisher whose mission is to inspire and support personal transformation and spiritual awakening. Founded in 1985 and located in Boulder, Colorado, we work with many of the leading spiritual teachers, thinkers, healers, and visionary artists of our time. We strive with every title to preserve the essential "living wisdom" of the author or artist. It is our goal to create products that not only provide information to a reader or listener, but that also embody the quality of a wisdom transmission.

For those seeking genuine transformation, Sounds True is your trusted partner. At SoundsTrue.com you will find a wealth of free resources to support your journey, including exclusive weekly audio interviews, free downloads, interactive learning tools, and other special savings on all our titles.

To learn more, please visit SoundsTrue.com/bonus/free_ gifts or call us toll free at 800-333-9185.